OPERATIONAL REVIEW

Maximum Results at Efficient Costs

THIRD EDITION

Rob Reider

JOHN WILEY & SONS, INC.

New York • Chichester • Weinheim • Brisbane • Toronto • Singapore

Library of Congress Cataloging-in-Publication Data:

Reider, Harry R., 1940–
    Operational review : maximum results at efficient costs / Rob Reider.—3rd. ed.
        p. cm.
    Includes index.
    ISBN 0-471-22810-9 (cloth : acid-free paper)
    1. Auditing, Internal.   2. Auditing.   I. Title.

    HF5668.25 .R45 2002
    657'.458—dc21

                                                                    2002004489

10 9 8 7 6 5 4 3 2 1

About the Author

Rob Reider, CPA, MBA, PhD, is the President of Reider Associates, a management and organizational consulting firm he founded in 1976, which is located in Santa Fe, New Mexico. Prior to starting Reider Associates, he was a manager in the Management Consulting Department of Peat, Marwick in Philadelphia. His area of expertise encompasses planning and budget systems, managerial and administrative systems, computer processing, financial and accounting procedures, organizational behavior and theory, management advisory services, large and small business consulting, management information and control techniques, and management training and staff development.

Rob has been a consultant to numerous large, medium, and small businesses of all types in the aforementioned areas (in both the private and public sectors). In addition, he has conducted many and varied operational reviews and benchmarking studies and has trained both internal staff and external consultants in these techniques.

He is the course author and nationally sought after discussion leader and presenter for more than 20 different seminars that are conducted nationally for various organizations and associations. He has conducted more than 1,000 such seminars throughout the country and has received the AICPA Outstanding Discussion Leader of the Year award.

Considered a national expert in the areas of operational reviews and benchmarking strategies, Rob provides specific consultation in the areas of general business management, development of internal and external consulting practices, organizational and management systems, and the development and conducting of continuing professional education (CPE) and other training programs.

Rob is the course author of nine Reider Associates self-study courses marketed nationally. He is also the author of the following books also published by John Wiley & Sons, Inc.

- *The Complete Guide to Operational Auditing*
- *Operational Review: Maximum Results at Efficient Costs*
- *Benchmarking Strategies: A Tool for Profit Improvement*
- *Improving the Economy, Efficiency, and Effectiveness of Not-for-Profits*

Rob has also been a presenter at numerous professional meetings and conferences around the country and has published numerous articles in professional journals. He has been a frequent commentator on the educational video programs produced by Primemedia Workplace Learning such as The CPA Report, The Governmental Update, and the Accounting and Financial Managers Network.

Rob has earned the degree of Bachelor of Science (BS) in Business Administration and Master of Science in Business (MBA) from Drexel University as well as Doctor Of Philosophy (Ph.D) in Organizational and Management Psychology from Southwest University. He is currently listed in *Who's Who in the East and West, Who's Who in the World, Who's Who in Finance and Industry, Personalities in America, International Biography, Who's Who of Emerging Leaders in America,* and *Who's Who in Executives and Businesses.*

For more information about Rob Reider and Reider Associates, visit his web site at www.reiderassociates.com/otp/ or e-mail him at hrreider@ reiderassociates.com.

Contents

CONTENTS

Chapter Four: Field Work Phase   209

Case Study: Mercy College, a College Business Office   239

Chapter Five: Development of Review Findings   299

Chapter Six: Reporting Phase   343

CONTENTS

Preface

The objective of this how-to guide to performing the operational review for results is to help the reader understand the basic principles involved in planning and conducting an operational review directed toward the continual implementation of best practices in an organized program of continuous improvements. In addition, it will provide the information and fundamentals the reviewer must know to use operational review concepts to enable the organization to operate most economically, efficiently, and effectively—that is, to maximize operating results at the least cost using the most efficient methods. This book is designed to meet the needs of the reviewer, regardless of any prior experience in performing operational reviews. Both basic knowledge for those with no previous hands-on experience, and reinforcement and additional learning for those who already have some prior operational review experience are provided.

Questions that will be answered include:

- What is an operational review?

- When should an operational review be performed?

- How can an operational review be performed effectively and efficiently?

- How can positive change be effected as a result of an operational review?

- How can operational review tools and techniques be used to maintain operations in an economic, efficient, and effective manner on an ongoing basis?

- How can best practices be identified and implemented in a formalized program of continuous improvements?

> *One Must Know the Questions*
> *before One Can Seek the Answers*

The materials presented in this book can be used by management and supervisors and other employees to perform operational reviews for their operational areas of responsibility. In addition, the tools and techniques presented can be used by others, such as internal and external consultants and auditors, to maintain operations in the most economical, efficient, and effective manner.

PURPOSE AND OBJECTIVES

In today's many-faceted and multidisciplined economic environment, organizational management has placed ever more emphasis on increasing results with fewer resources through evaluation of the economy, efficiency, and effectiveness of the organization's operations. The operational review is the tool used to perform such an evaluation, either singularly or as part of another procedure such as benchmarking, activity-based management, total quality management, reengineering, and so on. This book presents the basic principles of planning and conducting such an operational review, as well as the fundamentals the reviewer must be aware of to understand operational review concepts.

The objectives of this book are:

- To increase understanding of operational review concepts and the ability to use them effectively.

- To increase understanding of the purpose and mechanics of conducting operational reviews.

- To help identify the relationship and differences between operational reviews and other procedures such as benchmarking, activity-based costing/management, reengineering, and so on.

- To increase the skills and abilities needed to conduct operational reviews.

- To increase awareness of operational review opportunities and to help in their identification.

- To improve the reviewer's capability to perform operational reviews in his or her present situation.

> ### *Knowing the Purpose and Objectives*
> ### *Ensures Taking the Correct Path*

ORGANIZATIONAL SYSTEMS AS HELPERS

In many organizations today, top management is seeking ways to become competitive and maintain market position—or merely to survive. Managers have sensed that many of their organizational systems are detrimental to progress and have held them back from achieving organizational, departmental, and individual goals and objectives. These are the very systems that are supposed to be helpful; for example:

- Planning systems, long- and short-term, that resulted in documented plans but not in actual results.

- Budget systems that became costly in terms of allocating resources effectively and controlling costs in relation to results.

- Organizational structures that created unwieldy hierarchies, which produced systems of unnecessary policing and control.

- Cost accounting structures that obscured true product costs and resulted in pricing that constrained competitiveness.

- Management systems that produced elaborate computer systems and reporting without enhancing the effectiveness of operations.

- Sales functions and forecasts that resulted in selling those products that maximized sales commissions but may not have been the products management desired to produce and sell.

- Operating practices that perpetuated outmoded systems ("We've always done it that way") rather than promoted best practices.

Operational reviews, together with other techniques, are tools to make these systems helpful as intended and direct the organization toward its goals. Theoretically, organizations should operate in an economic, efficient, and effective manner at all times. If such was the case, operational review techniques would be applied on an ongoing basis. However, with the passage of time, good intentions and initially helpful systems tend to deteriorate. Operational reviews are then necessary to help get the organization back on track by pinpointing operational deficiencies, developing practical recommendations, and implementing positive changes.

> ### Helpful Systems
> ### Need to Be Helpful

Again, theoretically, managers at all levels should be held accountable for using the scarce resources entrusted to them to achieve maximum results at the least possible costs. Although management should embrace operational review concepts and apply them as they proceed, this is rarely the case. More typically, management has to be sold on the value of operational reviews. In selling the benefits of conducting operational reviews, it is important to stress that unlike other techniques that cost time and money for uncertain results, operational reviews pay for themselves. In effect, the operational review environment becomes a profit center instead of a cost center. Although there are no guarantees, a successful operational review should result in at least three to four times its cost in annual savings. These are not one-time savings, but ongoing, that is, savings year after year. With the success of an operational review, management may quickly realize that the more operational reviews done and the more recommended economies and efficiencies implemented, the greater the savings and results. In addition, the residual capability for performing operational reviews remains in the area under review, so operations personnel can continue to apply operational review concepts on an ongoing basis.

Keep in mind that the intent of the operational review is not to be critical of present operations, but to review operations and develop a program of best practices and continuous positive operational improvements by working with management and staff personnel. This can be accomplished most effectively by working with operations personnel in areas where they recognize deficiencies and are willing to cooperate. The concept of operational reviews should be sold as an internal program of review directed toward improved economies and efficiencies that will produce increased operational results.

> *Best Practices*
> *Provide Best Results*

OPERATIONAL REVIEW PROCESS: STARTING AT THE TOP

The operational review process should start at the top of the organization. Top management should define and communicate its strategic plans for the company, including areas of expansion, retrenchment, and status quo. At the same time, management members should identify the businesses they want to be in, the businesses they do not want to be in, their basic business principles and belief systems, and their desires for each function within the organization.

For instance, top management may define a desire for the sales function, which has historically sold whatever it could to customers, to become a more integral part of the planning process and other functions such as manufacturing and engineering. In defining their desires, members of management may identify attributes such as:

- Sales forecasts more realistically related to actual customers and products to be sold.

- A larger percentage of the sales forecast (at least 80 percent) matched by real customer orders.

- Sales efforts driven by management's identification in the planning process of what to sell, to whom, and at what quantity.

- A sales forecast with a high percentage of real customer orders that allows the company's production to be based on customer orders and expected delivery times, at a specified quality level.

- A sales function that is geared more toward providing customer service than toward making sales that maximize sales personnel's compensation.

- A sales function that works within the company's plans together with the other functions of the company, such as manufacturing, engineering, purchasing, accounting, and marketing.

With the clear identification and communication of management's desires, each function has a clear idea as to where it is heading and the basis for its evaluation The purpose of the operational review then becomes one of a helping agent, assisting each function to achieve its stated goals and objectives as related to management's desires. The performance of the operational review is thus less a critical evaluation of what a particular function is doing and more an appraisal of what needs to be done to help the function achieve its goals and become the best it can.

As the operational review team works with each function within the organization, it assists that function to understand what it needs to do to become what it should be. As best practices and improvements are recommended and implemented, each function moves toward its proper place within the organization and the company becomes a learning organization, both by function and overall.

In today's organizational atmosphere of cost cutting, downsizing, reengineering and so on, the operational review must be sensitive in its approach so as to maintain needed services in the most economical, efficient, and effective manner. Whereas management may be focusing on reducing costs, operations may be focusing on an increase in providing quality services. The review team must be careful to maintain a proper perspective so that it directs its efforts toward overall organizational goals as well as the individual requirements of each function.

> *Top Management's Desires*
> *Mirror the Organizational*
> *and Employee Direction*

WHO IS THE OPERATIONAL REVIEWER?

An operational review can be performed by anyone with the appropriate skills. However, internal and/or external consultants, because of their knowledge of the operations and their analytical skills, are typically requested to perform such services. In some organizations, a separate operational review unit trained in operational review concepts is established. The most effective way in which to implement such procedures is to assign overall responsibility for implementing organization-wide operational review procedures, which include the performance of operational reviews as well as training operations personnel in implementing these techniques in their areas.

The progress and ultimate success in achieving the benefits of operational reviews depend greatly on the reviewers' skills and what management and others think of them. Those assigned to an operational review engagement must possess the ability to review and analyze financial, management, and operational areas. The attributes of an effective operational reviewer include:

- Curiosity (imagination)
- Analytical ability
- Persuasiveness
- Good business judgment
- Common sense
- Objectivity
- Communication skills
- Initiative to develop techniques in such areas as work measurement, flowcharting, cost-benefit analysis, organizational analysis, information technology, and so on
- Independence
- Confidence

Beyond those previously listed, the successful operational reviewer should possess the following attributes:

- The ability to spot the trouble areas by looking at a given situation and quickly determining what is getting in the way.

- The ability to identify the critical problem areas, so as to avoid "chasing mice when one should be chasing elephants." The application of the 80/20 rule states that operational reviews require 80 percent common sense and 20 percent technical expertise; and that 80 percent of the trouble areas cause 20 percent of the problems, and 20 percent cause 80 percent of the problems.

- The ability to place oneself in management's position, to analyze the problem and ask questions from management's perspective. This is sometimes difficult, as often the reviewer has never been in an operations-related management position. Even when this is not true, the reviewer may have difficulty understanding the constraints under which the manager must work, in effect, what the manager can and cannot do.

- The skill to effectively communicate operational review results. The success of an operational review is measured by the degree to which recommendations are implemented, and implementation is a direct by-product of effective communication. A rule of thumb in operational reviews is that the reviewer has been successful if management can be persuaded to adopt more than 50 percent of the recommendations.

The Operational Review
Is Only as Good as the
Operational Reviewers

OPERATIONAL REVIEW SKILLS AND ABILITIES

The attributes described earlier would be helpful to any manager, but they are vital to an operational reviewer. Although managers should have analytical ability, they may use it primarily to perform repetitive tasks. Operational reviewers, however, use these skills and abilities to assess a user's situations and recommend positive operational improvements.

The difference between required attributes for operational personnel and operational reviewers is similar to the difference between the left brain and the right brain. The left brain, which controls thinking and calculation processes, is more important to operations personnel performing repetitive tasks; whereas the right brain, which controls creativity and perceptual skills, is more critical to the operational reviewer. Basically, the operational reviewer needs a good balance of both, yet with a greater emphasis on the creative and perceptual side. This is why the best manager or operating staff member does not always make the best operational reviewer—and why things tend to stay the same.

To render effective services, the operational reviewer must have substantial knowledge of the total environment of the organization being examined and a high degree of skill and experience with the analytical techniques and tools needed to solve problems. The operational reviewer should also have sensitivity to, and understanding of, the values and goals of all the various people that make up a going concern.

Those trained in operating systems and procedures need not spend many years learning new methods before engaging in operational reviews because the basic techniques are the same. They mainly need to sharpen the problem identification and analytical skills they already possess. Operational reviews can be viewed as 80 percent practical analysis and common sense and 20 percent technical know-how.

An operational review requires the reviewer to possess a number of varied tools and techniques which include:

- Planning and budget processes

- Cost analysis, such as direct, standard, and activity-based costing methods

- Preparation and analysis of systems flowcharts

- Development and/or analysis of computer systems and programs

- Evaluation of computerized procedures and results

- Statistical sampling procedures

- Development and understanding of forecasts and projections

- Interviewing skills

- Organizational planning development and analysis

- Creation of goals and objectives and other performance standards of measurement

- Development and analysis of organizational structures

- Identification of best practices, both internal and external, and development of a program of continuous improvements

- Verification of the accuracy of data

- Determination of compliance with laws and regulations

- Use of sophisticated analytical techniques such as matrix analysis, linear regression correlation, critical path method, and so on

- Cost versus benefit analysis

- Communication skills, both oral and written

- Knowledge of current thinking and procedures such as total quality management (TQM), benchmarking, reengineering, complexity theory, and so on

Success as an effective operational reviewer is based on what is accomplished, that is, recommendations made to management that are subsequently implemented. Operational reviews should be fascinating and rewarding to the reviewer as well as to operations personnel. The individual's stature as an operational reviewer, credibility of the entire review staff, management's and others' positive regard of the review staff—all will increase in proportion to the degree of success attained in the operational review.

Because of the number of different types and complexities of operational reviews and the varying skills required, supporting functional disciplines are often necessary to supplement the regular review staff's skills and abilities. However, it is not always practical to maintain personnel with all of the required skills on the operational review staff. Thus, consider the skills that are necessary for the successful conduct of each operational review, and either make sure that such skills are available on staff or contract for needed outside expertise.

> *The Success of the Operational Review*
> *Is Directly Related to the*
> *Skills of the Operational Reviewers*

OPERATIONAL AREAS TO BE ADDRESSED

In this book, we will be looking at conducting operational reviews of any and all organizational functions and activities that hinder or help the effort to maintain the company in the most economical, efficient, and effective manner possible. In this regard, the operational review team must be aware of basic business principles that help to enhance the organization's success as well as those that the company should avoid. With these principles in mind, the review team should analyze operations to identify areas for improvement in which best practices can be implemented that maximize the chances of success and minimize the risk of failure.

Although the primary focus of the operational review is on the manner in which scarce resources are used by the organization, considering the sources and uses of resources and the policies and procedures used to deal with over and under operational conditions based on expected results, the following specific operational areas need to be addressed:

1. Sales of Products or Services

- Are sales made to quality customers with the right products at the right time?

- Does each sale make a contribution to profits?

- Are all costs compared to the sale such as product costs (direct material and labor), assignment of product-related activity costs (e.g., manufacturing processes, quality control, shipping, and receiving), functional costs (e.g., purchasing, accounts payable, billing, and accounts receivable), and customer costs (e.g., marketing, selling, support services, and customer service)?

- Do sales relate to an agreed-upon sales forecast? Is the company selling the right products to the right customers?

- Do sales integrate with an effective production scheduling and control system?

2. Manufacturing or Production of Services

- Are sales orders entered into an effective production control system, which ensures that all sales orders are entered into production in a timely manner to ensure on-time, quality deliveries?

- Is work-in-process kept to a minimum so that only real customer orders are being worked on rather than building up finished goods inventory?

- Are the most efficient and economical production methods used to ensure that the cost of the product is kept to its realizable minimum?

- Are direct materials and labor used most efficiently so that waste, reworks, and rejects are kept to a minimum?

- Are nondirect labor (and material) costs such as quality control, supervision and management, repairs and maintenance, material handling, and so on kept to a minimum?

3. Billing, Accounts Receivable, and Collections

- Are bills sent out in a timely manner at the time of shipment or before?

- Are accounts receivable processing procedures the most efficient and economical?

- Is the cost of billing, accounts receivable processing, and collection efforts more costly than the amount of the receivable or the net profit on the sale?

- Is the number and amount of accounts receivable continually analyzed for minimization?

- Are any customers paying directly or through electronic funds transfer at the time of shipping or delivery?

- Are bills and accounts receivable in amounts exceeding the cost of processing excluded from the system?

- Has consideration been given to reducing or eliminating these functions?

4. Inventory: Raw Materials and Finished Goods

- Are raw material and finished goods inventories kept to a minimum?

- Are raw materials delivered into production on a just-in-time basis?

- Are finished goods completed in production just in time for customer delivery?

- Is the company working toward getting out of these inventory businesses?

5. Purchasing, Accounts Payable, and Payments

- Are all items that are less than the cost of purchasing excluding from the purchasing system with an efficient system used for these items?

- Are all repetitive high volume and cost items (e.g., raw materials and manufacturing supplies) negotiated by purchasing with vendors as to price, quality, and timeliness?

- Does the production system automatically order repetitive items as an integrated part of the production control system?

- Has consideration been given to reduce these functions for low and high ticket items leading toward the possible elimination of these functions?

- Does the company consider paying any vendors on a shipment or delivery basis as part of its vendor negotiation procedures?

6. Other Costs and Expenses: General, Administrative, and Selling

- Are all other costs and expenses kept to a minimum? Remember, an unnecessary dollar not spent is a dollar directly to the bottom line.

- Are selling costs directed toward customer service and strategic plans rather than maximizing salespeople's compensation?

- Is there a system in effect which recognizes and rewards the reduction of expenses rather than the rewarding of budget increases?

- Are all non–value-added functions (e.g., management and supervision, office processing, paperwork, and so on) evaluated as to reduction and elimination?

> ### *The Operational Reviewer*
> ### *Needs Direction*
> ### *to Know What to Look For*

Many other operational areas and concerns could be listed. Those listed above are only meant as examples of areas that should be considered in the operational review. In effect, the operational review may result in reviewing many of the company's major operations as most functions selected for review affect many other functions and activities. The operational review team needs to set their guidelines as to the extent of their study. Often the area selected (e.g., cash management) invades every activity of the company. To ensure that the company operates with effective operating procedures, the operational review team must understand that every dollar expended and every dollar collected by the company must be evaluated as to its appropriateness to the company's plans and operations.

> *Every Dollar Expended*
> *and Every Dollar Collected*
> *Must Be Evaluated*

CHAPTER ONE

Overview of
Operational Reviews

This chapter provides an overview of operational review concepts and principles and terminology. In an ever-changing economic and competitive environment, management is looking for more than historical financial data. Managers need and request information about the internal operations of their organization, and seek recommendations as to how they can manage and operate more economically, efficiently, and effectively. The operational review process is most helpful and beneficial in the following instances:

- Identifying operational areas in need of positive improvement—looking for best practices as part of a program for continuous improvements.

- Pinpointing the cause (not the symptom) of the problem—avoiding quick fix short-term solutions in favor of longer term elegant solutions.

- Quantifying the effect of the present situation on operations—identifying the cost of present practices and the benefits to be derived through implementation of best practices.

- Developing recommendations as to alternative courses of action to correct the situation—identifying best practices in a program of continuous improvements.

This chapter will:

- Introduce operational review concepts and principles.

- Provide an update of the current status of operational reviews.

- Familiarize the reader with commonly used operational review definitions and terms.

- Identify the purposes and components of operational reviews.

- Increase understanding of the benefits of operational reviews.

- Introduce the phases in which a typical operational review is conducted.

> *Pinpoint the Cause, Not the Symptom,*
> *of the Problem*
> *to Identify the Best Practice*

OPERATIONAL REVIEW CONCEPTS

Organizations have been in existence for thousands of years, some successful and long-lasting, others short-lived. Through the years there have been no clear cut criteria or formula for success. Many business organizations have been successful through such intangible attributes as luck, falling into a market niche, being the first, consumer acceptance, and so on. Other companies, even some using the best available business acumen and methods, have failed miserably.

Identifying, implementing, and maintaining the secrets of success is an elusive target. Banking on what has worked in the past and one's own internal Ouija board are ineffective substitutes for objective internal appraisal and external comparison and analysis—what is called an operational review. Operational reviews are becoming the tool of choice for gathering data related to programs of continuous improvement and to gain competitive advantage.

Operational review can be defined as a process for analyzing internal operations and activities to identify areas for positive improvement in a program of continuous improvement. The process begins with an analysis of existing operations and activities, identifies areas for positive improvement, and then establishes a performance standard upon which the activity can be measured. The goal is to improve each identified activity so that it can be the best possible, and stay that way. The best practice is not always measured in terms of least costs, but more often may be what stakeholders value and expected levels of performance.

> ### The Goal Is to Make Each Activity
> ### the Best Possible—
> ### And Keep It That Way

Operational review processes are directed toward the continuous pursuit of positive improvements, excellence in all activities, and the effective use of best practices. The focal point in achieving these goals is the customer or stakeholder (both internal and external) who establishes performance expectations and is the ultimate judge of resultant quality. A company customer is defined as anyone who has a stake or interest in the ongoing operations of the organization and anyone who is affected by its results (type, quality, and timeliness). Stakeholders include all those who are dependent on the survival of the organization, such as:

- Suppliers/vendors: external
- Owners/shareholders: internal/external
- Management/supervision: internal
- Employees/subcontractors: internal/external
- Customers/end users: external

Operational review results provide the company—owners, management, and employees—with data necessary for effective resource allocation and the strategic focus for the organization. The operational review process provides for those objective measures to determine the success of the company's internal goals, objectives, and detail plans, as well as external and competitive performance measures. Evaluating a company's performance against stakeholder expectations enables the company to pursue its program of continuous improvement on the road to excellence. Effective operational review procedures encompass both internal and external needs.

> *Stakeholder Expectations*
> *Are the Key to Evaluating*
> *the Company's Performance*

Managers or supervisors who are responsible for an operational area have traditionally maintained the operation as they found it; that is they primarily accepted the organization, personnel, and functions they inherited. They were not allowed or did not understand how to make their assigned area of responsibility more efficient. And many times, there were systems in effect (such as overcontrolling bosses) that prevented such positive changes. The purpose of the operational review is to assist managers and operations personnel in looking at their areas of responsibility from an operational viewpoint. This means that operations are viewed with an eye toward whether they can be improved so as to be performed more efficiently, effectively, or economically.

Given today's increasingly varied and competitive economic environment, management places more and more emphasis on the evaluation of the economy, efficiency, and effectiveness of the organization's operations. Managers and employees of an operational area are often too close to operations, too resistant to change, too enmeshed in daily operations, and so on, to review their own operations objectively. Because both internal and external consultants have the fact-finding and diagnostic skills needed to perform such operational reviews, they are frequently asked to do so. In some organizations, a separate unit is formed strictly to perform operational reviews.

Operational reviewing got its start when management stopped being concerned solely with reviewing the reporting of information and started wondering why a transaction was made in the first place and whether there was a better way to do it. Operational review is the process whereby the reviewer determines whether members of management are using the resources entrusted to them in the most economical and efficient manner, to achieve the most effective results of operations.

> *Why Was the Transaction*
> *Made in the First Place*
> *and Is There a Better Way?*

What are some of the reasons an operational review should be performed? The focus and scope of operations in both the public and private sectors have changed in recent years. Management has increased demands for more relevant information on the conduct of its operations and related results than can be found in strictly financial data. Both business and government management seek more information with which to judge the quality of operations and make operational improvements. That is why operational review techniques are needed to evaluate the effectiveness and efficiency of operations.

WHY BUSINESSES ARE IN EXISTENCE

Before even thinking about performing an operational review of an organization, it is necessary to determine why the organization is in existence. When clients are asked this question, invariably the answer is to make money. Although this is partly true, there are really only two reasons for a business entity to exist:

1. *The customer service business.* To provide goods and services to satisfy desired customers, so that they will continue to use the business's goods and services and refer it to others. An organizational philosophy that correlates with this goal that has been found to be successful is "to provide the highest quality products and service at the least possible cost."

2. *The cash conversion business.* To create desired goods and services so that the investment in the business is as quickly converted to cash as possible, with the resultant cash-in exceeding the cash-out (net profits or positive return on investment). The correlating philosophy to this goal can be stated as follows: "To achieve desired business results using the most efficient methods so that the organization can optimize the use of limited resources."

This means staying in business for the long term to serve customers and grow and prosper. A starting point for establishing operational review measurement criteria is to decide which businesses the organization is really in (such as the two above) so that operational efficiencies and effectiveness can be compared to such overall organizational criteria.

> *Being in the Customer Service*
> *and Cash Conversion Businesses*
> *Enables the Company to Make Money*
> *and to Survive*

BUSINESSES A COMPANY IS NOT IN

Once short-term thinking is eliminated, managers realize they are not in the following businesses and decision making becomes simpler:

- *Sales business.* Making sales that cannot be collected profitably (sales are not profits until the cash is received and all the costs of the sale are less than the amount collected) creates only numerical growth.

- *Customer order backlog business.* Logging customer orders is a paperwork process to impress internal management and outside shareholders. Unless this backlog can be converted into a timely sale and collection, there is only a future promise, which may never materialize.

- *Accounts receivable business.* Get the cash as quickly as possible, not the promise to pay. But remember, customers are the company's business; keeping them in business is keeping the company in business. Normally the company has already put out its cash to vendors and/or into inventory. It may even be desirable to get out of the accounts receivable business altogether. This is particularly true for small sales where the amount of the sale is less than the cost of billing and collections or where major customers (e.g., 20 percent of all customers equal 80 percent of total sales) are willing to pay at the time of shipping or receipt as part of price negotiations.

- *Inventory business.* Inventory does not equal sales. Keep inventories to a minimum (zero if possible). Procure raw materials from vendors only as needed, produce for real customer orders based on agreed-upon delivery dates, maximize work-in-process throughput, and ship directly from production when the customer needs the product. To accomplish these inventory goals, it is necessary to develop an effective organizational life stream that includes the company's vendors, employees, and customers.

- *Property, plant, and equipment business.* Maintain at a minimum: be efficient. Idle plant/equipment causes anxiety and results in inefficient use. If it is there, it will be used. Plan for the normal (or small valleys) not for the maximum (or large peaks); network to out-source for additional capacity and in-source for times of excess capacity.

- *Employment business.* Get by with the least number of employees possible. Never hire an additional employee unless absolutely necessary; learn how to cross train and transfer good employees. Not only do people cost ongoing salaries and fringe benefits, but they also need to be paid attention, which results in organization building.

- *Management and administration business.* The more an organization has, the more difficult it becomes to manage its business. It is easier to work with less and be able to control operations than to spend time managing the managers. So much of management becomes getting in the way of those it is supposed to manage and meeting with other managers to discuss how to do this. Management becomes the promotion for doing.

Knowing the Businesses Not to Be in
Keeps the Company in the Businesses
It Should Be in—
And to Grow and Prosper

If an organization accomplishes both of these goals successfully (paying attention to its business and staying out of the businesses it should not be in), it will more than likely (outside economic factors notwithstanding) grow and prosper through well-satisfied customers and keep itself in the positive cash conversion business in spite of itself.

Of course, a company also has to stay out of the numbers business—that is, looking at short-term reporting criteria such as the amount of sales, backlog, locations, employees, and the big devil, "the bottom line," that others judge as success.

The company must decide which of the above factors it wishes to embrace as organizational criteria, which ones it decides not to include as criteria, and which additional criteria to include. These criteria become the overriding conditions upon which the company conducts its operations and against which it is measured.

SOME BASIC BUSINESS PRINCIPLES

Each company must determine the basic principles which guide its operations. These principles become the foundation on which the company bases its desirable operational practices. Examples of such business principles include:

- Produce the best quality product at the least possible cost.

- Set selling prices realistically, so as to sell all the product that can be produced within the constraints of the production facilities.

- Build trusting relationships with critical vendors; keeping them in business is keeping the company in business.

- The company is in the customer service and cash conversion businesses.

- Do not spend a dollar that does not need to be spent; a dollar not spent is a dollar to the bottom line. Control costs effectively; there is more to be made here than increased sales.

- Manage the company; do not let it manage the managers. Provide guidance and direction, not crises.

- Identify the company's customers and develop marketing and sales plans with the customers in mind. Produce for the company's customers, not for inventory. Serve the customers by providing what they need, not by selling them what the company produces.

- Do not hire employees unless they are absolutely needed; and only when they multiple the company's effectiveness so that the company makes more from them than if they did it themselves.

- Keep property, plant, and equipment to the minimum necessary to maintain customer demand.

- Plan for the realistic, but develop contingency plans for the positive unexpected.

> ### *Basic Business Principles*
> ### *Guide the Company's Operations*

There seems to be an organizational trend toward empire building, particularly from the top, and the power and control that comes with it. Even with present movements toward downsizing, restructuring, reengineering, and so on, with their emphasis on getting by with less people and resources, those in power are trying to hold onto unnecessary empires of people and budget allocated resources. While management will agreeably reduce another manager's empire, there is considerable resistance when it comes to reducing the size of their own area. In many instances, even with short-term remedies at people reductions, there still remain unnecessary (non-value-added) individuals and layers of organizational hierarchy. Operational review principles, with its basic principle of doing the right thing, assists in building economic, efficient, and effective organizations, and maintaining them properly at all times using the correct techniques (best practices) for the situation. Operational review techniques assist the company in identifying its critical problem areas and then in treating the cause of the problems, not merely the symptoms of the problems. With sensible business principles as the hallmark for the company's operational criteria, the company can set a clear direction for positive movement and avoid merely improving poor practices. Clear business principles that make sense to all levels of the organization allow the company to identify and develop the proper organizational criteria. In this manner, everyone in the organization is moving in the same desired direction.

CRITERIA FOR ORGANIZATIONAL GROWTH

An organization may choose to implement numerous criteria in its program of continuous improvements leading toward organizational growth. As part of conducting an operational review, the reviewer must be aware of these criteria to be successful in addressing the company's desired direction, in total or by business segment or function. Some of these criteria include:

- Cost reductions
- Price increases
- Sales volume increases
- New market expansion

- New distribution channels

- Market share increases in existing markets

- Selling or closing a losing operation or location

- Acquire another company, division, operation, or product

- Developing a new product or service

- Efficiency or productivity improvements

- Non–value-added activities eliminated

- Making employees responsible

- Organizational structure revisions

Cost Reductions

Many times, costs can be reduced or eliminated without any appreciable diminishment of the organization's efficiency or effectiveness. These cost reductions should be aggressively pursued. Other times, management is strictly looking at short-term cost reductions to puff up the company's profitability. These cost reductions should be avoided because they typically only produce short-term gain for long-term pain. Remember the principle that a dollar of cost reduction produces a dollar increase to the bottom line net profits, but use this principle effectively.

Price Increases

Company management may decide at any time to increase the prices charged to customers for their goods and services. Such price increases may be justified in the marketplace (and part of a strategic plan) or just management's desire to increase revenues (hoping everything else stays the same). In this situation, a dollar increase in revenues will not produce a dollar increase in net profits. The best that can be achieved is the net profit margin of this additional sale (sales dollars less costs = net profit per sale). It is possible that if the costs of this additional sale exceed the revenues generated, that each additional sale results in a decrease in the bottom line. In addition, such price increases may create external competition that may cause fewer sales or increased costs to make each sale.

Sales Volume Increases

Part of the company's strategic plan may be to increase the level of sales to customers, both present and potential. It is usually easier to increase sales volumes with present customers than to prospect continually for new customers. If the company has been operating efficiently, their sales personnel should be close to its customers. They should know what each customer has purchased in the past, the sales trends over a period of time by product and/or product line, what their current and future needs are, whether the company has been making an adequate profit on its sales to the customer, and so on. If such things are not known about the customer, it may be an indication of poor sales practices and a performance gap between present practices and more desirable results. Part of the company's strategic plan should be to earmark specific present customers for increased sales: what products to sell to them, at what price and what amount, and how to sell to them.

The company may also decide to increase their sales volume to potential new customers. Again, such sales plans should be incorporated into the company's organizational plan. Overreliance on sales to new customers may be an indication of ineffective sales and customer service procedures with existing customers as well as costly sales practices for new customers.

Sales volume increases should always be part of overall company planning and integrated with other organizational functions such as sales and marketing, engineering, manufacturing, accounting, and so on.

New Market Expansion

As part of the organizational plan, the company may decide to expand its operations into new markets. It may decide to expand on a local basis, nationally, or internationally. It could decide to introduce new products, enhance present products, or expand the sales of its products into new markets. Each of these decisions should be part of an organized plan with its own criteria and scheme as to how to achieve such results and the method for evaluating successful progress. Such expansion may not always be positive. Management must be sure that this is the best course.

New Distribution Channels

As a criterion for organizational growth, company management may decide to develop additional channels for marketing and distributing their products.

For instance, if a company has traditionally sold its products directly to customers through their own internal sales force, it may decide to use outside sales groups, sales brokers, sales representatives, and the like. Such arrangements might supplement or reinforce their inside sales efforts or might replace the internal sales force in whole or in part. The company might also decide to distribute its products via additional distribution channels such as becoming an original equipment manufacturer (OEM), wholesaler, direct retailer, mail order house, internet seller, direct customer seller, and so on.

Market Share Increase in Existing Markets

The organizational plan may include specific steps designed to increase the company's market share in existing markets. The plan may include desired results by product line, product, or customer. Specific results should be clearly spelled out and those responsible for successful completion of each work step in the plan should be identified. The plan should be realistic and practical, with achievable results within the organization's methods of operations.

Selling or Closing a Losing Operation or Location

Sometimes an operation (product line, product, customer, etc.) or a plant or office location is deemed to be too costly in relation to the value (income or cost saving) added to the company. With the advisable information, company management can arrive at the proper decision to retrench. Without such an adequate information base, management may come to the opposite conclusion—to allocate more resources into the operation or location. In this instance, management would be more than likely allocating additional expenditures to a losing proposition. Management could establish a criteria of retrenchment, a criteria of developing an adequate information system, or both. The object of retrenchment is normally to reduce overall expenses while increasing net income, the bottom line. However, retrenchment will also decrease gross sales or income which may not be desirable to all of the stakeholders (e.g., owners or shareholders).

Acquire Another Company, Division, Operation, or Product

Company management may decide that the quickest method for reaching a desired result (such as increased sales, reduced costs, increased net income) is through acquisition. This could be accomplished by acquiring another company, a division of another company, a specific operation (e.g., research and development, information technology), a product line or product (e.g., a food company acquiring a complementary product), and so on. Such acquisitions should be considered using the concept of leverage. The resultant return on investment should exceed the cost of the investment. For instance, if the cost of the capital to make the acquisition is six percent, than the expected (and real) return on the investment should be sufficiently greater than six percent (e.g., over 10 percent) to cover the potential risk involved. Obtaining organizational growth through acquisition is not always positive as the company may acquire another's problems or may lack the expertise to take full advantage of the acquisition.

Developing a New Product or Service

Company management may decide that the best method for achieving organizational growth or reaching a specific result is to develop a new product or service. To do this effectively, the company should have a real vision of its marketplace, its existing products, its customer's requirements, the desired need for the new product, its effect on existing products, and so on. The decision to develop and market a new product should be based on integrated decisions between the company's major functions such as sales, marketing, engineering, manufacturing, accounting, and so on.

Efficiency or Productivity Improvements

The ability either to operate more efficiently at less cost or increase productivity at the same (or less) cost may also be a workable approach to reaching a company's organizational growth desired results. A dollar of costs saved (all other factors remaining the same) will produce an additional dollar of earnings to the bottom line. Increasing productivity produces more of the product or service at relatively the same cost, resulting in less cost per product or service produced. Both of these approaches can be implemented and controlled by internal management and operations personnel. There is usually more to be gained in the bottom line through cost efficiencies and productivity improvements than through the various methods of revenue or sales enhancements discussed above. Remember that a dollar in sales increase does not add a dollar to the bottom line, only the incremental amount of net income generated by the additional sale which could be a loss. Cost efficiencies and productivity improvements are two of the major areas to be considered in an operational review as part of the company's program of continuous improvements and best practices.

Non–Value-Added Activities Eliminated

Functions or activities which add no value to the product or service should be eliminated. As part of the operational review, such functions or activities should be identified. Company management should be able to identify those areas earmarked for elimination. For instance, they may identify all unnecessary quality control inspections or the preparation of purchase orders. They may express the desirability of eliminating an entire function, such as raw material storekeeping or credit and collections. This establishes the focus for those areas to be considered in the operational review. The review team can identify best practices and the most efficient methods for eliminating such functions or activities. They can also consider the resultant ramifications to remaining operations after the reduction or elimination of these non–value-added functions or activities. Typically, there is a multiplier effect, that is the elimination or reduction of one activity results in similar reductions or elimination of other activities.

Making Employees Responsible

Make employees responsible for meeting company expectations and results through motivating self-disciplined behavior. With an effective monitoring system, this eliminates the need for management personnel to exist mainly for policing and controlling these individuals with minimal value-added activities. Use of operating systems that make sense to the workers (where they have had input in developing such systems), who use them within a working together atmosphere (rather than a working for atmosphere) will increase productivity to the extent that fewer employees overall are needed. The trick is not to bring on unnecessary personnel as the company grows, so that the company is never in a position to have to cut back drastically. Many times a company penalizes the individuals being downsized or laid off for something out of their control. Operational reviews help to keep the company in focus regarding the types and levels of personnel required at any time.

Organizational Structure Revisions

There are many techniques for building an organization structure which are not dependent on the typical top to bottom military model that is based on policing and controlling those reporting to each higher level. Some other techniques for organizational structure include participative management, shared management, team management, self-motivated disciplined behavior (no manager), coaching and facilitative supports, and so on. There is no right answer for all situations. The company must learn to use a combination of these techniques as they fit the particular situation. The operational review process allows the company to achieve the best organizational structure overall, as well as within each function and activity. Operational review principles emphasize controlling results, not people; fixing the cause, not the blame; and doing the right job right, not just doing the job right.

> ### *The Operational Review*
> ### *Must Focus on*
> ### *the Company's Direction*

MENTAL MODELS AND BELIEF SYSTEMS

Many organizations operate on the basis of prevalent mental models or belief systems, usually emanating from past and present top management. These mental models and belief systems have an overriding effect on the conditions with which operations within the company are carried out. They can help to produce a helpful working environment or atmosphere or a hindering one. In effect, such mental models become performance drivers—those elements within the organization that shape the direction of how employees will perform their functions. Examples of such mental models and belief systems include:

- Hard work and doing what you are told are the keys to success for the individual and the company.

- The obedient child in the company survives and is promoted, while the rebellious child is let go or leaves the company.

- Only managers can make decisions.

- Power rises to the top—and stays there.

- Employees need to be watched to do their jobs.

- Power and control over employees is necessary to get results.

- Managers are responsible, employees are basically irresponsible.

- Those at the top of the organization know what they are doing.

- All functions should be organized in the same manner.

- Higher levels of organization ensure that lower levels do their jobs.

- Policing and control over employees ensures their compliance.

- All employees are interchangeable.

- Doing the job right is more important than doing the right job.

- Control the people, control the results.

- Organizational position is more important than being right.

- Top management has the right to set all policies and procedures.

- Managers create results. Employees do the job.

- Organizational hierarchies ensure that things get done.

- Employees cannot be trusted on their own.

- You cannot run a business without the proper organizational structure.

- Managers know more than employees.

- Managers have a right to be obnoxious.

- Management is the enemy.

- Each function needs its own organizational structure.

- The more employees reporting to you (and the larger your budget), the more important you are within the organization.

The accurate identification of organizational mental models, belief systems, and performance drivers is extremely important in the company's operating strategy. If these things are not changed, best practice changes will change only the system and not company results.

> *Mental Model Changes*
> *Create Best Practice Changes*

ORGANIZATIONAL CRITERIA EXAMPLE

As previously discussed, the first step in successful operational review planning is to define the company's desired criteria for results as related to their reasons for existence, basic business principles, mental models, belief systems, performance drivers, and so on. These organizational criteria typically encompass the company as an entity as well as its major functions. An example of such an organizational results criteria structure is:

Organization-Wide Criteria

- Operate all activities in the most economical, efficient, and effective manner possible.

- Provide the highest quality products to our customers at the least possible cost.

- Satisfy our customers so that they will continue to use the company's products and refer the company to others.

- Convert the cash invested in the business as quickly as possible so that the resultant cash in exceeds the cash out to the greatest extent possible.

- Achieve desired results using the most efficient methods so that the company can optimize the use of limited resources.

- Maximize net profits without sacrificing quality of operations, customer service, or cash requirements.

Sales Function

- Make sales to the right customers that can be collected profitably.

- Develop realistic sales forecasts that result in a present or future real customer order.

- Sell those products as determined by management to the right customers, at the right time, in the right quantities.

- Actual customer sales should directly correlate with management's long- and short-term plans.

- Sales efforts, and corresponding compensation systems, should reinforce the goals of the company.

- Customer sales should be integrated with other functions of the company, such as manufacturing, engineering, accounting, purchasing, and so on.

Manufacturing

- Operate in the most efficient manner with the most economical costs.

- Integrate manufacturing processes with sales efforts and customer requirements.

- Manufacture in the most timely manner considering processes such as customer order entry, timely throughput, and customer delivery.

- Increase productivity of all manufacturing operations on an ongoing basis.

- Eliminate, reduce, or improve all facets of the manufacturing operation including activities such as receiving, inventory control, production control, storeroom operations, quality control, supervision and management, packing and shipping, maintenance, and so on.

- Minimize the amount of resources such as personnel, facilities, and equipment that are allocated to the manufacturing process.

Personnel

- Provide only those personnel functions which are absolutely required as value-added activities.

- Maintain the levels of personnel at the minimum required to achieve results in each functional area.

- Provide personnel functions such as hiring, training, evaluation, and firing in the most efficient and economical manner possible.

- Develop an organizational structure that organizes each function in the most efficient manner for their purposes.

- Minimize the hiring of new employees by using methods such as cross training and interdepartmental transfers and other best practices.

- Implement compensation systems that provide for effective employee motivation and the achievement of company goals.

Purchasing

- Purchase only those items where economies can be gained through a system of central purchasing.

- Implement direct purchase systems for those items that the purchasing function does not need to process, such as low dollar purchases and repetitive purchases.

- Simplify systems so that the cost of purchasing is the lowest possible.

- Effectively negotiate with vendors so that the company obtains the right materials at the right time at the right quality at the right price.

- Maintain a vendor analysis system so that vendor performance can be objectively evaluated.

- Develop effective computerized techniques for economic processing, adequate controls, and reliability.

Accounting

- Analyze the necessity of each of the accounting functions and related activities, such as accounts receivable, accounts payable, payroll, budgeting, and general ledger.

- Operate each of the accounting functions in the most economical manner.

- Implement effective procedures that result in the accounting functions becoming more analytical than mechanical.

- Develop computerized procedures that integrate accounting purposes with operating requirements.

- Develop reporting systems that provide management with the necessary operating data and indicators that can be generated from accounting data.

- Eliminate or reduce all unnecessary accounting operations that provide no value-added incentives.

> *Organizational Criteria*
> *Focus Operational Review Criteria*

The development of such organizational and functional criteria provides the basis on which to focus the operational review and to evaluate current practices, identify critical problem areas, analyze detailed operations, identify best practices, and implement corrective solutions in a program of continuous improvements. Without the definition and communication of such organizational criteria, the company's operational review efforts may only succeed in developing best practices for functions and activities that in themselves are bad practices. The operational review process should not be an effort to improve bad practices but to develop procedures which bring best practices into the organization. Through the operational review process, operating functions and activities are evaluated as to their necessity as related to the achievement of organizational goals and objectives. If a function or activity is not necessary, it should be eliminated. If it is needed, it should be considered for improvement, looking for the best present practice, and continually analyzed in the company's program of continuous improvements. Through this process, the company starts to develop itself as a learning organization, with individuals responsible for achieving their own results. The operational review process becomes an ongoing integral tool, allowing the company to do things the right way and to keep doing them that way.

ECONOMY, EFFICIENCY, AND EFFECTIVENESS

Operational review procedures embrace the concept of conducting operations for economy, efficiency, and effectiveness. The following is a brief description of the "three Es of operational reviews."

1. *Economy* (or the cost of operations). Is the organization carrying out its responsibilities in the most economical manner through due con-

servation of its resources? In appraising the economy of operations and related allocation and use of resources, the reviewer may consider whether the organization is:

- Following sound purchasing practices

- Overstaffed as related to performing necessary functions

- Allowing excess materials to be on hand

- Using more expensive equipment than necessary

- Avoiding the waste of resources

2. *Efficiency* (or methods of operations). Is the organization carrying out its responsibilities with the minimum expenditure of effort? Examples of operational inefficiencies to be aware of include:

- Improper use of manual and computerized procedures

- Inefficient paperwork flow

- Inefficient operating systems and procedures

- Cumbersome organizational hierarchy and/or communication patterns

- Duplication of effort

- Unnecessary work steps

Note that economy and efficiency are both relative terms, and it is not possible to determine whether the area under review has reached the maximum practicable level of either. However, the reviewer and operations personnel are continually looking for best practices in a program of continuous improvements. Economy and efficiency are continually being appraised and improved upon; they are not put in place based on the operational review and then ignored.

Economy and efficiency are concerned with achieving the optimum balance between costs and results. In performing this part of the review, the reviewer evaluates cost minimization, emphasizing reduction of costs, but not to the point where results are not accomplished. In addition, productivity maximization may be analyzed, but not to the point where the costs become excessive. In evaluating economy and efficiency, the reviewer analyzes the use of resources: people, facilities, equipment, supplies, and money. For example, the reviewer might analyze the following:

- Allocation of responsibilities and authority within the organizational structure

- Physical deployment of distribution of resources

- Scheduling of resources: when people work, when facilities are used

- Segmentation of tasks into logical groupings

- Match between skill level, capacity, performance capability, and so on, and the way a resource is used

- Prices paid

- Charges levied

- Rate at which tasks are performed

- Number of tasks completed

Within the economy and efficiency concept, the reviewer does not ask whether the function is worthwhile in terms of what it accomplishes. The reviewer accepts that the function exists and asks whether that is the most economical and efficient way to get it done. Results are considered as part of the review of effectiveness.

3. *Effectiveness* (or results of operations). Is the organization achieving results or benefits based on stated goals and objectives or some other measurable criteria? The review of the results of operations includes:

   - Appraisal of the organizational planning system as to its development of realistic goals, objectives, and detail plans

   - Assessment of the adequacy of management's system for measuring effectiveness

   - Determination of the extent to which results are achieved

   - Identification of factors inhibiting satisfactory performance of results.

Although it is management's continuing responsibility to assess the results of operations, its objectives and measurement criteria are not always clearly defined. Without such clarification, the reviewer cannot meaningfully evaluate the results of operations. If management has not done so prior to starting the operational review, the reviewer should work with management to:

- State the objectives

- Establish measurement criteria

- Establish methods for accumulating the data necessary to measure achievement of operational results.

Effectiveness is concerned with results and accomplishments achieved and benefits provided. In evaluating the effectiveness of operations, the reviewer asks whether the activity is achieving its ultimate intended purpose. Analysis is qualitative rather then quantitative.

The relationship of economy and efficiency and their impact on results can be seen as a seesaw; that is, there is an attempt to balance them to achieve just the right amount of each. In a perfectly balanced situation, the cost of operations would be maintained at the lowest possible level without sacrificing efficiency (or the methods of operations) and effectiveness (or the results of operations), thus effecting economy. At the same time, the methods of operations would be performed at the least possible cost without sacrificing results, thus producing efficiency. Is it clear, then, why economy and efficiency are normally reviewed together as part of the operational review procedure? The three Es—economy, efficiency, and effectiveness—as well as the seesaw effect between economy and efficiency, are shown in Exhibit 1.1.

Economy, Efficiency, and
Effectiveness
(and Making Money)
Is Everyone's Business

EXHIBIT 1.1   The Operational Review Triangle: The Three Es: Economy, Efficiency, and Effectiveness

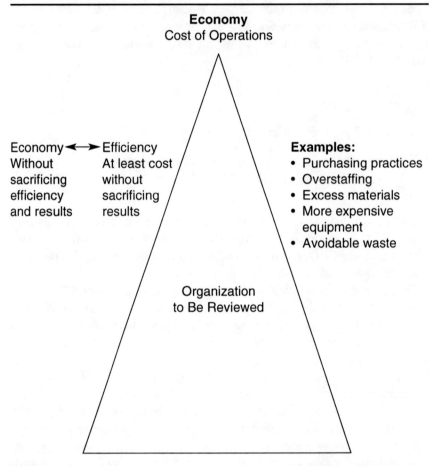

Economy
Cost of Operations

Economy ◄──► Efficiency
Without   At least cost
sacrificing   without
efficiency   sacrificing
and results   results

Examples:
• Purchasing practices
• Overstaffing
• Excess materials
• More expensive
  equipment
• Avoidable waste

Organization
to Be Reviewed

Efficiency
Methods of Operation

Examples:
• Manual vs. EDP
• Paperwork flow
• Systems and procedures
• Organizational hierarchy
  and communication
• Duplication of efforts
• Unnecessary work steps

Effectiveness
Results of Operations

Examples:
• Production/service
  provided
• Planning system:
  goals, objectives,
  and detail plans
• Results achieved
• Expectations

DEFINITION

Operational review is a widely used term encompassing many aspects and techniques. However, no uniform, commonly recognized definition has been unanimously accepted.

The definitions that have been given for operational reviews include the following:

1. An extension of the audit function into all operations of a business.

2. The application of internal auditing to operations rather than financial controls.

3. The identification of opportunities for greater efficiency and economy, or to improve effectiveness in carrying out operational procedures.

4. A control technique for evaluating the effectiveness of operating procedures.

5. Nothing more than a review of controls, now including nonfinancial controls.

6. Review of activities other than those pertaining to examination of financial data.

7. Review technique that involves evaluating the efficiency and economy with which resources are managed and consumed.

8. Review of operations with a management viewpoint.

9. Review of operations made for internal management, not for external third parties, with the results circulated internally rather than externally.

10. Combination of economy, efficiency, and effectiveness, or program results evaluation.

Combining these definitions, it could be said that operational review is a review of operations performed from a management viewpoint to evaluate the economy, efficiency, and effectiveness of any and all operations, limited only by management's desires.

> *Operational Review*
> *Evaluates Economy,*
> *Efficiency, and Effectiveness*
> *from a Management Viewpoint*

TERMS

In recent years various terms have been used interchangeably with operational review to describe this approach. Examples include:

1. Program review

2. Management review

3. Performance review

4. Performance review and evaluation

5. Departmental review

6. Nonfinancial audit

7. Compliance review

8. Cost-benefit analysis

9. Economy and efficiency evaluation

10. Effectiveness or results evaluation

11. Functional analysis

12. Full scope audit

13. Responsibility review

14. Comprehensive analysis and review

15. Internal benchmarking study

16. Activity-based costing/management review

17. Total quality management (TQM) study

18. Reengineering study

19. Organizational review

20. Value-added study (value-added vs. non–value-added activities)

Although the terms review, analysis, study, and evaluation are generally used to describe these procedures, as in the examples just mentioned, it is often a good idea to avoid the connotation that this is a procedure done by outsiders, which may have a negative impact upon the organization under review. To this end, internal review may be a better term to use with specific organizations. Often, the particular name given to the operational review procedure enhances internal management's trust and willingness to work with the reviewers (either internal or external), which is vital to the success of the operational review.

> ***Operational Review***
> ***Is an Internal Review***
> ***to Help Do Things Best***

FINANCIAL AUDITS VERSUS OPERATIONAL REVIEWS

Among the differences between financial audits and operational reviews, using operational review concepts, is that the reviewer is less concerned with determining whether purchase requisitions, orders, and suppliers' invoices reflect proper approvals, as in a financial audit, but more concerned with such operational aspects as whether:

- The materials were really needed

- Quantities used or purchased were reasonable

- There was avoidable waste and exposure to damage or loss

- Requisitioners exercised undue influence over purchasing by designating sources of purchase.

For example, a typical financial audit step may be to determine whether vendor purchase requisitions and invoices have been properly approved.

However, when looking at the operational aspects of vendor purchases, the reviewer may ask:

- *Were materials really needed?* For example, were materials mistakenly ordered that could not be used owing to changes in production specifications, because the product specifications unit failed to communicate with the purchasing department?

- *Were quantities used or purchased reasonable?* For example, assuming the materials were usable, were goods bought for inventory above calculated safety stock levels because of the fear of incurring a stock-out?

- *Was there avoidable waste and exposure to damage or loss?* For example, were steel components and parts that were susceptible to rust bought and stored in an outside yard, owing to an overcrowded inside storeroom?

- *Did the requisitioner exercise undue influence by stating specific sources or brands?* For example, did the requisitioner specify an IBM microcomputer or a Xerox copier when a less expensive brand would do just as well?

Some of the other differences between a conventional financial audit and an operational review are summarized in Exhibit 1.2.

A Financial Audit
Is Not an Operational Review

WHY PERFORM AN OPERATIONAL REVIEW?

What are some of the reasons an operational review should be performed? The focus and scope of many operations in both the public and private sectors have changed in recent years. Management has increased demands for more relevant information on the conduct of their operations and the related results than can be found solely in financial data. Both business and government management seeks more information with which to judge the quality of operations and make operational improvements. That is why op-

EXHIBIT 1.2 Financial Audit Versus Operational Review

Characteristic	Financial Audit	Operational Review
1. Purpose	Express opinion on financial condition	Analyze and improve methods and performance
2. Scope	Fiscal financial records	Business operations
3. Skills	Accounting	Interdisciplinary
4. Time orientation	To the past	To the future
5. Precision	Absolute	Relative
6. Audience	Stockholders, public	Internal management
7. Necessity	Legally required	At option of management
8. Standards	GAAP, GAAS*	Economy, efficiency, effectiveness
9. Opinion	Required	Not required
10. Audit results	Opinion, financial statement	Recommendations to management
11. Focus	Financial statement presented fairly	Operational positive improvements
12. Viewpoint	Financial	Management
13. Success	Unqualified opinion	Management adoption of recommendations

*GAAP = generally accepted accounting principles;
GAAS = generally accepted auditing standards

erational review techniques are needed to evaluate the effectiveness and efficiency of operations.

Management, with the assistance of others, both internal and external, is being asked more frequently to evaluate an organization's operations. Although this is not a new service for internal management to provide, requests by top management for such specific operational reviews have increased as a result of the greater emphasis on the economy, efficiency, and effectiveness of operations and related results. In many cases, members of operations management do not possess the specific skills necessary for an objective evaluation of those activities reporting to them; they may be too close to the operations or they may be part of the problem. The technical skills that internal and external consultants possess, particularly those of analysis, fact finding, and reporting, make them excellent choices for performing such operational reviews.

An operational review involves a systematic review of an organization's activities in relation to specified objectives. The general purposes of the operational review could be expressed as follows:

- *Assess performance.* To assess performance is to compare the way an organization conducts its activities with (1) objectives established by management, such as organizational policies, standards, goals, objectives, and detail plans, (2) comparisons with other similar functions or individuals within the organization (internal benchmarking), and (3) comparisons with other organizations (external benchmarking).

- *Identify opportunities for improvement.* Increased economy, efficiency, or effectiveness are the broad categories under which most improvements are classified. The reviewer may identify specific opportunities for improvement (best practices) by analyzing interviews with individuals (within or outside the organization), observing operations, reviewing past and current operational data, analyzing transactions, making internal and external comparisons, and exercising professional judgment based on experience with the particular organization or others.

- *Develop recommendations for improvement or further action.* The nature and extent of recommendations developed in the course of operational reviews vary considerably. In many cases, the reviewer may be able to make specific recommendations. In other cases, further study outside the scope of the review may be required. The reviewer should be continually looking for best practices (both internal and external) in a program for continuous improvements. It may seem that operations personnel would be involved in establishing and implementing recommendations. However, in most instances such procedures are set by management, causing operations personnel to resist and often sabotage them and work against their being successful. Organization structure tends to evolve over a period of time; with minimal regard to economy, efficiency, and effectiveness.

In most organizations there are built-in incentives to increase organizational levels; such as budget systems that reward larger organizations and politicking to build empires. It is the reviewer's role to identify such organizational inefficiencies and recommend improvements. However, the reviewers do not put themselves in the position of recommending specific individual cuts. Assuming that the organization's personnel are all good employees (and hiring, orientation, training, and promotion policies and procedures are adequate), the reviewer may recommend achieving desired results with less overall personnel. However, it is then management's responsibility to decide what to do with extraneous personnel, through such measures as departmental transfers, retraining, lateral moves, and so forth. It is usually more desirable to use existing good personnel somewhere else in the organization than to terminate them.

**The Operational Review
Is Performed to
Maintain Organizational Excellence**

SPECIFIC OBJECTIVES

There are many reasons why management might desire to have an operational review of their operations performed, such as those given in the following list. Keep in mind that management may be looking for a single objective (i.e., operational efficiency), a combination of objectives (i.e., least cost but most efficient systems—best practices), or their own specific agenda (i.e., achievement of results on the basis of cost versus benefits).

Financial and Accounting

- Adherence to financial policy
- Performance of accounting procedures
- Procedures performed by individuals with no incompatible functions
- Adequateness of existing audit trail
- Observability of right procedures

Adequacy of Internal Controls

- Accounting controls

  Safeguarding of assets

  Reliability of financial records

  System of authorizations and approvals

  Separation of duties

  Physical controls over assets

- Administrative controls

  Operational efficiency

  Adherence to managerial policies

  Adequacy of management information and reporting

  Employee competency and training

  Quality controls

Procedural Compliance

- Laws and regulations: federal, state, and local
- Adherence to administrative policy
- Performance of authorization and approval
- Evidence of action to achieve stated goals and objectives
- Adherence to long-range/short-term plans
- Achievement of management objectives
- Effective recruiting and training
- Evaluation of organizational policies

Organizational Efficiency

- Clear understanding of responsibilities and authority
- Logical nonconflicting reporting relationships

- Current job/functional descriptions

- Separation of duties

- Productivity maximization (internal benchmarking)

- Staffing levels compared with those of similar organizations (external benchmarking)

- Elimination of non–value-added functions and activities

- The right number of people to do the right job

Operational Results

- Organizational planning: goals, objectives, and detail plans

- Detail plan development and implementation; considering alternatives, constraints, cost/benefit, and resource allocation

- Evaluation of operational results

  Appropriateness of measurement criteria

  Feedback on success or failure

  Adjustment of goals, objectives, strategies

- Doing the right job, the right way, at the right time

**The Operational Review
Ensures Doing
the Right Job, the Right Way,
at the Right Time**

SPECIFIC PURPOSES

In conducting an operational review, the reviewer should be aware of the purpose for the review. Prior to the start of the operational review, the reviewer should communicate clearly his or her understanding of the purpose(s) to appropriate management personnel and the purpose(s) should be mutually agreed upon from the start. The purpose may be one or more of the following seven listed items:

1. To review and evaluate the adequacy of the accounting system and related internal accounting controls (including both accounting and administrative controls).

2. To analyze systems and controls, as related to internal controls, functional operations, and legal compliance.

3. To analyze the capability to accomplish agreed-upon stated goals, objectives, and results in management's approved plan.

4. To compare actual accomplishments/results with the goals and objectives established in management's plan for the period; and to determine reasons that established goals and objectives were not met.

5. To analyze and explain cost overruns or high unit costs for each function/activity for which such data can be quantified.

6. To assess and evaluate compliance with federal, state, and local laws and regulations; ensuring at least minimal compliance.

7. To identify and report deficiencies and areas for improvement and to provide technical assistance and follow-up where necessary.

BENEFITS OF OPERATIONAL REVIEWS

Depending on its scope, an operational review can be of significant benefit to top management and staff, in some or all of the following 13 ways:

1. *Identifying problem areas, related causes, and alternatives for improvement.* This is a major purpose of operational reviews. Although often aware of a problem, management cannot always define its dimensions exactly. The reviewer's third party objective viewpoint helps to achieve the proper focus on operational problems. To define a problem in some instances, the reviewer need merely talk to operations personnel and then share their viewpoints with management. Keep in mind that people in operations are usually more aware of problems and their causes than management personnel.

The reviewer's role is also to identify the actual causes (not the symptoms or believed causes) of problems, which may be the result of management policy or actions. Finally, the reviewer must formulate realistic, practical solutions to these problems. This is where the reviewer's experience in working with numerous other departments and/or organizations is valuable. Remember to always look for best practices (internal or external) that can be practically implemented in your situation as part of a program of continuous improvement. A good rule for reviewers to follow is not to recommend any course of corrective action that they could not assist in implementing.

2. *Locating opportunities for eliminating waste and inefficiency; that is, cost reduction.* Keep in mind that each dollar of cost reduction (without sacrificing efficiency or effectiveness) contributes dollar-for-dollar to the bottom line. Cost reduction is a significant element in operational reviews. However, be wary of short-term cost reductions causing long-term problems (for instance, downsizing of operations and/or personnel when business falls off). It is the role of the reviewer to assist the company to operate at the lowest possible cost in relationship to adequate plans. Costs should always be at the correct level, and when costs need to be cut, proper decisions are made so as not to adversely impact operations. This is in contrast to typical cost cutting across the board, which not only constricts all operations, but also fails to provide for the necessary resources for those operations which actually need increased funds.

3. *Locating opportunities to increase revenues, that is, income improvement.* Increasing revenues also has an effect on the bottom line, yet only to the extent of profit margins for this additional amount of revenue. Increasing revenues may, in fact, be detrimental in terms of profits and operating efficiencies (both short term and long term). Often revenues or sales are increased to present a more favorable sales picture in the short term or to fill plant or service capacity, rather than on the basis of sound planning. Note that in most organizations a greater amount of resources and emphasis is devoted to revenue improvement than to cost economies, even though effective cost cutting offers greater rewards.

4. *Identifying undefined organizational goals, objectives, policies, and procedures.* It would be nice to think that all organizations are doing

effective long-term and short-term planning. However, in reality this is usually more the exception than the rule. Therefore, the reviewer will have to assist management in recognizing undefined goals, objectives, and detailed plans and developing such plans prior to starting the operational review. Without defined plans, there are no yardsticks or milestones against which to measure the organization's effectiveness.

5. *Identifying criteria for measuring the achievement of organizational goals.* As mentioned previously and there is great likelihood that plans and related goals and objectives do not exist and even when they do, there may not be appropriate criteria for measuring their achievement, thus requiring the reviewer to assist management in the development of such criteria.

6. *Recommending improvement in policies, procedures, and organizational structure.* The reviewer may find instances in which the cause of the problem lies with existing policies or procedures. Policies should be set by senior management and relate to the rules by which the organization conducts its business (e.g., service to the customer). However, many times either such policies get in the way of operations personnel performing their functions (e.g., excessive controls and paperwork to process a customer credit) or insufficient authority is delegated to allow them to be most effective (e.g., sending a service representative to the customer to investigate a complaint). In these instances, the policies may be wrong and in need of correction.

Procedures are the ways in which functions are performed based on stated policies. As such procedures refer to operations, it might seem that operations personnel would be involved in establishing and implementing them. However, in most instances, procedures are set by management, causing operations personnel to resist them (and many times sabotage them) and work against their success. Organizational structure tends to evolve over a period of time, with minimal regard to economy, efficiency, or effectiveness. In most organizations there are built-in incentives to increase organizational levels, such as budget systems that reward the growth of organizations and encourage politicking to build empires. It is the reviewer's role to identify such organizational inefficiencies and to recommend improvements. However, when reviewers do this, they do not recommend specific individual cuts. Assuming that the organization's personnel are all good employees (and that hiring, orientation, training, and promotion procedures are adequate), the reviewer may recommend achieving desired results with fewer overall personnel. It is then management's responsibility to decide what to do with extraneous personnel, possibly effecting departmental transfers, retraining, lateral moves, and so on. It is usually more desirable to use existing good personnel elsewhere in the organization than to terminate them. In most organizations that have a policy of termination, their personnel departments are hiring at the same time, often for similar positions.

7. *Providing checks on performance by individuals and by organizational units.* Assuming that proper results have been defined for individuals and work units, it is the reviewer's responsibility to ensure that adequate checks or measurement criteria have been established to monitor progress toward their achievement.

8. *Reviewing compliance with legal requirements and organizational goals, objectives, policies, and procedures.* The reviewer makes sure that the organization complies with the laws and internal rules under which it performs its functions. If there is a lack of compliance, the reviewer defines the consequences.

9. *Testing for existence of unauthorized, fraudulent, or otherwise irregular acts.* Such testing is normally a requirement for operational reviews, particularly where such acts have an adverse effect on operations.

10. *Assessing management information and control systems.* The reviewer will address a number of concerns in this area:

    - Are such reporting systems adequate to provide management and operations personnel with the information necessary to effectively operate all aspects of the organization?

    - Is the level of detail commensurate to the level of operations (i.e., more detail at lower levels; less detail at higher levels)?

    - Is information lacking that should be present?

    - Are all key indicators being considered (e.g., units shipped as well as items rejected and returned)?

11. *Identifying possible trouble spots in future operations.* Many times the reviewer senses a future problem based on troubles in the past. For instance, problems with past computer conversions may indicate future troubles with an extensive computer processing upgrade.

12. *Providing an additional channel of communication between operating levels and top management.* In many organizations there is a clear (or unclear) separation between management and operations— management makes the decisions and operations personnel carry them out. One of the most important benefits of the operational review is the reviewer's ability to convey operational concerns to management in those instances when such concerns are not being communicated on an ongoing basis.

13. *Providing an independent, objective evaluation of operations.* Both management and operations personnel are often too close to what is going on within their own operations to evaluate their results effectively. The independent operational reviewer can do this objectively, pointing out those areas in need of improvement as well as those that are being performed well.

Operational Review Benefits
Help to Sell the Review

OPERATIONAL REVIEW PHASES

Operational reviews consist basically of gathering information, making evaluations, and developing recommendations where appropriate. An operational review is essentially the evaluation of an activity for potential improvement. Management has the primary responsibility for proper planning, conduct, and control of activities. Thus, review and evaluation of the way management itself plans, conducts, and controls the activities become a major consideration and focal point in the conduct of the review. In addition, the review includes analyzing results and being alert to problems. These also provide insights into the effectiveness of management and the potential for improvements.

The five phases through which an operational review progresses are:

1. Planning

2. Work programs

3. Field work

4. Development of findings and recommendations

5. Reporting

The operational reviewer may perform two types of reviews: preliminary and in-depth. Both types include all five phases. The difference between the two is the degree of emphasis, the specific techniques chosen, and the objectives of a particular phase.

In the preliminary review, for example, field work may consist of limited transaction testing and interviewing, and the report may be a briefing to management. In an in-depth review, field work may consist of detailed examination, using techniques such as work measurement, workload analysis, cost-benefit analysis, and so on, and the report may be formally written, with wider distribution. The type and objectives of the review to be performed will determine the nature of the work to be done.

Planning

The reviewer obtains general information about the kinds of activities performed, the general nature of those activities and their relative importance, and other general information to help plan the early portions of the review.

Work Programs

The reviewer prepares the operational review work program for the preliminary review of those activities selected for review in the planning phase. Well-constructed work programs are essential for conducting efficient and effective operational reviews. Such programs must be individualized for each situation, and each work step must state clearly the work to be done and why.

Field Work

The reviewer analyzes operations to determine the effectiveness of management and related controls. Such functions and controls are tested in actual operation, with particular emphasis on areas that are difficult to control and have high potential for weakness. The purpose of this phase is to determine whether a situation needs improvement, whether it is significant, and what should be done about it.

Development of Findings and Recommendations

Based on the significant areas identified during the field work phase, specific findings are developed according to the following attributes:

- Condition: What did you find?
- Criteria: What should it be?
- Effect: What is the impact on operations?
- Cause: Why did it happen?
- Recommendation: What needs to be done to correct the situation (based on present best practices, and always subject to change)?

Reporting

The reviewer prepares the report based on the results of the review in order to bring these results to the attention of those having an interest in, or responsibility for, the findings. In reality, the majority of findings, if not all, should have been reported to management with remedial action already being taken or completed prior to the formal report. The report becomes a summary of the results of the review.

> *Operational Review Phases*
> *Cover All of the Bases*

WHAT FUNCTIONS TO REVIEW

The most critical question for an organization to answer is what function(s) to include in the operational review. Where shall it review? Does it perform the operational review for all functions of the organization or only for selected areas? A good starting point is to list the organization's major functions, to check off those where operational review would be most helpful, and then to prioritize each function as to its criticalness and/or the desired order of review. Exhibit 1.3 is a sample checklist.

One way to decide which functions to review is to determine how critical each function is to the overall organizational operation. For instance, for a manufacturing business, the most critical area may be the inventory or production control functions. For a service-oriented concern, where personnel

EXHIBIT 1.3   Checklist of Major Organizational Functions

Board of Directors

Management
Organizational
Departmental
Reporting and control

Planning Systems

Organizational
Departmental
Detail planning

Personnel

Hiring procedures
Evaluation procedures
Staffing levels
Payroll procedures

Accounting

Assets
Liabilities
Budget procedures
Payroll and labor distribution
Accounts payable
Accounts receivable
Billing and collections
Financial reporting

Cost accounting procedures
Borrowing and debt outstanding
General ledger and journal entry
system

Computer Processing

Systems design and analysis
Programming and software
development
Equipment and hardware
Operating procedures
Data control
Reporting

Operations

Purchasing
Personnel administration
Plant and/or office operations
Manufacturing and/or service
delivery controls
Production control
Inventory control
Marketing and sales
Engineering
Property, plant, and equipment
Fixed assets
Insurance and risk management

costs approximate 70 percent of total expenditures, the personnel function would be more critical. Normally, reviewers work with a limited budget in terms of hours allocated to the operational review, so they are greatly concerned with spending these hours on functional areas that offer the greatest potential for operational improvements in return for their effort. Criteria for determining a company's critical areas include:

- Areas with large numbers in relationship to other functions; such as revenues, costs, percentage of total assets, number of sales, units of production, and personnel.

- Areas where controls are weak; for instance, there may be a lack of an effective manufacturing control system, management reporting system, or organizational planning and control system.

- Areas subject to abuse or laxity; for example, inventory and production controls that allow transactions to go unreported and undetected, uncontrollable time and cost reporting, and ineffective personnel evaluation procedures.

- Areas that are difficult to control; for example, ineffective storeroom, shipping, or time recording procedures.

- Areas where functions are not performed efficiently or economically; for instance, ineffective procedures, duplication of efforts, unnecessary work steps, inefficient use of resources such as computer equipment, overstaffing, and excess purchases.

- Areas indicated by ratio, change, or trend analysis characterized by wide swings up or down when compared over a number of periods. Examples include sales changes by product line, costs by major category, number of personnel, inventory levels, and so forth.

- Areas where management has identified specific weaknesses or needs for improvement, such as personnel functions, manufacturing procedures, computer operations, and management reporting.

Another factor to consider in choosing the critical operational area to review is the willingness of the personnel in the area to cooperate in the performance of the review. First, those in operational management should want to have their operations reviewed and be willing to work with the reviewer in the improvement of their operations. Without such top management commitment, the operational review is not likely to succeed. Second, staff and operating personnel must be willing to work with the reviewer both in performing the operational review and in the subsequent implementation of operational improvements. Cooperation at all levels of the organization is essential to a successful operational review.

The reviewer must enlist the cooperation of all personnel: members of management to ensure top commitment to the review, and operations personnel to help in identifying areas to review and proposed improvements. Normally, in most operations, the staff or operating personnel know precisely what is going on day by day and, with firsthand knowledge of operations, can help the reviewer to identify the most critical areas to review.

> *Any and All Functions*
> *Should Be Subject*
> *to an Operational Review*

BUDGET

In addressing the number of critical areas to be covered in the operational review, it is important to understand the relationship between budgeted review time and the scope of operational review work desired to be accomplished. In many situations, the budget hours are established first and then the scope of the operational review is made to fit within the budget. While this procedure may work from an internal standpoint in regard to budget and staffing, it does not fully take into account the aspect of such reviews that require flexibility and expandability of formulated operational review work programs. In addition, it is important for the reviewer and management to consider the cost against the expected benefits of the specific operational review. This is a significant concept in helping to determine how much time to allocate to the operational review.

In performing an internal or external type financial audit, the audit group is budgeting staff time and related costs. In effect, the financial audit becomes a cost center. In an operational review, on the other hand, operational benefits and dollar savings should greatly surpass the cost of the review (savings should be at least three times its cost). In effect, the operational review becomes a profit center. Theoretically, the more operational reviews are done, the greater the savings realized by the organization. In reality, however, some guidelines are needed to establish the extent of an operational review in a given functional area, once the critical areas for review have been identified.

There are a number of factors to consider in establishing the operational review budget:

- *Scope of the operational review.* For example, are all significant operational areas to be reviewed, or only the major ones identified?

- *Frequency of the operational review.* Is the operational review to be done on a one-time basis, which requires more up-front planning and research; or is it to be performed for an area that is reviewed on a regular basis and requires minimal up-front efforts?

- *Nature of the business operations.* A service business dealing primarily with selling staff time, such as a medical, legal, or CPA practice, normally requires less time for an operational review than a manufacturing business that produces, ships, sells, and services a fairly wide product line.

- *Degree of management effectiveness.* Functional areas that are ineffectively managed normally require more operational review time than those that are more effectively managed.

- *Expectation of benefits.* Those areas that afford the greatest expected benefits, in terms of the number of potential recommendations or savings, should be the areas reviewed first. However, these areas will take more time to review than those with lesser expectations.

Operational reviews, to be most successful, require a large amount of preplanning, fact gathering, and research. This can make the costs of conducting an operational review considerable. However, when compared with the potential benefits and savings, costs become less significant. That is why, when determining how much time to spend on the operational review, it is best to use a cost-versus-benefit approach, tempered, of course, with the reality of available staff and hours. In effect, an effort should be made to cover competently as many of the major critical areas as possible within the limited staffing constraints.

> *The More Operational Reviews*
> *that Are Performed,*
> *the Greater the Savings*

INITIAL SURVEY

To achieve the greatest results from limited operational review resources, the reviewer identifies those areas of major importance and those offering the greatest potential savings or benefits as part of an initial survey, either prior to or as part of the planning phase of the operational review. If performed before the planning phase, either because the client requests it, because of a relatively small scope or budget, or for some other reason, the survey usually consists of some type of management and operational questionnaire. The purpose of the questionnaire is to determine what functions are performed, who performs each function, and why and how each is performed.

Answers to these questions should provide insight into the organization's objectives, activities, work performance, systems and procedures, limits of authority, and so on. The reviewer uses the questionnaire as a guideline and does not rely solely on yes or no responses. This is a quick review tool to help identify critical areas for further review when it is not feasible to implement the more desirable, but time-consuming, full planning phase. However, a survey of this kind should not be used in lieu of the planning phase, as it is still the reviewer's responsibility to substantiate, with adequate evidence, the identification of critical operational areas to be reviewed.

Exhibit 1.4 is a sample operational review initial survey form. The purpose of the initial survey is to identify areas of major importance in the total organization or specific operations to be reviewed. Improper identification results in spending unnecessary effort on less significant activities and insufficient effort in more important areas. The survey should provide for more detailed answers, rather than simple yes or no responses. The same questions are reviewed with various personnel, such as departmental management, functional supervision, and operations and support personnel. The reviewer thus isolates patterns of agreement and disagreement, as well as various interpretations and perceptions that lead to the correct conclusions.

EXHIBIT 1.4   Sample Operational Review Initial Survey Form

Planning and Budgeting

1. How does the company plan? Describe the system of planning.
2. Does a long-range plan exist? Attach copy.
3. Do current short-term plans exist? Attach copy.
4. What are plans for expansion or improvement?
5. What are plans for physical plant development?
6. What are plans for future financing?
7. What are personnel plans?
8. How does the organization budget? Describe the budgeting system.
9. Does a current budget exist? Obtain or prepare copy.
10. Do budget versus actual statistics exist for the last five years of operations? Obtain or prepare copy.

Personnel and Staffing

1. Does an organizational chart exist? Obtain or prepare copy.
2. Do functional job descriptions exist for each block on the organization chart? Obtain or prepare copies.
3. Do staffing statistics by functional area exist? Obtain or prepare copy.
4. Is there a system of employee evaluations? Describe procedures.
5. How are employees recruited, hired, evaluated, and fired? Describe procedures.
6. How are new employees oriented and trained? Describe.
7. What are promotional policies? Describe.
8. How are raises and promotions determined? Describe.
9. Is there a grievance mechanism? Describe.
10. What type of personnel records are maintained? Obtain copies.

Management

1. Does a board of directors exist? Attach list of names and credentials.
2. Who is considered top management? Attach list of names and credentials.
3. Who is considered middle management? Attach list of names and credentials.
4. Who is considered lower management? Attach list of names and credentials.
5. How adequate are existing reports in furnishing information for making management decisions? Describe.

EXHIBIT 1.4   (*Continued*)

6. Are there tools for internal downward communication to the staff? Attach copies.
7. Is authority effectively delegated to management and lower levels? Describe.

Policies and Procedures

1. Do written policies exist? Obtain copy.
2. Are written policies current?
3. Are systems and procedures documented? Obtain or provide copy.

Accounting System

1. What is the chart of accounts used? Obtain or prepare copy.
2. Is the accounting mechanized? Obtain documentation.
3. What financial reports are produced? Obtain documentation.
4. Is there an internal audit function? By and to whom?
5. Are internal operating reports produced? Obtain copies and determine uses.

Revenues

1. What are the sources of revenue for the last five years? Obtain or prepare statistics.
2. Have there been any substantial changes during this period? Document any that have been made.
3. Are actual versus budgeted data available? Obtain or prepare copy.

Expenses

1. What are the major expense accounts used? Obtain or prepare copy.
2. What are actual expenses for these accounts for the last five years? Obtain or prepare copy.
3. Have there been any substantial changes during this period? Document any that have been made.
4. Are actual versus budgeted data available? Obtain or prepare copy.

Computer Processing

1. Where is computer processing presently located in the organization? Obtain or prepare copy of information technology organization.

EXHIBIT 1.4 (*Continued*)

2. What computer equipment is used? Obtain or prepare copy of equipment list and locations.
3. What is total cost of equipment rental or purchase price?
4. What are the major applications computerized? Obtain or prepare copy of list of applications, with general systems applications.
5. Are management, operational, control, and exception reports provided? Describe.

Purchasing

1. What is purchasing authority? Obtain or prepare copy of policy relative to purchasing authority.
2. Is purchasing centralized or decentralized? Describe operations.
3. How are purchase requisitions initiated? Describe general procedures.
4. Who determines quality and quantity desired?
5. Are purchase orders used? Describe procedure.
6. Are competitive bidding procedures used? Describe procedure.

Manufacturing Systems

1. Is a computerized manufacturing control system being used? Describe operation.
2. What type of manufacturing processes are being used? Describe processes.
3. How are jobs controlled in manufacturing? Describe procedures.
4. Is a manufacturing cost system used by job? Describe system.
5. Are operational and management reports provided to control manufacturing operations? Obtain or prepare copies.

Production Control

1. Is a manufacturing control system being used? Is it computerized? Obtain or prepare copy of general procedures.
2. What types of manufacturing processes are being used? Describe.
3. What is location(s) of manufacturing facilities? Document.
4. Are production control cost centers used to control the routing of manufacturing orders? Obtain or prepare copy of cost centers.
5. Is a manufacturing cost system used? Obtain or prepare copy of cost accounting procedures.
6. Are operational and management reports provided to control manufacturing operations? Obtain copies.

EXHIBIT 1.4 (*Continued*)

Inventory Control

1. Is an inventory control system being used? Is it computerized? Obtain or prepare copy of general procedures.
2. What types of inventory control procedures are being used? Describe.
3. Where are inventory storeroom locations? Obtain or prepare copy of locations and describe storeroom procedures.
4. How are inventory records maintained? Describe procedures.
5. Are inventory statistics and data maintained? Obtain data as to items in inventory, dollar value, usage, on-hand balances, etc.
6. What is basis for reordering inventory items, and how are reorder quantities determined? Describe procedures.

Responsibility and Authority

1. Are responsibilities clearly defined and understood by managers and staff personnel? Describe procedures.
2. Has authority been delegated effectively to managers and lower levels within the organization? Describe process.

Where necessary, each question is supported by available documentation. This form could also be used as part of the more formal planning phase, but should be more specific to a departmental or functional area.

ENGAGEMENT DEVELOPMENT

An operational review could be conducted by an external consulting firm, an internal review group, an independent in-house unit, departmental personnel, or a combination of staff from these entities. Whichever organization has primary responsibility for conducting the operational review, the major steps in its development and performance should be similar. These steps are summarized in Exhibit 1.5.

Recognize and Define the Problem

The first step is to recognize and define the problem. Normally, it is management's prerogative to identify the major problem area(s) to be addressed

EXHIBIT 1.5   Operational Review Engagement Development

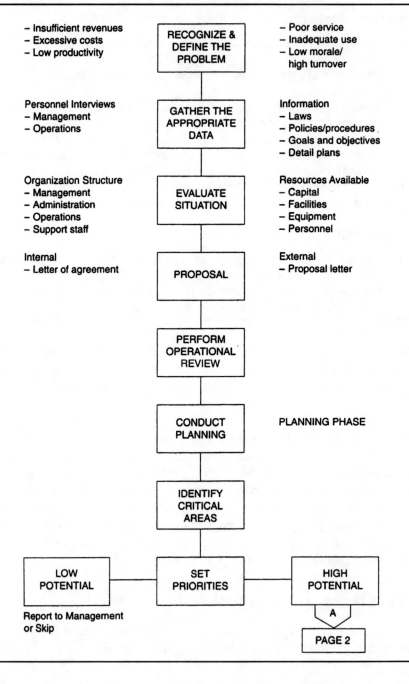

EXHIBIT 1.5 (*Continued*)

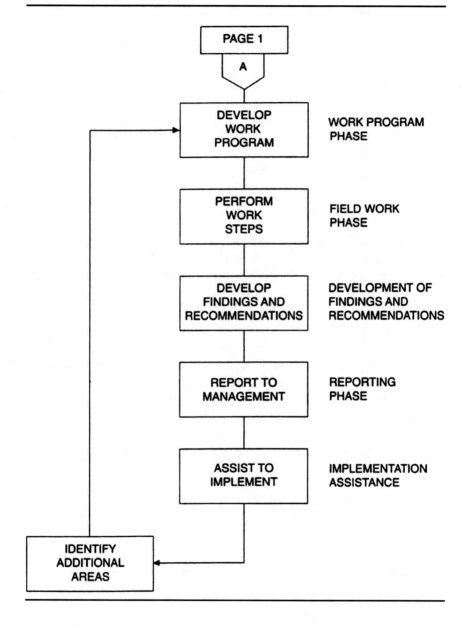

in an operational review. However, if requested by management, the reviewer can either assist in the problem definition described previously or perform a preliminary survey to identify significant operational areas to be reviewed.

Gather Appropriate Data

The second step is to gather the appropriate supporting data a function usually performed by the operational reviewer. The purpose of this data gathering is to provide background information relative to the problem areas defined in the first step, so as to substantiate the problem situation.

Evaluate the Situation

The next step is to evaluate the situation within the organization to determine the organizational structure and resources available. These are the factors on which the reviewer bases the proposal to management for conducting the operational review.

Proposal Letter

When the reviewer has gathered sufficient background data on the operational problem areas identified for review and has decided on the review plan, a written proposal or engagement letter must be submitted. The proposal clarifies for management such considerations as:

- Background of the situation describing the need for the operational review

- Operational review engagement objectives

- Scope of the review engagement or which operational areas are to be included.

- The reviewer's approach to conducting the operational review

- Proposed general work steps to be included in the conduct of the operational review

- Operational review staff and client personnel who are expected to participate in the operational review, including each one's responsibilities and expectations as well as time commitments

- Reporting requirements to management, such as progress meetings and final reporting, including a description of all deliverable output

- Benefits to be provided as a result of conducting the operational review

- Estimates of time and cost

Although an external consulting firm usually submits the proposal letter to management, it is also good practice for an internal group to submit a similar proposal prior to the start of the operational review engagement. The major purpose of an internal proposal letter is to ensure clear communication, as to the purpose and scope of the operational review, between the review group and management. In this context, the internal proposal becomes a letter of understanding between the internal review group and management. The contents of the internal proposal letter would differ somewhat from an external proposal, and would only include those areas necessary to the situation.

Exhibit 1.6 provides an example of an operational review proposal, or engagement letter, for the Example Company, as well as sample time and cost budget estimates for the planning and field work phases. These cost estimates are for the reviewer's use in determining the cost of the engagement and are not given to operations management. An external consulting firm proposing to perform an operational review for a client may have to estimate time and costs before starting an engagement. To enable the reviewer to estimate accurately requires sufficient initial survey work and adequate prior experience on similar engagements. Although it is obviously advantageous to estimate the amount of field work required after completion of the planning phase, the client normally wants to know these amounts up front. The samples provided are for a relatively sizable operational review. In a situation where potential operational review engagements may be smaller in scope, the two phases may be combined and the numbers scaled down.

Perform the Operational Review

Once the proposal letter has been submitted and accepted by management, the actual operational review begins, using the proposed phase approach of planning, work program, field work, development of findings and recommendations, and reporting. Should management request it, the reviewer might also help to implement the recommended operational improvements,

EXHIBIT 1.6   Samples Operational Review Proposal Letter: The Example Company

Dear Mr. Worthington:

It was a pleasure meeting with you on January 23 to discuss how Reider Associates might assist the Example Company in the review and analysis of Purchasing Department operations. This proposal letter summarizes our understanding of your situation, the assistance to be provided by us, our approach to providing such assistance, and an estimate of our time and fees.

Background
You have expressed some concern relative to the quality of present systems and methods that your Purchasing Department personnel are currently using. In addition, you are concerned about implementing more sophisticated operating and data processing techniques, so that Purchasing Department personnel can better manage their operations and provide the necessary services in an economical and efficient manner.

In response to these and other situations, you have recognized the need to provide system review and analysis assistance addressing these concerns. Accordingly, you have requested that Reider Associates submit this proposal relative to how we might assist your efforts in designing and implementing such an operational improvement to meet your needs.

Objectives
The objectives of the operational review of Purchasing Department operations would be to:

1. Determine which systems and procedures would be best to improve Purchasing Department effectiveness.
2. Design operating systems and data processing procedures to enable Purchasing Department functions to operate more efficiently and economically.
3. Identify opportunities for operational improvements within the Purchasing Department.
4. Review and analyze present data processing procedures to determine their effectiveness and to recommend improvements, for greater efficiency of operations.

Scope of the Engagement
This engagement is to be confined to those Purchasing Department areas reporting to the vice-president of operations, located at your central headquarters. Therefore, the engagement will exclude all non-Purchasing Department operating areas reporting to the vice-president of operations located at central headquarters, as well as Purchasing Department functions at other sites.

EXHIBIT 1.6 *(Continued)*

As we discussed, we would plan to review operating systems and procedures, as well as interview selected management/supervisory and operating personnel in the following Purchasing Department work units:

- Purchasing
- Purchasing Supervisor
- Buyers I & II
- Clerk Supervisor
- Clerical Supervisor
- Clerk Typist
- Standard Specifications Unit
- Standard Specifications Unit Supervisor
- Procurement Technician
- Management Trainee
- Clerk Stenographer
- Clerk

Our Approach
We propose to assist you in the review and analysis of present Purchasing Department operating procedures and methods, which will encompass techniques and procedures needed presently, as well as provide for flexibility for growth and adaptation to changed circumstances. Accordingly, we plan to provide our assistance in the following steps:

1. General review of existing operational methods and procedures to provide us with a clear understanding of your Purchasing Department functions so that we can provide effective consulting assistance in developing and implementing improved procedures. This would include a review of management/administrative practices and procedures, as well as related operating systems and methods.

2. Interviews of a number of Purchasing Department management/ supervisory and operating personnel so that we can assess individual needs and concerns as well as incorporate such concerns into overall considerations.

    We will, of course, discuss the findings of our general review and interviews with you so that we can jointly agree as to the major issues for change to be included in our detailed review and analysis.

3. Detailed operational review and analysis of those critical areas identified in our general review. We will perform sufficient analytical work to fully determine the present condition of each area, what it should be, the effect on operations, the cause of the condition, and recommendations for improvement.

EXHIBIT 1.6 (*Continued*)

4. Development of detailed findings of recommendations for improvement, which will be developed in a manner that will optimize each Purchasing Department function's achievement of its individual goals and objectives, as well as deal with issues identified by us in our general operational review and participant interviews.

   These findings and recommendations will be documented for your review in both an oral and a written report.

5. Assistance to you and your staff in the implementation of recommendations that can be accomplished during the course of this consulting assistance. Other longer-term recommendations will be reviewed with you at the oral presentation at the conclusion of our field work and subsequently documented in the final report summarizing the results of the consulting engagement.

Our Participation
Mrs. Betty White, manager in our operational review consulting department, will be personally responsible for the technical conduct and successful completion of this operational improvement program. She has provided similar assistance to numerous clients.

We plan to assign Mr. Bill Brown, supervisor, and Mr. Joe Super, senior, of our consulting staff to this engagement. Both of these people are uniquely qualified to perform the tasks required in this engagement. They will be responsible for the performance of the work steps, as described in this section "Our Approach." We will assign other personnel as necessary, with your approval. We also plan to utilize the services of Mr. Mike Clark, an independent consultant, in the areas of his expertise, which are systems and procedures, flowcharting, facilities layout and work flow, and data processing.

We are attaching to this proposal resumes for each of these people.

Client Participation
Based on our experience, we consider client participation to be essential for such an operational improvement program to be effective and successful. Accordingly, we recommend that a management member be assigned as part of a task force to work along with us in formulating the details of the operational improvement program. We would expect this person to participate in the engagement as necessary, to be available to attend progress meetings as scheduled, and to provide us with necessary input (particularly related to his or her functional area) as required. We would recommend Mr. Cliff Chambers, purchasing supervisor, to assume the overall client management responsibility.

EXHIBIT 1.6 *(Continued)*

In addition, we would suggest assigning an operations staff member from both the Purchasing and Standards Specifications work units to this engagement to work along with us. We would not expect either one of them to be assigned duties that would consume more than two days per week during the course of the engagement.

Progress Meetings
Progress meetings will be held at least every three weeks, at which time we will discuss such things as (1) progress to date, (2) specific findings and recommendations, (3) decisions to be made, (4) implementation efforts, and (5) ongoing plans. We will, of course, document these progress meetings in brief written reports.

Reporting
At the conclusion of this engagement, we will submit our findings and recommendations to you at an oral presentation, which will provide you with an opportunity to review and discuss these findings and recommendations. As a follow-up to the oral presentation, we will subsequently document our findings and recommendations in a formal, written report.

Benefits to Be Provided
The benefits to be derived from the conducting of an operational review for your Purchasing Department are many and varied. However, you should expect at least the following:

- Identification of operational problem areas, related causes, and alternatives for improvement.
- Effective reduction of unnecessary costs through the identification of opportunities for eliminating waste and inefficiency.
- Identification of undefined organizational goals, objectives, policies, and procedures.
- Assessment of the existing management information and control system.
- An independent, objective evaluation of operations.

We believe the assistance to be provided by us will also ensure a positive and effective method of implementing improved operating techniques, which will enable all levels of Purchasing Department personnel to:

- Understand their basic roles and functions so that all individuals can implement such operational techniques and principles within their own areas,
- Develop meaningful operating procedures that will enable them to better control, monitor, and evaluate the results of their operations,

EXHIBIT 1.6 *(Continued)*

- Perform their current job responsibilities more effectively with a greater level of competency, a better understanding of operational procedures, and a greater ability to apply their knowledge in their particular situations, and
- Develop a greater sense of teamwork and working together, which should make operations more effective and efficient.

Time and Cost
We recommend that the operational review be conducted in two phases to be most effective and to optimize the benefits to be derived by your organization, as follows:

Phase I: Planning
The planning phase would consist of a general review of your purchasing operatings to provide us with a working knowledge of your operations, as well as to identify those significant areas offering the greatest payout in operational improvements that we believe should be analyzed in greater depth during the Phase II field work. We would, of course, bring to your attention all operational improvements and related recommendations identified by us during Phase I so that you will be able to implement immediate or short-term positive changes.

Phase II: Field Work
As a result of the Planning Phase, we will identify those critical operational areas where we believe further review and analysis will result in substantial improvements which will far outweight the costs of conducting the operational review. Based on our mutual agreement, we would then develop an operational review work program directed toward further review and analysis of each of these critical areas, resulting in the development of findings which would improve the reporting of specific recommendations for improvement.

Our fees are based on the amount of time expended on the engagement, extended by our standard billing rates. Based on our experience in similar engagements, our initial survey of your operations, and discussions with you, we estimate our time participation and related costs to be as follows:

Phase I: Planning
Three weeks of elapsed time, at an estimated cost of $10,000 to $12,000

Phase II: Field Work
From 10 to 12 weeks of elapsed time, at an estimated cost of $28,000 to $32,000.

EXHIBIT 1.6 (*Continued*)

Our estimated costs for the Field Work phase are based on our present knowledge of your situation and what we believe is necessary at this time. However, should the situation change, based on what we find out in the planning phase, we will inform you immediately as to the need to change our time and cost estimates either upward or downward.

In addition, we are to be reimbursed for out-of-pocket expenses incurred for travel, lodging, subsistence, and the like. We will, of course, attempt to minimize both fee and expenses and will bill you only for actual time and expenses incurred.

It is our practice to submit progress billings at two-week intervals.

We are ready to being this engagement within one week of your acceptance of this proposal. However, to meet your desired timetable, we suggest starting no later than March 1.

*   *   *   *   *   *   *   *   *   *   *

We appreciate the opportunity to submit this proposal and look forward to working with you on this important and challenging project. If the arrangements described above meet your approval, you man indicate your acceptance by signing and returning the enclosed copy.

Very truly yours,

_____

Rob Reider, President
Reider Associates

Approved
by_____

George Worthington, Vice-President Operations

Date _____

EXHIBIT 1.6   (*Continued*)

Work Program and Operational Review Engagement
Budget Estimate (in hours)

Client Name: The Example Company   Date: February 2, 20XX
Phase I: Planning

Engagement Work Program

	Mgr.	Supv.	Out. Staff	Cli. Cons.	Time	Total
1. Goals & Objectives						
a. Review legislative/ internal materials					6	6
b. Planning systems & procedures		26				26
2. Budgets		11				11
3. Organizational Chart and Procedures Manual	14					14
4. Flowcharts				28		28
5. Reports					18	18
6. Personnel			21		12	33
7. Facilities			4	12		16
8. Review Planning Phase Results	10					10
Total Time	24	37	25	40	36	162
Other:						
9. Prepare Work Program	12				12	24
10. Review Management	24				16	40
Total Other Time	36				28	64
Grand Total Time	60	37	25	40	64	226
Standard Billing Rates	$80	$60	$30	$75	—	
Total Estimated	$4,800	$2,220	$750	$3,300	—	$10,770
Contingency: 10%						1,230
Grand Total						$12,000
Proposed Fee Quoted						$10,000 to $12,000

EXHIBIT 1.6   (*Continued*)

Work Program and Operational Review Engagement
Budget Estimate (in hours)

Client Name: The Example Company   Date: February 2, 20XX
Phase II: Field Work

Engagement Work Program

	Mgr.	Supv.	Staff Sr./Jr.	Out. Cons.	Cli. Time	Total
1. Company Policy & Organization						
a. Organization Status of Purchasing		50				50
b. Responsibility for Purchasing		20				20
c. Authority for Purchasing				10		10
d. Decentralized Purchasing			20			20
2. Purchasing Department Operations						
a. Proceedings Flowcharts				50		50
b. Department Forms					20	20
c. Physical Facilities					12	12
d. Value Analysis Program					8	8
e. Collateral Operation				16		16
3. Review of Purchase Transactions						
a. Selected Transactions			8	12		20
b. Examination of Purchasing Transactions			12	18		30
4. Records & Reports				34		34

EXHIBIT 1.6   (*Continued*)

	Mgr.	Supv.	Staff Sr./Jr.		Out. Cons.	Cli. Time	Total
5. Review Field Work Results	24	24				12	60
6. Development of Findings	8	8		22		32	80
7. Oral Reporting	10					10	20
8. Written Report	12	20				8	40
Total Time	54	132	40	112	50	102	490
Other							
9. Prepare Work Program	12	8	4	6	2	8	40
10. Review Management	80					20	100
Total Other	92	8	4	6	2	28	140
Grand Total	146	140	44	118	52	130	630
Standard Billing Rates	$80	$60	$40	$30	$75	—	
Total Estimated Fees	$11,690	$8,400	$1,760	$3,540	$3,900		$29,290
Contingency: 10%							$2,720
Grand Total							$32,000
Proposed Fee Quoted							$28,000 to $32,000

but client personnel may feel confident enough to implement the agreed-upon recommendations on their own. As part of the reporting process, it is also important to identify other significant operational areas in which the operational review approach could offer specific improvements and quantifiable benefits. This could lead to a follow-up operational review engagement for the external consulting firm, particularly if it has proven its worth in the current operational review. For the internal review team, it may result in management 's asking for additional operational reviews. Not only is such an approach productive in selling the entire operational review concept, but it reinforces the concept of the internal review group existing as a profit center in conducting operational reviews. The "profit center" concept is based on convincing management that the benefits to be derived from operational reviews far exceed the costs involved. This is where the quantification of findings is extremely important.

Another aspect to consider is that if the operational review is performed properly with the help of departmental personnel, the department retains the residual ability to perform operational review procedures in other areas. As the operational review team cannot normally cover every operational area that could be improved within the scope of the original operational review, the team should identify those additional areas for further review and, possibly, for review by the department. Management then decides whether to pursue these areas on their own or with the operational reviewer's help.

One of the goals in acquainting an organization with the operational review approach is to multiply the effectiveness of operational reviewers. In other words, while performing the operational review, reviewers are also training client personnel. In this way, operational review procedures and results are quickly multiplied throughout the organization, and the reviewers can then spend their time on the most significant areas and tasks.

> *The Operational Review*
> *Is a Learning Process*
> *for the Individual,*
> *the Work Unit,*
> *and the Organization*

CHAPTER TWO

Planning Phase

This chapter discusses the planning phase of an operational review. The planning phase is where the reviewer first learns about the organization's operations through various techniques such as review of planning and budget systems, interviewing, review of organizational structure and management, gathering and analyzing information, analysis of financial data and statements, physical inspection of facilities and work procedures, and so forth. Through the performance of these work steps, the reviewer identifies possible critical operational problem areas to be analyzed in more depth in the field work phase, through the development of an operational review work program. In addition, the proper steps to be taken in the planning phase to ensure successful results from an operational review are fully discussed in this chapter.

This chapter will discuss the following five topics:

1. Increase understanding of the purpose of the planning phase in an operational review.

2. Introduce information that must be obtained during the planning phase and related sources of information.

3. Increase knowledge of how to use planning phase information in the identification of critical operational areas.

4. Increase understanding of planning and budget concepts and their expansion into operational areas and related principles of good operational controls.

5. Introduce a sample operational review planning phase work program.

PLANNING PHASE OVERVIEW

The starting point for the operational review is management's decision as to which operational area(s) are to be reviewed, and whether the operational review is to be preliminary or in-depth. Based on management's decision, the operational reviewer then starts the planning phase of the operational review. The primary purposes of the planning phase are to:

• Gather information about the operational area

• Identify possible operational problem areas

• Start to develop the basis for the operational review work program.

In the planning phase, general working information on all important aspects of the organization's operations is obtained in a relatively short time. This is usually accomplished on site at the company's facilities. However, if this is a first time review of the company or a new area of review, the reviewer may have to do some additional on-site research and learning, such as reviewing the company's planning and budget systems and its organizational structure and management.

It is important to get this information quickly. The information gathering need not be a long, drawn-out process, with laborious readings of manuals and other materials. Time-consuming efforts to show the existence of significant deficiencies should not be undertaken. However, if any indications of serious deficiencies are found, the reviewer should document them so that they will be considered in deciding on areas for additional work. This procedure provides for an orderly approach to the planning phase and directs operational review effort to those areas with the greatest payout in terms of significant improvement.

Remember the 80/20 rule. Its application in this case states that 20 percent of the problems cause 80 percent of the critical impact, and 80 percent of the problems cause only 20 percent of the impact. So the reviewer is advised to chase the elephants, the 20 percent, and not the mice, the 80 percent.

At the end of the planning phase the reviewer should have adequate working knowledge of the objectives and controls of the reviewed area. The reviewer should be familiar with the organization: its objectives, its problems, its physical layout, and the relative significance of the various responsibilities it has been assigned or has assumed. This enables the reviewer to determine at the outset how much time is required to perform the remaining phases of the review.

> *Proper Planning*
> *and the Planning Phase*
> *Pays for Itself*

INFORMATION TO BE OBTAINED

All of the documents gathered during the planning phase are used to start the permanent files for the operational review. The planning phase can be performed efficiently and systematically if the reviewer has a clear idea of what is needed. The records and information that could be required may include:

- Laws and regulations that apply to the activities being reviewed

- Material on the organization

- Financial information

- Operating methods and procedures

- Management information and reports

- Problem areas

Laws and Regulations that Apply to the Activities Being Reviewed

An understanding of the basic legal authorities governing the area and its activities is needed. The satisfactory performance of an operational review requires that the reviewer ascertain the purpose, scope, and objectives of the activities being reviewed, the way those objectives are to be achieved, and the extent of authority and responsibility conferred. In addition to the basic legislation relating to the area, the reviewer needs to obtain information on all important laws that specifically apply to the area or activity, including related regulations and legal decisions. As to each law, the reviewer should find out:

- Its history and background
- The objectives sought
- The authority vested to achieve the objectives
- The responsibilities imposed
- The nature of any restrictions imposed
- Any other significant requirements

In operational reviews in which related legislation is a major consideration, the reviewer should be aware of the following factors:

- Management may justify certain activities on the basis of general authority contained in basic laws. Whenever general authority is relied on for conducting an activity, the reviewer obtains complete and clear explanations as to such reliance. The reviewer determines and reports on the extent to which such general authority has been used, and makes full disclosure of unused authority, if significant.

- Legislation may impose various restrictions on an organization in carrying out an activity. Compliance with these restrictions is a basic responsibility of management. The reviewer should be familiar with the nature of these restrictions and determine specifically how management provides for ensuring compliance.

Material on the Organization

The second area in which the reviewer needs to gather information involves the organization and its activities. Primary emphasis should be on the activities that are within the scope of the operational review. This information should include the following:

- Division of duties and responsibilities
- Principal delegations of authority

- Nature, size, and location of each operational entity (i.e., any field offices)
- Number of employees by organization segment and location
- Nature and location of physical assets and accounting records

Among the reviewer's primary concerns is to determine how the company is organized to carry out its functions and how duties and responsibilities are assigned. In addition, the reviewer must determine where the area being reviewed fits into the organizational pattern of the whole company and its relationship to other areas. This knowledge is necessary for a full understanding of the organization's operations.

Financial Information

The third area of interest to the reviewer is all pertinent financial information, such as:

- Cost of operations by periods
- Year by year record of income from revenue-producing operations
- Budget versus actual data for the present and past periods
- Cash flow analysis
- Cost accounting data

Operating Methods and Procedures

Normally, the reviewer is more concerned with operating data than with the data typical in a financial statement. A fourth area is investigated to obtain a general description of the organization's operating methods and procedures. The reviewer analyzes and documents the operating methods and procedures by which activities being reviewed are performed. In the planning phase, the reviewer should obtain information as to the general methods and procedures top management prescribes for operating in the area under consideration. In this phase, the review of methods and procedures should not extend below the management level. If it is necessary to get accurate information on which to base a conclusion of how certain systems and procedures actually work, the reviewer may want to talk with a limited number of operations personnel. However, the information obtained may be generalized and may require further development later in the review to determine the precise methods and procedures at the operating level.

Management Information and Reports

A fifth category of interest is management information and reports. The reviewer should identify all available management information as well as the nature, content, and timing of all reporting. The reviewer should also look for management information that should be present, but is not. It is extremely important to identify the key operating indicators that management has singled out for reporting purposes and those items subject to exception reporting.

Problem Areas

Finally, the reviewer gathers information regarding any problem areas. The reviewer identifies and documents all important problem areas relative to the activities to be reviewed. Areas of major deficiency and those that lend themselves to the greatest improvements are to be emphasized. Remember, these are the items to be pursued in the work program and field work phases. To spend review time most efficiently, it is important to analyze those operational areas with the largest potential payout in terms of improvements. Again, the organization's "elephants" should be identified in terms of present problem areas, and the "mice" considered only for in-house correction.

Chase the Elephants,
Not the Mice

SOURCES OF INFORMATION

What are the sources of the information to be gathered in the planning phase? Such information could come from various sources; however, the following are the most usual sources:

- Effective interviewing
- Organizational data

- Financial data
- Policies and procedures
- Operating and management reports
- Physical inspection

Effective Interviewing

One of the major sources of information about the organization's activities, procedures, and systems is an effective interview. The purpose of the interview is to find out what is going on and why. Interviews in the planning phase should normally be limited to management, to obtain an overview of the operations without becoming involved in the time-consuming details of interviewing the technical personnel more directly engaged in the operation. In practice, however, limited interviews with operations personnel are usually conducted to ensure that a full and accurate picture is obtained.

Organizational Data

Organizational data may include such things as copies of organization charts, functional job descriptions, and position charts. The reviewer should be sure to ascertain actual duties, responsibilities, and levels of authority for each individual; written job descriptions should not be automatically accepted at face value. This could entail talking to selected management and operations personnel and/or having them prepare a description of their perceived job duties and responsibilities.

Financial Data

Another source of planning phase information is financial data, such as financial statements over a number of years, budget versus actual reports (present and past), cost of operations by period, revenues year by year by source, cash flow analysis, cost accounting data, and ratio, change, and trend analysis.

Policies and Procedures

Existing policies and procedures, which should be documented in procedures manuals, policy pronouncements, directives, and regulations are yet another source of information. For many small organizations, such materials will probably not exist, except in the heads of management personnel. In this case, the reviewer would then interview these persons to determine what they believe to be existing policies and procedures, and then test them to determine whether they are actually being followed.

Operating and Management Reports

A further source of information are operations and management reports submitted either internally or externally, prior and related review and audit reports and workpapers, and, if available, internal audit and review reports. The reviewer would also determine whether management has responded to any findings identified in these reports and whether any action has been taken.

Physical Inspection

Finally, the reviewer makes a physical inspection of the operation, including a tour of all pertinent operational areas and the observation of significant activities being performed. A physical review of the operations area, whenever appropriate, should be made relative to the nature of the activities to be examined. The purpose of this physical review is to improve understanding of the activity in physical terms, and to provide support for information about the activity obtained during interviews.

> *Operational Information*
> *Comes from Many Sources*

REVIEW OF ORGANIZATIONAL PLANNING AND BUDGET SYSTEMS

A good starting point for the reviewer in the planning phase is to understand the organization, why it is in existence, and what it is trying to accomplish, that is, its goals and objectives. To accomplish this, the reviewer needs to understand the organization's long-term and short-term planning methods and related budgeting and control processes. The reviewer should focus on the organization's approach to planning and its integration with the budgeting process. The organization's planning and budgeting techniques should be a means of achieving improved organizational effectiveness. The reviewer should also be aware of the elements of an effective planning/ budgeting system to compare to the practices of the organization under review.

There should be interaction and interdependence of the strategic (long-term) planning, short-term planning, detail planning, budgeting, and monitoring processes. The planning process should be an essential first step in the preparation of an effective budget for the organization. By learning effective planning and budgeting procedures, reviewers will be able to review and analyze such procedures more effectively as part of their organization-wide, departmental, or specific function operational review.

Although organizations may plan and budget, many consider these processes as separate. In reality, they should be one process. Planning comes first until the organization defines its goals and objectives. Knowing where to allocate resources constitutes the budget process. All organizations plan and budget. Some do it formally, others informally (or even furtively); some are effective, others ineffective or even counterproductive in their methods—but all organizations do it! The advantages of formalizing and throwing open the planning and budgeting process provides an open, integrated, and reasonably structured process that significantly benefits the long-term visibility of the organization. It is for these benefits that this area is considered a critical function to include in the planning phase of an operational review.

Every organization, whether a manufacturer, service provider, or not-for-profit, must plan for its future direction if it desires to achieve its goals and objectives. The organizational plan is an agreed-upon course of action to be implemented in the future (short- and long-term) and directed toward moving the organization closer to its stated goals and objectives. The planning process, if exercised effectively, forces the organization to:

- Review and analyze past accomplishments

- Determine present and future needs

- Recognize strengths and weaknesses

It also enables the organization to:

- Identify future opportunities
- Define constraints or threats that may get in the way
- Establish organizational and departmental goals and objectives
- Develop action plans based on the evaluation of alternatives
- Prioritize the selection of action plans for implementation based on the most effective use of limited resources

The first step in the planning process is to determine why the organization is in existence as discussed in Chapter 1. Once the organization has identified all of the reasons that it is in existence and has articulated them by means of an organizational "mission statement," the next step is to define related organizational goals, both long and short term. These organizational goals are typically formulated by top management, although it is a good practice to obtain feedback from lower level managers, supervisors, and operating personnel within the organization as to the appropriateness, practicality, reasonableness, and attainability of the stated organizational goals. A good rule to keep in mind in the development of an effective organizational plan is that in most organizations it is the employees closest to day-to-day operations who usually know most about present problems and what needs to be done to correct them. Accordingly, the organization that wishes to be most successful over the long term must have "everyone" (i.e., representatives from many levels) in the organization involved in the planning process from the beginning to end. Many organizations have been unsuccessful in their planning efforts and their ability to survive because of lack of foresight and their inability to use employees' input creatively.

In addition, operating personnel need to know how to plan properly and operate according to such plans by putting them into action in order to conduct their operations successfully as part of an integrated organizational plan. Operations personnel cannot plan for their own areas effectively unless they understand and agree with the organization's long- and short-term goals—and have had the opportunity to provide significant input and feedback concerning these plans. It is not sufficient that operations personnel be allowed merely to provide input and feedback; top management must also encourage their input and seriously consider it in the finalization of organizational goals. The development of organizational goals must be internalized as a system of top to bottom agreement for it to be most successful.

Yet the reviewer must also understand that members of top management have the ultimate decision-making power and therefore may still decide to do whatever they desire, regardless of operations personnel input. The result of such exclusive top management decision making, however, is organizational goal setting by directive rather than by participation. If operations staff see this organizational goal setting as top management's and not their own, they will not only be less inclined to direct their efforts toward achievement of those goals, but may also tend to sabotage or work openly against the accomplishment of the goals. In an effective planning system, it is extremely important to have everyone in the organization working toward the same goals. In this manner, management and operations staff are far more likely to make decisions that are consistent with the organization's overall plans and direction.

Within this framework, how then does an organization plan effectively for its future? A schematic of the organizational planning process is shown in Exhibit 2.1. Note that in the development of long- and short-range plans, which includes the development of detail plans and related budgets, a "top to bottom" approach is used, whereby top management and operations management and staff interact and communicate, resulting in an agreed-upon set of organizational plans (strategic plans, corporate goals, and corporate objectives) and departmental/segment goals, objectives, detail plans, and budgets.

The organizational long-range goals established by top management then have to be translated into more specific departmental/segment goals and objectives. Definitions of goals and objectives are presented in Exhibit 2.2. Note that goals are broad directions or targets that the organization or department desires to move toward. They may or may not be achievable. On the other hand, objectives are specific desired results, relating to one or more goal, that can be attained within a given time frame. Normally, short-term goals and objectives are developed for a specific planning cycle (usually a one year annual cycle) for both the organization and each departmental unit. As top management is responsible for developing the long-term organizational goals, so operating managers and staff are responsible for developing and implementing the short-term goals and objectives within the framework of the overall long-term plans.

The following example demonstrates the relationship between long-term goals and short-term goals and objectives. The long-term goal of an

EXHIBIT 2.1   Organizational Planning Process

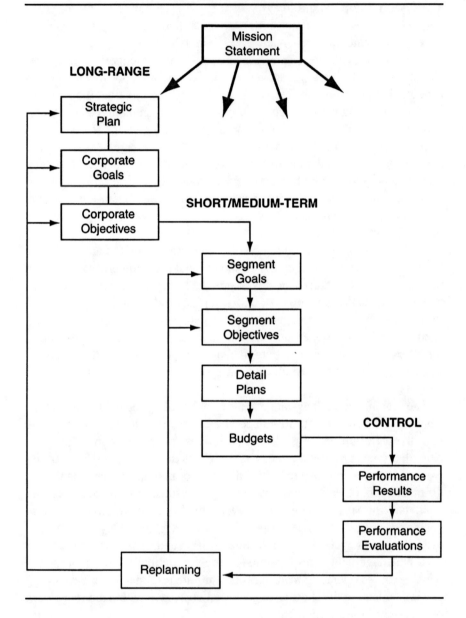

EXHIBIT 2.2   Planning Definitions

GOALS
   —Statements of broad direction
      —that describe future states or outcomes of the organization to be attained or retained.
      —that indicate ends toward which the organization's effort is to be directed.

OBJECTIVES
   —Measurable, desired accomplishments related to one or more goals.
   —Attainment is desired within a specified time frame and can be evaluated under specificable conditions.

CHARACTERISTICS OF OBJECTIVES
- MEASURABLE—attainment (or lack thereof) can be clearly identified.
- EXPLICIT—clear indication of who, what, when, how
- TIME-SPECIFIC—to be accomplished within a stipulated period of time.
- REALISTIC—capable of being attained within the time frame specified and with the expenditure of a reasonable and cost-effective amount of effort and resources.

---

organization is "To become the industry sales leader for product line YY." The related short-term goal is "To increase sales in units of product line YY." The specific objective for this planning cycle is "To increase sales in units of product number 3 of product line YY by at least 10 percent over last year." This specific objective can then be translated into specific detail plans (i.e., how to go about achieving the specific objective) and related performance expectations for the sales manufacturing and finance departments, and other affected areas of the organization.

These short-term performance objectives can then be translated into levels of production, inventory to be carried, labor requirements, manufacturing capacity, and other short-term decisions. In effect, these short-term objectives and related detail plans become the starting point for the budget process. The beginning budget will then reflect what is necessary (in terms of labor, materials, facilities, equipment, and other costs) to meet agreed-upon short-term objectives. When each budget is approved by top management, it will reflect the authorized level of expenditures needed to fulfill the objectives by following through on agreed-upon plans. At this point, each manager/supervisor has theoretically been delegated the authority to incur the expenditures to make each detail plan workable. Finally, managers/ supervisors can be evaluated based on their ability to work their plan effectively to achieve the short-term objectives.

It would be nice to think that every organization to be reviewed has an effective planning system as described above. However, the reviewer will find that very few organizations come close to planning and budgeting in this manner. In cases where such planning systems do not exist or are found to be deficient, the reviewer must superimpose such concepts on the organization or area under review to establish desired results prior to commencing the operational review. The reviewer must also keep in mind that his or her task is not merely to determine the existence of such planning systems, but their effectiveness in moving the organization in the right direction. To be most effective, the planning system must be continually attended to and the related budget flexible so that it supports the plan rather than making it more difficult to achieve results. If such planning does not exist, the reviewer must establish with management what desired results relate to the area under review.

> *The First Step in Planning*
> *Is to Determine Why*
> *the Organization or Work Unit*
> *Is in Existence in the First Place*

ORGANIZATIONAL STRUCTURE AND THE ROLE OF MANAGEMENT

Theoretically, organizations are put together so that the entity can conduct its business more efficiently, and so that the owners and/or top management can multiple their effectiveness, that is, maximize their desired results. Organizing is intended to be a helping process to enable us to conduct our business better. However, for many organizations it has become a costly process that just ends up getting in the way. As part of the planning phase, the operational reviewer must ascertain whether the organization is properly organized or whether improper organization is the cause of its problems.

Adequate organizational control requires that all employees clearly know their role and function in the organization, and exactly what authority and responsibility have been assigned. It also requires proper separation of duties so that the same individual is not charged with the responsibility for recording and reporting on how a particular task has been accomplished.

Those who have ever been managers know that it is usually easier to just do a task themselves rather than spend the time necessary to make sure the person they have assigned to do the task has done it correctly (i.e., their way). The main reason for having people reporting to a manager is to accomplish the organization's and the management area's mission, goals, and objectives more effectively. However, very rarely is this found to be the case. In many instances, the organization itself, not the accomplishment of results, has become the reason for being.

Typically, the organization and individual departments or work units spend more time on internal goings-on—who got promoted, who reports to whom, who is more important in the hierarchy, and so on—than on the reasons they exist in the first place. Organizing and reorganizing and implementing the latest organizational panaceas (such as total quality management and benchmarking) become their goals, as if the structure of the organization were causing the problems. Many times, the type of organization is not the cause of the problem or even the symptoms; it is just easier to shuffle people around than to do the right thing.

So why do organizations in the private and public sectors place more emphasis on the organizational structure of their operations? The answer, in most cases, is that this is how it has always been. If people were not required to report to other people, they would not know what to do and how could they be trusted to do their jobs without someone else to watch them? It has become standard procedure to departmentalize people without maintaining individual responsibility. When there is trouble within the organization, it is simple to get rid of an entire department or the departmental scapegoat or troublemaker (usually the one who asks the right questions when management does not have the right answers) and avoid facing the real cause of the problem. Many times the real problem is ineffective top management and rather admit to that, management consultants are called in to do what management should have been doing in the first place.

The real answer to why organizations should organize is so that they can accomplish their desired results (be most effective) in the most economical manner (with optimum use of limited resources) using the best available methods of operations (being most efficient). These are, of course, the three Es of operational reviews: economy, efficiency, and effectiveness. If an organization were able to accomplish the goals of the three Es in the first place, and keep things that way, it would not need the quick fixes (i.e., downsizing, reengineering, and so forth) and outside consultants. So, rather than admit its mistakes and make the necessary corrections (i.e., do the right thing), it hires consultants.

The organizational structure is the tool that is supposed to enable the organization to conduct its business in the desired manner. The purpose of both management and the organizational structure is the same, namely, to use the limited resources entrusted to them to accomplish agreed-upon results using the most efficient methods of operation available. If a business used this principle when it put organizations together and made managers and other employees accountable for their results, it would avoid many of the present pitfalls of unwieldy organizational structures.

Theoretically, the organizational structure and management's goals should be the same, and each should support the other in the efforts toward making the organization successful. That this has not happened is evident by what is occurring in many organizations, both large and small today: downsizing, reengineering, layoffs, cost cutting, total quality management, and its ilk. Rather than using one of these new management miracles, hoping for quick, short-term fixes that often result in longer term problems, it may be time to go back to organizational basics whereby all those working for the organization take responsibility for the organization's success.

> *Ask Why the Organization Organizes*
> *and How It Helps to Achieve Results*

Organizational Structure Examples

Exhibit 2.3 depicts a representative top level organization chart graphically, showing the reporting relationships from the president down through departmental levels. This typical structure would fit most organizations. It is based on a hierarchical pyramid concept in which the ultimate power starts at the top and is delegated down through the pyramid. This model originates from the military, specifically from Napoleon's time. Its purpose was to maintain control within the organization through a chain of command, demanding obedience from each level of the organization that reported to a higher level. To this day, many business organizations still function in

EXHIBIT 2.3   Top Level Organization Chart

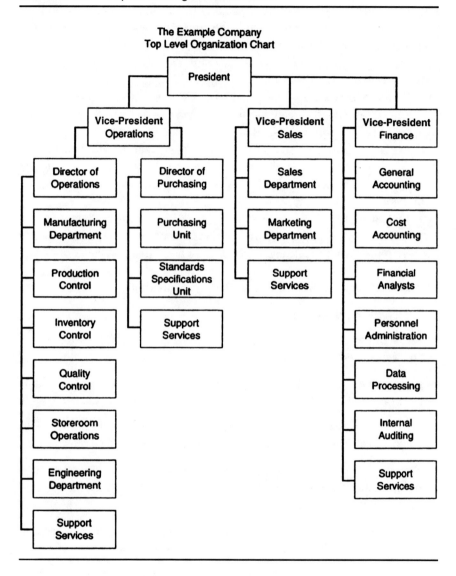

this manner, whereby the purpose for the organizational hierarchy is to police and control those reporting to them to make sure they do their jobs.

The structure is also set up with the intrinsic message that those in a higher position on the chart know more. Hence, much of their time is spent on reviewing the work of those under them and having them redo it so it looks more like what the manager would do. These policing and control, review and redo processes make many supervisors and managers superfluous (non–value-added) organizational overhead, and often more hindrance than help. If these non–value-added processes are eliminated, management will be strictly limited to necessities, and the organization will create an atmosphere that encourages the motivation of self-disciplined employee behavior. If so, many of these layers of unnecessary organization can be eliminated.

A look at Exhibit 2.3 may raise many questions and reveal areas for review related to making this organization more effective and efficient and, as a result, more economical. The following are areas that may be considered:

- The need for vice-presidents and their real functions.

- Directors' level and their purposes.

- The number of functions reporting to the vice president of operations and the related control structure.

- The number of department levels and breakdowns, such as the manufacturing and finance areas.

- Which departments or units are necessary, combined, eliminated, could be provided more economically in another manner, and so on.

- Reporting relationships throughout the organization, such as between the president and vice presidents, the vice presidents and directors/department heads, and so on.

- The degree of value-added management/supervision, as opposed to policing and control, and review and redo procedures.

- The ability of personnel in general to perform their functions in a motivated self-discipline mode without the need for close supervision or management.

- The purpose of support services for each branch and their related functions.

Exhibit 2.4 shows a further breakdown of the functional areas reporting to the vice-president of operations.

A review of this organizational chart, with particular attention to the purchasing function, reveals some areas for further review, such as:

• Why does the purchasing department report to the vice-president of operations?

EXHIBIT 2.4 Further Breakdown Organization Chart

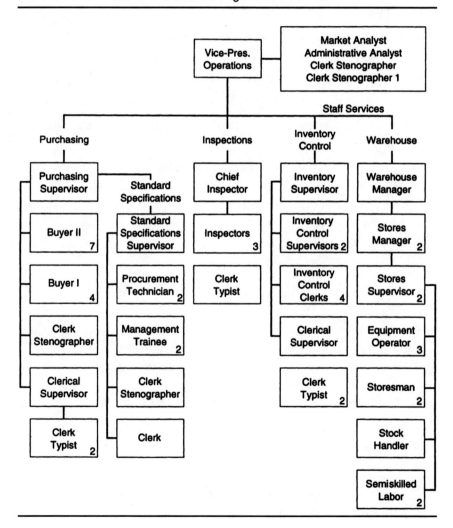

- What are the functions, responsibilities, and authority of staff functions such as market analyst and administrative analyst?

- Why are two clerk stenographers reporting directly to the vice president of operations? What do they do?

- What is the function and authority of the purchasing supervisor? (Note: This position was listed as Director of Purchasing on the top level organization chart).

- What are the buyers' functions and how are they used within the purchasing department?

- What is the difference between a Buyer II and a Buyer I?

- Are all the buyers necessary, based on division of the workload?

- What is the function of the clerk stenographer and how does it differ from those of the clerical supervisor and clerk typists?

- What does the clerical supervisor do, and is supervision of the two clerk typists necessary?

- What are the functions of the two clerk typists, and is the work load appropriate?

- What is the function of the Standards Specifications Unit? Is it needed to this extent or at all? Can its functions be eliminated or outsourced?

- Is the personnel complement within the Standards Specifications Unit appropriate to the present work required?

- What are the specific functions of the Standards Specifications Unit personnel, and are they necessary?

- Should other units such as Inspections, Inventory Control, and Warehouse be reporting to the same individual, vice president of operations, as the Purchasing function? To what extent are these functions necessary?

Sample Planning Phase Organizational Work Program

The following are 14 work steps that may be included in a planning phase operational review work program for the organization represented in Exhibit 2.4:

1. Secure or prepare an organization chart with descriptions of each department's and work units' specific functions.

2. Determine formal and informal reporting relationships from top to bottom, bottom to top, and across functional lines.

3. Analyze actual operations to determine whether such reporting is proper in relation to how the organization actually functions and whether it results in operational concerns and problems.

4. Analyze each work unit's functions to determine whether they are appropriate.

5. Document the duties and responsibilities of each employee. Obtain copies of existing job descriptions or prepare them through the use of user-provided data such as a Job Responsibility Questionnaire.

6. Interview the president, vice-presidents, managers and supervisors, and each employee, to validate their functions.

7. Observe actual work being performed to determine the necessity of all duties and responsibilities.

8. Obtain or prepare company policies and procedures relating to each function under review.

9. Determine that authority and responsibility relationships are clearly defined and understood by all personnel.

10. Ascertain that all employees know their delegated authority and responsibilities; ensure that the responsibilities are proper for the function and do not overlap or duplicate another area.

11. Look for functions and individuals that either are not providing value-added services or are not being cost effective. Examples may be isolates, dispatchers, controllers, unwieldy hierarchies typified by policing and control, and management/supervision that gets in the way.

12. Review hiring, orientation, training, evaluation, promotion, and layoff/firing practices.

13. Question inefficient practices such as management policing and controlling, reviewing and employee redoing, inappropriate following of policies, and so on.

14. Ascertain the level of self-motivated disciplined behavior.

Various operational review tools are used to assist in gathering and analyzing information about an organization. Sample tools include the survey form in Exhibit 2.5, which stresses management roles and responsibilities.

EXHIBIT 2.5   Organizational Initial Survey Form

Planning

1. How does the company plan? Describe the system of planning.
2. Does a long-range plan exist? If so, attach copy.
3. Do current short-term plans exist? If so, attach copy.
4. What are plans for expansion or improvement? How will they affect the organization?
5. What are plans for physical plant development? How will they affect the organization?
6. What are personnel plans?
   - Positions to be added
   - Positions to be eliminated
   - Functions to be changed
7. How does the organization budget? Does it encourage the increase of personnel costs and positions? Are personnel positions and costs part of the budget justification process?

Personnel and Staffing

1. Does an organization chart exist? If so, provide copy.
2. Do job descriptions exist for each block on the organizational chart? If so, provide copies.
3. Are job descriptions of a general nature by position, or specific functional descriptions for each employee?
4. Do staffing statistics by functional area exist? If so, provide copy. Are there areas where such statistics do not exist?
5. How are employees recruited, screened, interviewed, and hired?
6. Is there a system of employee evaluations? Describe.
7. Is there a process of justifying a new position? Describe.
8. How are employees disciplined, laid off, and fired? Describe.
9. How are employees oriented and trained? Describe.
10. What are salary increase and promotion policies? Describe.
11. How are salary increases (and decreases) determined? Who makes these decisions?
12. Is there an employee personnel manual? Obtain copy.
13. Is there a wage and salary policy and adopted schedule? Is it shared with employees? Obtain copy.
14. Is there an employee grievance procedure? Describe.
15. What types of personnel records are maintained?
16. Are staffing patterns established based on operational requirements justified by the three Es or by some other means?

EXHIBIT 2.5 (*Continued*)

17. Are employees cross-trained, or do they remain in the same area throughout their employment with the company?
18. Are personnel adequately capable and competent for their jobs?

Management

1. Is there a board of directors? If so, provide list of names, addresses, and credentials.
2. What are the functions of the board? How often does it meet?
3. Who is considered top management? Provide list of names.
4. Who is considered middle management? Provide list of names.
5. Who is considered lower management (supervision)? Provide list of names.
6. How adequate are existing reports in furnishing information for making management decisions?
7. Are there internal downward communication tools for the staff?
8. Are authority and related responsibilities effectively delegated to management and lower levels?
9. Is there an effective mechanism for upward communication from the staff to levels of management? Describe.
10. Is management performing the functions of managing entrusted resources in the most economical, efficient, and effective manner? Describe how this is accomplished.
11. What are the criteria for management promotion? Describe system.

Authority and Responsibility

1. Has authority been delegated effectively to managers and lower levels within the organization? Describe the process.
2. Are responsibilities clearly defined and understood by managers and staff personnel? Describe the process.
3. Are there written policies and procedures relating to personnel and other functions? If so, provide copies.
4. Do employees know clearly what is expected of them and exactly what authority and responsibility have been assigned to them?

Note: When completing this initial survey form or having client personnel provide the responses, make sure that answers encompass the entire organization, individual departments, specific job positions, and individuals performing each function. All exceptions to the norms should be noted.

IDENTIFICATION OF CRITICAL PROBLEM AREAS

Now that needed information has been obtained, how should it be used? The planning data gathered provide the background and general working information for the operational review staff. These data should also be used to help decide which specific areas of activity to examine in the field work phase. In most operational reviews, the review staff decides which specific areas to review. The general objective is to direct attention to those matters that most urgently need it. Identifying these critical areas is an important component of each operational review.

Techniques for preliminary identification of critical areas vary with the type of engagement. They require a reviewer's ingenuity and judgment. Such techniques include:

- Identification of key activities

- Use of management reports

- Examination of past reviews and reports

- Physical inspection of the activities

- Discussions with responsible personnel

Identification of Key Activities

The information obtained may disclose key activities or aspects of an activity that appear to be difficult to control or susceptible to abuse or laxity. For instance, in a purchasing operation, the key critical areas might be:

- Determinations of quantities and qualities to be purchased

- Methods used in obtaining the most advantageous price

- Methods of determining whether the correct quantities and qualities are actually received

Use of Management Reports

Examining the reports management uses to assure itself that work is progressing within established time and cost goals should provide valuable information in selecting areas of inquiry. Examples of such reporting are operational exception reporting and actual versus plan reporting, which compare actual results with goals and objectives. The reviewer should look closely at those items management has selected as critical for exception reporting, such as inventory levels, productivity measures, sales analysis, and so on. Indications of critical areas to look at will surface if major deviances are found between the plan and actual results. Keep in mind that the plan could be all right and the operational results critical, or vice versa.

Where such reports are not being used effectively, the reviewer should inquire about the methods by which control is exercised. This inquiry may point up a lack of effective control with related administrative weakness or it may disclose other less formal control procedures, which may, in turn, disclose operational weaknesses. Similar considerations would apply if proper performance yardsticks have not been established.

Examination of Past Review and Audit Reports

Past review and audit reports (internal and external) may be a valuable source of information in determining the direction of effort. There should be an examination not only of reports prepared by the internal or external review or audit groups, but also of those of other internal review organizations, as well as supervisory groups, where applicable, such as bank examiners. The reviewer should determine whether management agrees with specific review or audit findings, particularly if mentioned by more than one review or audit group, and whether any action has been taken to correct the situation.

Physical Inspection of the Activities

A physical inspection of activities requires alertness for signs of ineffectiveness or inefficiency, such as bottlenecks, excess accumulations of equipment or material, and idleness of personnel. Such inspections may disclose serious weaknesses warranting inquiry, or they may depict a pattern prevalent throughout the organization.

Discussions with Responsible Personnel

Finally, discussions with responsible officials and personnel directly concerned with an activity may assist in the identification of critical areas. Sometimes valuable leads can be obtained through discussions with responsible officials and others directly concerned with the activities performed. These individuals can often identify troublesome areas or request that the reviewer look into specific matters that they are concerned about, but for which they lack information regarding the actual conditions.

> **The Critical Areas Are Those**
> **that Most Urgently Need Review**

REVIEW OF ADMINISTRATIVE AND OPERATIONAL CONTROLS

Certain key areas are part of the operational reviewer's review of internal administrative and operational controls in the planning phase:

- Organization
- Policies and procedures
- Accounting and other records
- Performance standards
- Information systems and internal reports

Organization

Adequate organizational control requires that all employees know clearly what their role and function is in the organization, and exactly what authority and responsibility have been assigned. It also requires proper separation of duties so that the same individual who is assigned a function is not charged with the responsibility for recording and reporting on how the particular task has been accomplished.

Policies and Procedures

Policy sets forth the organization's operating guidelines and specifies what is required, and procedures outline how the policies will be carried out.

Accounting and Other Records

The results of business operations must be recorded promptly, accurately, completely, and in conformity with both operating responsibilities and generally accepted accounting principles. Accounting and other records must accurately reflect the financial condition of the organization and provide the means for making future business decisions, based on past results.

Performance Standards

Performance standards are used to measure results and highlight conditions or trends for management's actions. The reviewer will determine the existence and appropriateness of any performance standards established and what actions have been taken.

Information Systems and Internal Reports

Major tools in the management control process are information systems and internal reports. They must be economically viable, timely, accurate, concise, and complete, and must provide adequate control over the organization's resources, revenues, and expenditures. That is why the appraisal of the effectiveness of internal reports and communications is so important. The task of appraising the effectiveness of internal reports involves determination of three factors:

1. The purpose of the report or the primary communication function management intends the report to perform (the intended function)

2. The way in which the report affects supervisees (the actual function)

3. The correlation or degree of correspondence between the report's intended effect and the actual effect on the function

The reviewer's task is to determine that the intended function and the actual function (how the report's recipient perceives his or her function) are the same. If they are not, there is a lack of effective communication. If, on the other hand, such reports are not used, the reviewer should ask about the methods by which control is exercised, which may point to a lack of effective control, with related laxity and administrative weakness.

> ### *Administrative and Operational Controls Set the Tone for Operations*

PLANNING PHASE WORK PROGRAM

After the gathering of operational data and information and the preliminary identification of critical operational problem areas, a planning phase work program can now be constructed. This work program provides guidance and direction as to which additional work steps must be performed to finalize the areas to be included in the in-depth operational review. A sample of such a work program is shown in Exhibit 2.6. Note that the items included in this work program are based on the initial review previously described.

> ### *The Planning Phase Needs to Be Planned*

FINANCIAL STATEMENT ANALYSIS

Because members of the operational review team usually have some financial expertise, a good place to start in determining critical operational areas is to analyze the organization's financial data and statements. Keep in mind that financial statements, produced from a financial accounting standpoint, are essentially historical documents that present the organization's assets, liabilities, and equity in a balance sheet and its revenues and expenses in an income statement. These financial statements tell what has happened within the organization during a particular period or series of periods.

These same financial statements can be used from an operational review standpoint to help identify present and future critical areas for review. The use of certain analytical tools can effectively help to analyze the financial statements, determine how the organization is doing, and zero in on critical

EXHIBIT 2.6   Planning Phase Work Program

1. *Goals and Objectives*
   a. Review legislative and internal materials that define the general goals and objectives of the area.
      Find out it auditee has elaborated on legislative goals and objectives. Does the area have a formal procedure for doing this?
   b. Planning Systems and Procedures
      - Document the planning procedure either with a narrative or with a flowchart plus narrative.
        Relate to copies of forms and reports.
        Note: Planning must be a coordinated effort between upper- and lower-level management—lower management levels incorporating broader objectives of upper management, as well as defining their own specific objectives.
      - Determine the extent of planning: use of short-term (current year) and long-term planning (five years forward).
        Do objectives and goals coordinate with those of other related and unrelated functions?
        Is there a formal procedure for identifying needs for operating improvements?
        Do planning procedures include a formal statement of justification and a statement of impact?
      - Review present plans and related goals and objectives.
        Substantiate definition of needs incorporated in the planning process through a review of documentation, such as minutes of meetings and correspondence files.
        Note: Goals and objectives should be?
           clearly stated.
           communicated to various management levels.
      - Review detail plans of action and procedures involved in administering the plan.
        Are the steps clearly outlined?
        Are the program responsibilities assigned?
        Are progress review dates established and slippages in schedules promptly reported and corrected?
        Are budget (plan) versus actual dollars controlled?
        Sometimes there are alternative courses to achieve program objectives. Have alternatives been analyzed in terms of effectiveness and cost?

EXHIBIT 2.6 (*Continued*)

2. *Budgets*
   a. Review budget process as related to planning procedures.
      - Are budget procedures integrated with the planning process?
      - Are budgets justified in terms of plan?
   b. Budget Justification Procedures
      - Review justification for all budget levels and measures these against actual conditions. Evaluate soundness of budget allocations.
      - Review justification and evaluate soundness for new and increased funding, and measure against actual conditions.
      - Relate one aspect of budget to another aspect. Some may be realized, others may not.
         Example: An expanded program requires:
         additional personnel.
         more equipment.
         more furniture.
         more supplies.
      The employees are not hired, but the department, meanwhile, has gone ahead and purchased the equipment, the furniture, and the supplies.
         Example of other areas where correlation is helpful:
         higher postage expenses with increased correspondence (e.g., billings).
         more equipment with increased supplies or paper.
         increased activities in one department matched by an increase in another department.
         request for fixed assets, if not for an expanded area, should alert the auditor to ask about asset retirement, scrap or surplus sales.
   c. Analyze budget reporting procedures and their effectiveness?
      - Budget versus actual reporting.
      - Use of flexible budgeting (relating budget to actual conditions).
      - Effective monitoring and control.
3. *Organization Chart and Procedures Manuals*
   a. Obtain copy or prepare organization chart, and analyze as to possible inefficiencies, such as:
      - One-on-one administration or supervision.
      - Span of administration much too wide for one person. This should be evaluated by competence of the administrator, capability of supervisees, complexity of functions performed.

EXHIBIT 2.6 (*Continued*)

- Overlapping, so that personnel report to more than one person.
- Apparent illogical placement of units within the organization.
- Administrative positions that do not appear to be commensurate either with extend to responsibilities or with numbers supervised.

b. Obtain copies of procedures manuals and review for:
  - Absence of definitions of jobs and responsibilities.
  - Existing but outdated or inadequate procedures.

4. *Flowcharts*
   a. Prepare for flowcharting by becoming familiar with the department and its operations.
      - Review the budget detail.
      - Review the procedures manual.
      - Review the organizational charts.
      - Review all reports.
      - Review analysis of expenditures and revenues.
      - Obtain copies of all forms used.
      - Discuss operations in a general way with auditee personnel.
   b. Prepare general systems flowcharts of major systems and procedures.
   c. Analyze flowcharts to identify such things as:
      - Weaknesses in internal control.
      - Work-flow bottlenecks or uneven distribution of work.
      - Unnecessary handling of documents.
      - Inefficient routing of documents.
      - Unnecessary document copies or records or unused information.
      - Duplication of efforts.
      - Insufficient use of equipment.

5. *Reports*
   a. Obtain copies of management and operating reports.
   b. Discuss reports with appropriate personnel and prepare written description of contents and purpose of each report.
      - Do reports provide usable information based on the auditor's understanding of the operation?
      - Are users really using the reports? If not, discuss and document reasons.
      - Prepare list of distribution of reports and frequency of their issuance.

EXHIBIT 2.6 (*Continued*)

Quantify exceptions on the basis of the amount of time used, and the salary levels of personnel using them.

d. Analyze the department's general operating procedures. Are they:
  • Manual when automated would be better?
  • Automated when manual would be better?
  • Automated, but not fully utilized?

e. Review fixed assets used in operations and related records. Some idea of the care the department lavishes or does not lavish on its fixed assets can be gleaned from these results.

---

areas that need attention and improvement. These tools are summarized as follows:

• Comparisons

• Trend percentages

• Common-size statements

• Financial ratios

Comparisons

Financial statements are primarily static historical documents showing data related only to a specific period of time. Operational reviewers are concerned with the period being reported, and what the trend of events has been and will be over longer periods of time. Accordingly, comparing financial statement data with the results of other periods, or of other organizations, provides a better understanding of trends and helps in making proper decisions as to their relative significance. Comparisons can be made with the historical performance of the company, a competitor's performance, performance of other organizations within the same general industry, and organizational goals, objectives, and detail plans. Comparison within the same organization is also known as internal benchmarking, which looks for best results and related best practices. Comparison outside of the organization (competitors, industry, and best in class) is also known as external benchmarking, which looks for best practices that can be incorporated into the company's operations in a program of continuous improvement.

In making such comparisons, it is important to be reasonably sure that the data are comparable; that is, that they are calculated on a consistent basis between or among years, companies, and so on. If not, incorrect or misleading conclusions may be drawn, resulting in the expenditure of a substantial amount of operational review time on the wrong functional area.

An initial analytical procedure in financial statement analysis is to format the company's statements comparatively. This may entail comparing this year with last year or comparing a number of years' data, arriving at numerical and/or percentage differences. Preparing statements in such comparative form can disclose valuable information as to present conditions and what to expect about future financial and operating performance.

Comparison of two or more years' data is known as "horizontal analysis," which identifies changes over time by displaying data changes from year to year in both dollars and percentages. Dollar changes help to identify key factors having an impact on future operations, financial position, or profitability. The Example Company's comparative financial statements for the last three years are shown in Exhibits 2.7 through 2.9.

These statements should be reviewed and possible critical areas of the Example Company's operations to be considered for operational review should be listed. A list of such critical areas is shown in Exhibit 2.10.

The review team then presents such critical areas to management so as to mutually agree on which areas to include in the present operational review, which ones can be dealt with by departmental personnel, and which ones need to be considered for a future review.

Looking at changes in percentage between years also can provide proper perspective regarding changes. For example, a different conclusion is reached when sales increase by $2 million over a previous year's sales of $4 million (a significant increase of 50 percent), than when the previous year's sales were $100 million (an increase of only 2 percent). In the Example Company's Comparative Balance Sheets there are other examples in which the combination of dollar and percentage changes provide a more complete analysis and help to determine a future trouble spot. For instance, an Accounts Receivable increase from $1,600 in 20X8 to $1,900 in 20X9 does not appear very critical; however, expressed as an 18 percent increase (and as 7 percent of sales of $12,500) it takes on greater significance. As seen in the Example Company's Comparative Income Statements, sales increased by $500,000 from 20X7 to 20X8; however cost of goods sold also increased by $500,000, exactly offsetting the change in sales and adding nothing to profitability.

EXHIBIT 2.7 Comparative Balance Sheets as of December 31: The Example Company

	20x9	20x8	20x7	20x6
	\$\$ in 000s)			
	\$	\$	\$	\$
Assets				
Cash	100	450	400	400
Marketable securities	-0-	500	300	200
Accounts receivable	1,900	1,600	1,700	1,500
Inventory	2,000	1,500	1,500	1,300
Prepaid expenses	200	150	100	100
Current Assets	4,200	4,200	4,000	3,500
Property, plant, & equipment	7,700	3,500	3,000	2,800
Less accumulated depreciation	(1,800)	(1,000)	(800)	(700)
Net Property, Plant, & Equipment	5,900	2,500	2,200	2,100
Intangibles & miscellaneous	600	600	600	500
Total Assets	10,700	7,300	6,800	6,100
Liabilities & Stockholders' Equity				
Notes payable	100	100	100	100
Accounts payable	700	300	250	350
Accrued expenses	550	500	400	350
Income taxes payable	400	350	500	200
Current maturity, long-term debt	250	150	150	150
Current Liabilities	2,000	1,400	1,400	1,150
Long-term debt	3,000	950	1,100	1,250
Total Liabilities	5,000	2,350	2,500	2,400
Preferred stock	100	100	100	100
Common stock (1 million shares)	1,000	1,000	1,000	1,000
Additional paid-in capital	1,100	1,100	1,100	1,100
Retained earnings	3,500	2,750	2,100	1,500
Total Stockholders' Equity	5,700	4,950	4,300	3.700
Total Liability & Stockholders' Equity	10,700	7,300	6,800	6,100

EXHIBIT 2.8   Comparative Income Statements for Years Ended December 31: The Example Company

	20X9	20X8	20X7
	($$ in 000s)		
	$	$	$
Net Sales	12,500	11,000	10,500
Cost of Goods Sold			
Material	3,500	2,400	1,600
Labor	2,200	2,700	3,200
Manufacturing expenses	2,400	2,200	2,000
Total Cost of Goods Sold	8,100	7,300	6,800
Manufacturing Profit	4,400	3,700	3,700
Selling Expenses	1,100	900	900
General & Administrative			
Expenses	1,200	1,300	1,200
Total Operating Expenses	2,300	2,200	2,100
Operating Profit	2,100	1,500	1,600
Other (income) Expenses			
Interest, net	150	140	160
Other	(50)	10	40
Total Other	100	150	200
Profit before Income Taxes	2,000	1,350	1,400
Provision for Income Taxes	800	450	500
Net Income	1,200	900	900

Trend Percentages

Financial statement analysis can also be accomplished through the use of trend percentages, which are used to state a number of years' financial data in terms of a base year. The rule in using trend percentages is that at least three data points must be examined before a trend can be identified.

EXHIBIT 2.9 Statement of Cash Flow for Years Ended December 31: The Example Company

	20X9	20X8	20X7
	($$ in 000s)		
	$	$	$
Operating Activities			
Net income	1,200	900	900
Depreciation	800	200	100
Changes in assets and liabilities			
Accounts receivable	(300)	100	(200)
Inventory	(500)	0	(200)
Prepaid expenses	(50)	(50)	0
Other assets	0	0	(100)
Accounts payable	400	50	(100)
Accrued expenses	50	100	50
Income taxes payable	50	(150)	300
Total Cash Provided by Operating Activities	1,650	1,150	750
Investing Activities			
Plant and equipment	(4,200)	(500)	(200)
Financing Activities			
New borrowing	2,200	0	0
Repayment of debt	(150)	(150)	(150)
Increase in short-term debt	100	0	0
Preferred stock dividends	(10)	(10)	(10)
Common stock dividends	(440)	(240)	(290)
Total Cash Provided (Used) by Financing Activities	1,700	(400)	(450)
Increase (decrease) in cash	(850)	250	100
Beginning Cash Balance	950	700	600
Ending Cash and Marketable Securities Balance	100	950	700

EXHIBIT 2.10   Financial Statement Analysis, Comparative Statements: Suggested List of Critical Areas

BALANCE SHEET

Assets

Cash Management: Decrease in cash (from $400 to $450 to $100) with corresponding sell-off of marketable securities.

Accounts receivable: Increase of 18% from $1,600 to $1,900. Also, could be large in relation to sales ($12,500/$1,900 = 6.58%). Could also indicate ineffective billing and collection procedures.

Inventory: Increase of 33% from $1,500 to $2,000. Could indicate weaknesses in inventory control and related purchasing procedures.

Property, plant, and equipment: Large increase of 120% from $3,500 to $7,700 indicates large recent expansion which may have been unnecessary, controlled ineffectively, or used improperly.

Liabilities

Accounts payable: Increase of 133% from $300 to $700, which could indicate unnecessary purchasing, overextension or expenditures, and weakened ability to pay.

Long-term debt: Large increase of 226% from $950 to $3,000, which indicates substantial changes in the organization resulting in increased property, plant, and equipment with corresponding decrease in the company's cash position.

Stockholder's Equity

Retained earnings: Increase of $650 and $750 for the two years, which indicates that the company has increased its net income as the result of changes noted above. However, is this significant expected change and should the company have been able to do even better?

INCOME STATEMENT

Sales: Sales have increased from $10,500 to $11,000 to $12,500 over the past few years. Analysis by product line should be made to determine the causes for such an increase in sales.

Cost of goods sold: Cost has increased in total from $6,800 to $7,300 to $8,100. However, material costs are the major contributor to this increase—indicating a possible major critical operational area. In addition, labor costs have greatly decreased over the last three years (from $3,200 to $2,200). This indicates a possible shift in manufacturing and products produced, which could also be a major area for consideration. It appears that the company is becoming less labor intensive.

Consider the Example Company:

	20X9	20X8	20X7
Sales	$12,500	$11,000	$10,500
Net Income	$ 1,200	$ 900	$ 900

Analyzing the dollar data alone, it could be concluded that both sales and net income have increased over the three-year period. However, it cannot readily be concluded how fast sales have increased and whether the increases in net income have kept pace with sales increases. Using dollar data alone may make it difficult to conclude adequately. Now assume that the base year 20X7 is equal to 100 percent; the other years can be stated as a percentage of the base year:

	20X9		20X8		20X7	
	Dollars	%	Dollars	%	Dollars	%
Sales	$12,500	119%	$11,000	105%	$10,500	100%
Net Income	$ 1,200	133%	$ 900	100%	$ 900	100%

By using these trend percentages as well as the differences in real dollars (or numbers), the increase in sales and net income can be put into proper perspective. It can now be clearly seen that the relative growth in sales has been surpassed by the growth in net income; sales in 20X9 are 19 percent greater than the base year, but net income is 33 percent greater. Sales growth was better than net income growth in 20X8, and growth in sales in 20X9 over 20X8 was considerably below the growth in net income for the same year. Such an analysis could indicate major operational areas for review, such as sales analysis, cost of goods sold analysis, selling price procedures, and cost analysis.

Common-Size Statements

A common-size financial statement shows the line items as percentages in addition to absolute dollars. Each line item on the financial statements is shown as a percentage of some total, such as assets or sales. The preparation and presentation of common size statements is known as "vertical analysis" revealing changes in the relative significance of each line item. Common-size balance sheets and income statements for the Example Company for the past three years are shown in Exhibits 2.11 and 2.12.

EXHIBIT 2.11 Common-Size Balance Sheets as of December 31: The Example Company

Assets	20X9 $	20X9 %	20X8 $	20X8 %	20X7 $	20X7 %	20X6 $	20X6 %
				($$ in 000s)				
Cash	100	0.9	450	6.2	400	5.9	400	6.6
Marketable securities	-0-	0.0	500	6.9	300	4.4	200	3.3
Accounts receivable	1,900	17.8	1,600	21.9	1,700	25.0	1,500	24.6
Inventory	2,000	18.7	1,500	20.5	1,500	22.0	1,300	21.3
Prepaid expenses	200	1.9	150	2.0	100	1.5	100	1.6
Current Assets	4,200	39.3	4,200	57.5	4,000	58.8	3,500	57.4
Property, plant & equipment	7,700	71.9	3,500	48.0	3,000	44.1	2,800	45.9
Less accumulated depreciation	(1,800)	(16.8)	(1,000)	(13.7)	(800)	(11.7)	(700)	(11.5)
Net Property, Plant, Equity	5,900	55.1	2,500	34.3	2,200	32.4	2,100	34.4
Intangibles & miscellaneous	600	5.6	600	8.2	600	8.8	500	8.2
TOTAL ASSETS	10,700	100.0	7,300	100.0	6,800	100.0	6,100	100.0
Liabilities & Stockholders' Equity								
Notes payable	100	0.9	100	1.4	100	1.5	100	1.6
Accounts payable	700	6.6	300	4.1	250	3.7	350	5.7
Accrued expenses	550	5.2	500	6.9	400	5.9	350	5.7
Income taxes payable	400	3.7	350	4.8	500	7.3	200	3.3
Current maturity long-term	250	2.3	150	2.0	150	2.2	150	2.5
Current Liabilities	2,000	18.7	1,400	19.2	1,400	20.6	1,150	18.8
Long-term debt	3,000	28.0	950	13.0	1,100	16.2	1,250	20.5
Total Liabilities	5,000	46.7	2,350	32.2	2,500	36.8	2,400	39.3
Preferred stock	100	0.9	100	1.4	100	1.5	100	1.6
Common stock (1 million shares)	1,000	9.4	1,000	13.7	1,000	14.7	1,000	16.4
Additional paid-in capital	1,100	10.3	1,100	15.0	1,100	16.2	1,100	18.1
Retained earnings	3,500	32.7	2,750	37.7	2,100	30.8	1,500	24.6
Total Stockholders' Equity	5,700	53.3	4,950	67.8	4,300	63.2	3,700	60.7
TOTAL LIABILITY & STOCKHOLDERS' EQUITY	10,700	100.0	7,300	100.0	6,800	100.0	6,100	100.0

EXHIBIT 2.12   Common-Size Income Statements for Years Ended
December 31: The Example Company

	20X9		20X8		20X7	
	($$ in 000s)					
	$	%	$	%	$	%
Net Sales	12,500	100.0	11,000	100.0	10,500	100.0
Cost of Goods Sold						
Material	3,500	28.0	2,400	21.8	1,600	15.2
Labor	2,200	17.6	2,700	24.6	3,200	30.5
Manufacturing						
expenses	2,400	19.2	2,200	20.0	2,000	19.1
Total Cost of						
Goods Sold	8,100	64.8	7,300	66.4	6,800	64.8
MANUFACTURING						
PROFIT	4,400	35.2	3,700	33.6	3,700	35.2
Selling expenses	1,100	8.8	900	8.2	900	8.6
General &						
administrative						
expenses	1,200	9.6	1,300	11.8	1,200	11.4
Total Operating						
Expenses	2,300	18.4	2,200	20.0	2,100	20.0
OPERATING PROFIT	2,100	16.8	1,500	13.6	1,600	15.2
Other (income)						
expenses						
Interest, net	150	1.2	140	1.2	160	1.5
Other	(50)	(0.4)	10	0.1	40	0.4
Total Other	100	0.8	150	1.3	200	1.9
PROFIT BEFORE						
INCOME TAXES	2,000	16.0	1,350	12.3	1,400	13.3
Provision for income						
taxes	800	6.4	450	4.1	500	4.7
NET INCOME	1,200	9.6	900	8.2	900	8.6

An analysis of financial statements on a common size basis could disclose such areas as:

Balance Sheet:

	% Of Total Assets		
	20X7	20X9	Change
Current assets	58.8%	39.3%	−19.5%
Property, plant & equipment	32.4	55.1	+22.7
Intangibles	8.8	5.6	−3.2
Current liabilities	20.6	18.7	−1.9
Long-term debt	16.2	28.0	+11.8
Stockholders' equity	63.2	53.3	−9.9

Comments: There has been a major shift into property, plant, and equipment, financed by reduction of current assets and additional long-term debt. The reason for this major investment needs to be investigated.

Income Statement:

	% Of Total Sales		
	20X7	20X9	Change
Material	15.2%	28.0%	−12.8%
Labor	30.5	17.6	−12.9
Manufacturing expenses	19.1	19.2	− .1
Cost of Goods Sold	64.8	64.8	-0-
Selling expenses	8.6	8.8	+ .2
G & A expenses	11.4	9.6	− 1.8
Operating expenses	20.0	18.4	− 1.6
Operating Profit	15.2	16.8	+ 1.6

Comments: The switch between labor and material indicates a major change from in-house manufacturing to outside sourcing of parts, or some other significant change in product. The drop in general and administrative (G & A) expenses is also significant, but may be the result of increasing volume. Other changes are not material. The change away from in-house manufacturing when related to the investment in property, plant, and equipment raises a disturbing conflict that needs to be explained.

Financial Ratios

Proper financial analysis of an organization's results provides for the measurement and evaluation of its progress toward accomplishment of financial goals and objectives, for example, earning an adequate return on investment or maintenance of a satisfactory financial position. The organization's financial position usually involves two fundamental considerations:

- Potential for survival: measured by short-term liquidity (ability to meet short-term financial obligations) and long-term solvency (ability to meet long-term financial obligations).

- Performance (toward meeting financial and operational goals): measured by asset management and profitability results.

Financial ratios, which represent a mathematical relationship between two quantitative conditions, are the primary means used for such financial analysis. Measured over a period of time, these ratios can be used to identify changes or trends in operations. They can also be used to provide information for identifying operational trouble spots. By analyzing changes and trends using ratios, and comparisons between time periods of various accounts (such as inventory, sales, expenses, and so on), they can also provide advice and insight into the client's operations as well as indicate where the most critical problems might lie. Presented on the following pages are some specific financial ratios derived from the data on the Example Company financial statements. The specific examples of survival and performance ratios provided in Exhibits 2.13 and 2.14 indicate the possible conditions and risks to the Example Company. These ratios should be analyzed in combination, as well as related to specific operations.

IDENTIFYING CRITICAL AREAS

As a result of the initial survey and analysis of financial statement data of the Example Company, the operational reviewer should be able to help management identify its critical operational areas where operational review procedures would provide the most benefits. This step is not always required, as quite often management has already decided which areas would provide the biggest payout through operational review procedures. However, based on the reviewer's analysis of the Example Company financial

EXHIBIT 2.13   Survival Rations

Survival ratios address the prospective ability of a company to continue as an economically viable entity.

Liquidity Ratios   Liquidity measures the organization's ability to meet current obligations in the short term (one year or less), or the ability to convert noncash assets into cash or otherwise to obtain cash to meet current liabilities. These ratios are of particular interest to short-term creditors of the company—banks, vendors, and other suppliers of goods and services.

Working Capital   is determined by subtracting current liabilities from current assets. It provides a safety cushion for the company and creditors. Relatively higher levels of working capital may be desirable if the firm has difficulty obtaining short-term borrowed funds. In the following illustration from the Example Company, the decrease in working capital is a negative sign, as the organization has reduced its capacity for meeting its short-term obligations by more than 20 percent.

	Current Assets —	Current Liabilities =	Working Capital
20X9	$4,200	$2,000	$2,200
20X8	4,200	1,400	2,800
Decrease in Working Capital			$ 600

Current Ratio   is calculated by dividing current assets by current liabilities. It measures the organization's ability to pay off current liabilities by use of its current assets. Within reason, the higher the current ratio, the more safety and security the company's balance sheet demonstrates for short-term purposes. However, the ratio may be misleading if, for example, an organization has merely improved its cash position by selling off fixed assets, resulting in an improved current ratio but possibly adverse long-range effects. Moreover, a too high current ratio indicates that the company may not be employing its resources to maximum advantage. The Example Company's current ratios follow:

	20X9	20X8	20X7
Current Assets	4,200	4,200	4,000
Current Liabilities	2,000	1,400	1,400
= Current Ratio	2.10:1	3.00:1	2.86:1

Quick (Acid-Test) Ratio   is calculated by dividing cash plus marketable securities plus accounts receivable by current liabilities. This is a more rigorous test of liquidity in that it eliminates inventory and prepaid expenses from the analysis. This

EXHIBIT 2.13   (*Continued*)

ratio represents a comparison of the most liquid assets (cash, marketable securities, and receivables) to current liabilities. The quick ratios for the Example Company are as follows:

	20X9	20X8	20X7
Quick Assets	2,000	2,550	2,400
Current Liabilities	2,000	1,400	1,400
= Quick Ratio	1.00:1	1.82:1	1.71:1

An analysis of the Example Company liquidity ratios shows that the organization appears to be in a deteriorating liquidity position. Possible areas for improvement could be cash management, better collection procedures, or tighter control over expenditures. A current ratio of at least 2.0 and a quick ratio of 1.0 or better are considered acceptable as rough rules of thumb. However, every situation must be evaluated on its merits before any definitive conclusions are drawn, because each industry may have entirely different standards of acceptability for its liquidity status, and the rules of thumb may be totally inapplicable for the specific company being evaluated.

Leverage Ratios (long-term solvency)   These ratios measure the long-term solvency of the organization—its ability to meet long-term obligations as they come due. Long-term lenders and creditors may have a particular interest in these ratios.

Debt to Equity Ratio   is calculated by dividing total liabilities by total equity, and measures the amount of long-term debt in relation to the amount of shareholder equity the company has in its capital base. Too much debt may cause difficulty for an organization in meeting current interest charges and principal payments as they come due and may cause lending institutions to be wary of lending additional money. The following data are from the Example Company:

	20X9	20X8	20X7
Total Liabilities	5,000	2,350	2,500
Stockholders' Equity	5,700	4,950	4,300
= Debt to Equity Ratio	0.88:1	0.47:1	0.58:1

This means, for every dollar of equity capital outsiders have supplied, respectively, 88, 47, and 58 cents of financing for the three years. Here the organization seems to be fairly well balanced in its capital structure, although 20X9 shows a substantial jump in external financing, which may be some cause for concern. As a general

EXHIBIT 2.13 *(Continued)*

rule of thumb, the company's debt to equity ratio is likely to fall within the range of 0.50 to 1.00. Below that range, the company is not making adequate use of the leverage available to it through use of borrowed funds; yet a company's being above that range may cause lending institutions to feel there is too much leverage and thereby too much risk. Each industry, however, will have different ranges of acceptable ratios, which will be much more useful measures of what is acceptable or not.

Debt to Assets Ratio is calculated by dividing total liabilities by total assets. It is a variation of the debt to equity ratio and measures similar characteristics of the company's financial position—namely, how much of the company's total financing needs is being supplied by lenders and creditors. The range of ratios is likely to fall between 0.33 and 0.50, with variations again depending on the nature of the particular industry in which the company operates. The Example Company results follow:

	20X9	20X8	20X7
Total Liabilities	5,000	2,350	2,500
Total Assets	10,700	7,300	6,800
= Debt to Assets Ratio	0.47:1	0.32:1	0.37:1

The increase in 20X9 indicates that the Example Company has increased its borrowing at a faster rate than its equity. This conclusion can be verified by examining the underlying dollar amounts in the balance sheet or by reviewing the debt to equity ratio.

Interest Coverage Ratio is determine by dividing earnings before interest and taxes (EBIT) by interest expense, and it shows the number of times pre-tax earnings cover the interest expense. It provides a safety margin indicator as it shows how much of an earnings decline can be absorbed before the company is unable to meet interest expenses out of current earnings. For the Example Company:

	20X9	20X8	20X7
EBIT	2,150	1,490	1,560
Interest Expense	150	140	160
= Interest Coverage Ratio	14.3 ×	10.6 ×	9.8 ×

While the increase in the ratios seems a positive indicator since more earnings are available to meet interest expenses, existence of substantially more debt on the balance sheet warns of a possible future decline in this ratio.

EXHIBIT 2.14 Performance Ratios

Performance ratios measure how well an organization performed in terms of resource management and profits.

Activity Ratios   These ratios, also referred to as turnover ratios, measure the organization's use of assets to generate revenue and income. Generally, the higher the turnover, the more efficiently the organization is managing its assets, although too high a turnover may cause problems in that the operating needs of the business may not be met.

Accounts Receivable Collection   There are two accounts receivable ratios that should be examined:

- **Accounts Receivable Turnover,** which provides the number of times accounts receivable are collected in the year. Turnover is calculated by dividing total sales by the average accounts receivable (beginning balance plus ending balance divided by 2). The higher the accounts receivable turnover, the better the organization is at collecting more quickly from customers. The funds are thus available for use in the company's operations. However, if the turnover is too high, it can be a signal that the company is overstrict in its credit policies and may thereby be losing valuable business. The Example Company results show:

	20X9	20X8	20X7
Credit Sales	12,500	11,000	10,500
Avg. Accts Receivable	1,750	1,650	1,600
= Accts. Receivable Turnover	7.14 ×	6.67 ×	6.56 ×

  The increase in the accounts receivable turnover ratio is not enough to be significant, but a turnover ratio in the range of seven times per year may be too low, as will be more clearly explained in the next ratio calculation.

- **Accounts Receivable Collection Period,** which measures the number of days it takes the company to collect its receivables. The calculation is made by dividing the average daily sales (credit sales divided by 365 days) into the accounts receivable balance. The Example Company calculations indicate the following:

	20X9	20X8	20X7
Accounts Receivable	1,900	1,600	1,700
Average Daily Sales	12,500/365	11,000/365	10,500/365
= Days Collection	55.5 days	53.1 days	59.1 days

EXHIBIT 2.14 *(Continued)*

This means that it is taking over 55 days for a sale to be converted to cash by the company in 20X9, which seems to be a rather long time unless the industry standard is this long or the company's credit terms allow more than 50 days to pay. The increase from the prior year is another cause for concern, raising the possibility that the company's collection effort is not being pursued vigorously enough, or that the credit policy is too loose and too many sales are being made to marginal customers. The latter raises the possibility of future collectibility problems for the company.

Inventory Turnover The inventory turnover ratio is a measure of how efficiently the company is using its inventory resources. It is frequently calculated by dividing the inventory balance into the sales to generate an annual turnover amount, but a more useful measure is to divide the cost of goods sold for the year by the inventory balance, since this relates two comparably calculated numbers. Inventory turnover for the Example Company can be shown as follows:

	20X9	20X8	20X7
Cost of Goods Sold	8,100	7,300	6,800
Average Inventory	1,750	1,500	1,400
= Inventory Turnover	4.63 ×	4.87 ×	4.86 ×

The average age of the inventory can be calculated by dividing the turnover rate into 365 (days in the year).

	20X9	20X8	20X7
Days/Turnover	365/4.63	365/4.87	365/4.86
= Average Age	78.8 days	74.9 days	75.1 days

An inventory turnover rate of just under five times per year indicates an organization with possibly slow-moving inventory. When examining the change in this figure over time—in this instance a reduction from 4.86 to 4.63—the analyst may conclude that the company is stocking more inventory or that the inventory is becoming less sellable. It is also possible that slow-moving or obsolete inventory is building up. Under these circumstances management may wish to consider doing a product-mix analysis or implementing more effective inventory control procedures. The longer the inventory needs to be held, the more expensive it is for the company, since carrying costs and risk the loss, obsolescence, or deterioration become higher. On the other hand, it is also possible that in comparison with other similar companies the inventory turnover is within reasonable limits.

EXHIBIT 2.14 *(Continued)*

Asset Turnover This is the ratio of sales divided by total assets. It measures the level of capital investment relative to sales volume and provides an indication of how well the company is managing its assets and how efficiently those assets are being utilized to generate sales and profit. Once again, consider the Example Company:

	20X9	20X8	20X7
Sales	12,500	11,000	10,500
Average Assets	9,000	7,050	6,450
= Asset Turnover	1.39 ×	1.56 ×	1.63 ×

The decrease in asset turnover may indicate too heavy an investment in fixed assets or too low a utilization of the investments the company has made. The absolute number is meaningful only in relation to other companies in the same line of business—some capital-intensive businesses such as steel making work on very low asset turnover ratios, while other types of businesses, such as supermarkets, have extremely high asset turnover rates.

Profitability Ratios These ratios measure an organization's ability to earn a satisfactory profit and return on investment. They can be extremely important, as investors may avoid companies with poor earnings potential and creditors may be wary of insufficient profitability because of the increased risk of loss.

Net Profit Margin is probably the most commonly used measure of performance, though it may not be the most useful. It measures how much of each dollar of sales is retained as profit. If compared with that of other similar companies or with the company's past performance, this ratio provides an effective measure of performance, but results can vary significantly from industry to industry. The Example Company results show:

	20X9	20X8	20X7
Net Income	1,200	900	900
Net Sales	12,500	11,000	10,500
= Net Profit Margin	9.6%	8.2%	8.6%

EXHIBIT 2.14 *(Continued)*

In this instance the net profit margin has increased favorably over the three-year-period, indicating that the company is improving its profitability relative to sales volume.

Gross Profit Margin   is a related profitability measure which calculates gross profit as a percentage of sales to determine the profitability of a company's manufacturing or processing activity. The Example Company results are as follows:

	20X9	20X8	20X7
Gross (Mfg.) Profit	4,400	3,700	3,700
Net Sales	12,500	11,000	10,500
= Gross Profit Margin	35.2%	33.6%	35.2%

Here again the increase in the return, even though small, from 20X8 to 20X9 indicates the company's ability to maintain the profitability of its principal activities. A negative trend in either the gross or net profit margin percentages or a significant drop from one year to the next may indicate to management the need for a cost study or for an intensive look at productivity.

Return on Investment (ROI)   is an exceedingly important measure to review, in that it indicates how effectively the company has utilized its invested funds. "Return on Investment" is a generic term inasmuch as there are numerous ways in which it can be calculated, and it is necessary for the reviewer to be fully aware of the particular ROI calculation being utilized before any evaluations can be made. There are two basic measures that are commonly used:

• **Return on Assets (ROA)** measures the profit-generating *efficiency* of the total assets of the company. For instance, the Example Company ROA can be calculated as follows:

	20X9	20X8	20X7
Operating Profit	2,100	1,500	1,600
Average Total Assets	9,000	7,050	6,450
= Return on Assets	23.3%	21.3%	24.8%

EXHIBIT 2.14   (*Continued*)

- **Return on Equity (ROE)** measures the *effectiveness* of the investment made by stockholders in the company. It is a measure of the overall return to the share-holders, which they can use to compare with alternative investment opportunities. ROE for the Example Company:

	20X9	20X8	20X7
Net Income	1,200	900	900
Average Equity	5,325	4,625	4,000
= Return on Equity	22.5%	19.5%	22.5%

Considering alternative rates of return available in financial and capital markets, both ROA and ROE seem to be rather attractive. The subjective factor that needs to be taken into account is the element of risk and how much extra return is appropriate to compensate for that risk. There is no single answer to that question, since risk is a factor that must be evaluated by each analyst personally. Needless to say, however, a higher return would be appropriate for a business than for an investment in a government Treasury bill, because the possibility for loss is certainly greater in the former than in the latter, and there should be appropriate compensation for that greater risk.

statements, a list of 12 potential areas for operational review were developed as follows:

1. Cash management
2. Billing and collections
3. Inventory control procedures
4. Purchasing
5. Capital expenditures (property, plant, and equipment)
6. Financing/borrowing
7. Sales and pricing analysis
8. Manufacturing and production control procedures
9. Cost accounting

10. Marketing

11. Storeroom operations

12. Computer procedures

Although all of the operational areas recommended for operational review should produce beneficial results and adequate payout, the Example Company's management has decided to review the purchasing function first. Its rationale is that purchasing is responsible for the economy of operations related to additions to inventory; manufacturing material costs; additions to property, plant, and equipment; expediting on-time vendor deliveries; and overall vendor relations. Because the Example Company has become increasingly material dependent in its manufacturing operations, with resultant increases in inventory, this does appear to be a good place to start. In addition, the initial survey disclosed that Purchasing Department systems and procedures were antiquated and quite ineffective.

**Areas Selected for Review
Should Produce Beneficial Results
and Adequate Payout**

AREAS NOT SELECTED FOR REVIEW

The other operational areas for which it is determined that additional operational review work will not be performed at this time are not to be merely put aside. They should all be mentioned to organizational and departmental management in an oral and/or written report, recommending further action, such as:

- *Immediate action.* For example, facility changes can be made so that buyers have privacy when talking with vendors, and a set schedule established for vendor appointments.

- *Further analysis and review by organizational and departmental management.* For example, management might consider changing the Purchasing Department reporting to the vice-president of operations, as well as other conflicting units such as inspections, inventory control, and warehouse.

- *Future operational review by the operational review team or internal departmental personnel.* For example, the review of special approval procedures such as capital expenditures, over budget limitations, and special projects.

**Areas Not Selected for Review
Are Not Merely Put Aside**

CONCLUSION

As a result of the work steps conducted in the planning phase as described above, a properly indexed and organized planning phase workpaper file should have been developed for all the materials gathered and work steps performed. The workpaper file is then used as a resource in developing the in-depth work program and the corresponding field work. A number of critical operating areas should also have been developed where more in-depth review procedures need to be performed in the work program phase leading toward development of a significant operational review finding.

For example, the following areas may have been identified for more in-depth analysis from the planning phase described in this section.

- Inadequate planning procedures, resulting in no identification of goals, objectives, and detail plans
- Sales trends on a downward spiral in certain product lines
- Overall expenditures increasing, particularly:
  - Cost of goods sold, including production labor and materials
  - Production support functions such as inventory and quality control
  - General and administrative personnel
  - Material and supplies

- Repairs and maintenance

- Increased inventories, with an increase in obsolete inventory

- Increase in the number of administrative positions

- Increase in employee turnover

- Inefficient use of computer equipment

- Crowded working conditions, in both production and office

The in-depth operational review work program should also have been started. Based on the identification of possible critical operational areas, each member on the review team should have begun thinking about and have documented suggested work steps to be incorporated into the in-depth work program. This is the starting point for developing the operational review work program.

> **The Planning Phase**
> **Is the Starting Point**
> **for the Operational Review**

An Operational Review
Case Example:
The Accounting Function

In the current business environment, the accounting function in many organizations is perceived as a prime candidate for cost reduction, and in extreme situations, for elimination. Many of its functions (e.g., preparing customer bills, collecting payments, processing vendor payments, preparing payrolls) are viewed by company management as necessary but of non–value-added operations. In other words, these things may have to be done, but can the company accomplish them with as little cost as possible (none, it hopes)? It is within such a framework that the review team may be working. Rather than review how present functions can be performed in a better manner, the review team may be asked to look at how such functions can be severely reduced or eliminated.

With the nature of most businesses changing from a predominantly mechanical operation to a more customer service-oriented function, the review team must also appraise the accounting function from this perspective. That is, the review team must not only review and appraise the accounting function's present activities, but must also be aware of the benefits the accounting function should be providing to the company.

Accordingly, the review team must work with each function within the organization to assist in redefining its role as desired by top management and the most effective way to get there. The reviewers must also consider the impact of each function on others within the company and how best for all functions to work together in an integrated fashion. The review team must possess the knowledge of the overall direction of the company, management's desires for the function under review, and the manner in which the two can be coordinated.

This case example addresses an operational review of the accounting function. In reading these materials, the reader should be aware of the changing face of those activities making up the accounting function. To make the changes that are necessary for an organization to stay competitive in today's marketplace, old belief systems—of both the organization and the reader—must be challenged. Quick fixes and static solutions are no longer sufficient. The operational review must spur the ability for the company to maintain its own program of continuous improvements. The review team must be a catalyst for change and trainers of others working within the framework of a true learning organization. This is the real test of the success of the operational review.

LOOKING AT THE ACCOUNTING FUNCTIONS

Operational review is an effective process to use in looking at a company's operations to measure current economies, efficiencies, and effectiveness of results. In addition, the operational review process assists in the identification of performance gaps—the difference between present and desired operating results as compared with internal goals and external competitors. A thorough understanding of such performance gaps enables company and departmental management to seize opportunities for improvement. There has always been a demand, and perhaps more so today, to decrease costs and improve product/service/customer quality, all directed toward increasing profits.

Ironically, many companies see the accounting function as strictly non–value-added overhead (in many cases unnecessary), and such companies are constantly moving to cut these costs. The operational review process can assist in reducing accounting function costs through the use of more efficient systems and procedures, along with a clear identification of desired results for each such accounting function. At the same time, the quality of the accounting/financial value-added services can be greatly enhanced. In effect, the accounting function can be an active value-added function that contributes effectively to the company's profit.

An operational review of the accounting functions begins with the analysis of existing practices within the various accounting areas of the company to identify activities, performance drivers, and areas that can be improved with regard to best practices. Performance drivers are the causes of work (e.g., all vendor invoices must be verified by recalculation) or triggers (e.g., a customer order) that set in motion a series of activities.

The operational review process focuses on questioning such performance drivers and triggers as to their elimination and to the ultimate elimination of the corresponding activities. Significant positive improvements can be made as review team members ask questions such as:

- Is this activity needed?
- Why is this activity performed?
- Is this position/material really needed?
- Can the activity be done better in another way?
- Is this step necessary? Does it provide added value?

The operational review process can also entail the comparison of similar operations, functions, or activities within an organization to identify opportunities for improvement and best practices within a common environment. For an organization to maximize the benefits to be derived from an operational review, it is best for it to fully understand and document its existing systems and procedures.

The various operational review steps help to identify critical areas of the company's activities, related performance drivers, and opportunities for positive improvements. Improvement opportunities may arise from one part of the company, division, or work unit learning from another. In this manner, overall communication processes improve, areas of excellence are identified, and operating procedures are changed to reflect best practices.

Once the critical areas within the accounting function are identified, an initial operational review planning phase is performed to obtain data on activities such as:

- Who is involved and how do they relate to the activity, its desired results, and each other? Document such things as the number of individuals, relative positions, method of organization and management.

- Why each individual is involved and his or her value or non–value-added activities. Does each one perform necessary operations, have special expertise, or bear responsibility or are some just excess structure?

- What activities are being done and does each one have to be done, can it be done more efficiently, or is it being done well (a best practice)?

- Why each activity is being done. Does each of the activities relate to desired goals and objectives, and is each one being performed most effectively?

- What resources are allocated to each activity? Is the allocation most economical, and are resources excessive, or deficient, to achieve desired results?

When the operational review team members have a clear understanding of how the area under review operates, including performance drivers; organizational, departmental, and work unit belief systems; and basic business principles for conducting activities within the area, they can begin to conduct the review by developing a specific work program. The focus of the operational review work steps to be performed in the field work phase is to provide understanding and to document existing practices and procedures clearly by:

- Identification of key aspects of the accounting function's activities and performance results.

- Identification of inherent, structural, and performance drivers.

- Identification of critical operational areas and opportunities for improvement (one part learning from another).

- Establishment of channels of communication within the company.

- Identification of pockets of good, desirable practices (best practices and areas of excellence).

- Establishment of standards for good practices to reflect the adoption of best practices.

Defining the elements of each activity and determining whether it is a value-added or non–value-added activity and what each individual does in the process, as well as why it is done, is the basis for analysis as to positive improvements. Questions to be addressed in the operational review are:

People

- Who is involved and why?

  Number of people

  Number of positions

  How organized and managed

  Current personnel resource demands

- Are all personnel needed?

  Reasons for involvement

  What are they doing

  Value-added or non–value-added

  Vital operation or task

  Special expertise

- Who has responsibility for outcomes?

  Hierarchical pyramid: power and control

  Management oriented: review and redo

  Employee self-motivated disciplined behavior

  Delegation of authority to lowest operational levels

  Empire building: work continues—reason no longer valid

Procedures

- Why is the task performed? (e.g., It has always been done this way)
- Necessary or unnecessary? (e.g., That is the way we do it)

- Adding value to customer? (internal vs. external viewpoint)

- Unnecessary bureaucracy? (e.g., unwieldy hierarchy)

- Ineffective, inefficient, or redundant procedures?

- What does each one do, and why? (foundation for internal improvements)

- What are the bundles or groups of value- and non–value-added procedures and activities?

CHOOSING WHAT TO STUDY

The operational review team, in consultation with management, decides which critical areas it will include in the operational review and which areas are to be addressed by management and operations personnel. For instance, the operational review of the accounting and financial functions can be looked at in a number of ways, such as:

- Functional: Accounting, computer processing, treasury, reporting

- Process: accounts payable, accounts receivable, payroll, general ledger, budget, cash management

- Industry: Specific manufacturing, retailing, banking

- Business cycle: Based on the concept of closed loop activities such as:

  - Sales cycle: Sales order, shipping, billing, accounts receivable, collections

  - Purchase cycle: Purchase requisition, purchasing, receiving, vendor invoicing, accounts payable, cash disbursements

  - Payroll/Labor distribution cycle: Time and job verification, data entry, payroll/labor distribution processing, pay distribution, record keeping

  - General ledger/financial statement cycle: Subsystem data collection, journal entries, general ledger posting, financial reporting

  - Cost accounting cycle: Material/labor/overhead data collection, computer processing, operating reports, off line action, reporting by task, job, and period

The accounting functions (e.g., accounts payable, accounts receivable, payroll, and general ledger) cannot be isolated on a linear basis from those other functions that are supported and integrated with the specific accounting function (e.g., accounts payable and the purchasing, receiving, and manufacturing functions). This thinking has allowed such accounting functions to be drastically cut back in many organizations to the detriment of the aforementioned supported operating functions. In reality, a business operates in a circular or cyclical basis, with each component of the cycle equally important as the others. Therefore, to perform an operational review of one of the accounting functions most effectively, it is best to look at it as part of its business cycle. For the purposes of this example of the operational review of the accounting function, each of these functions is considered as a part of its corresponding business cycle.

IDENTIFYING GOALS AND BASIC BUSINESS PRINCIPLES

Prior to the start of an operational review of the accounting functions, the review team should be clear about management's goals and desires for each of these functions. For the management team to identify such goals and desires, they have to be clear as to the purpose of each of the functions and the results that will be most beneficial to the overall operations of the company. There must be more than just a desire to eliminate unnecessary costs; there must also be a full understanding of why each of these functions should be in existence. For example, management may identify goals and desires for each of the major accounting functions as follows:

Accounts Payable

- The elimination of the function, to the extent possible, where the cost of processing vendor payments exceeds the value to the company in delaying such payments.

- The elimination of processing vendor payments where the cost of processing exceeds the amount of payment.

- The least costly and most efficient methods of processing the remaining vendor payments.

- The ability to computer integrate accounts payable data with other sub-systems such as cost accounting, vendor statistics, manufacturing controls, inventory controls, production controls, and cash management.

- An economic balance between necessary controls and the cost of implementing such controls.

Accounts Receivable

- The elimination of the function, to the extent possible, where the cost of billing, collecting, and processing customer payments exceeds the value to the company of extending credit to such customers.

- The elimination of processing customer billings and collections where the cost of processing exceeds the amount of billing.

- The least costly and most efficient method of processing the remaining customer bills.

- The ability to computer integrate accounts receivable data with other subsystems such as credit controls, sales forecasts, customer and sales statistics, collection controls, and cash management.

Payroll Processing

- The least costly and most efficient methods for processing payroll and maintaining necessary records.

- The ability to integrate payroll data with other subsystems such as cost accounting, personnel records, and planning and budget systems.

- The ability of a computerized payroll system to automatically process labor distribution labor costs to production jobs (e.g., production employees time processing at their pay rates to job costs), maintain personnel records (e.g., leave records), and post to the budget system as it processes payroll transactions.

General Ledger

- Full computer integration with all other subsystems so that the general ledger is automatically updated on a real time basis.

- Automatic generation of all repetitive journal entries, allowing for minimal manual journal entries.

- Ability to produce financial statements (balance sheet, income statement, and statement of cash flows) on demand.

Accounting and Financial Reporting

- Automatic generation of all accounting and financial reports, showing exceptions to key operating indicator criteria.

- Integration of accounting and financial reporting with operating statistics.

- Ability to analyze and interpret all such reports so that each report is most useful for both management and operational purposes.

- Use of real-time reporting via computer screens, and the requirement for positive action to be taken in all areas.

In addition, management must clearly state its basic business principles, such as the following five points:

1. Produce the best quality product at the lowest possible cost.
2. Set selling prices realistically, so as to sell all the product the company can produce within the constraints of production capabilities.
3. Build trusting relationships with critical vendors because keeping them in business keeps the company in business.
4. The company is in the customer service and cash conversion businesses.
5. The survival of the company allows it to serve its customers, take care of its employees, and achieve its goals.

Members of top management should also define their agreed-upon basic business principles as related to the accounting functions. The following are examples of such principles:

- The cost of processing should always be less than the price at which the item is sold.

- All unnecessary or non–value-added accounting functions should be eliminated.

- All redundant or duplicate activities should be eliminated.

- All necessary accounting functions should be accomplished in the least costly and most efficient manners.

- All accounting processing and data should be fully integrated with all other applicable subsystems.

- Accounting and financial reporting should be fully integrated with operational reporting so that management and operations personnel can make the best decisions.

- The accounting functions (accounts payable, accounts receivable, payroll, and general ledger) should be fully integrated into the operations of the company.

- The accounting functions should be value-added providers of financial and operational data so that the value provided exceeds the cost of their operations.

- Accounting function personnel must be able to design, develop, and implement effective reporting systems that assist the company in reaching its operational and profit goals.

- Accounting function personnel must become analyzers and interpreters of data for management decisions, rather than mere processors of data and transactions.

PRIORITIZING ACTIVITIES

One of the first tasks for the operational review team is to identify and prioritize those activities, related to the selected accounting functions, to include in the review. The areas selected should be the most critical to the company as identified in the operational review planning phase and in feedback from management and operations personnel via such tools as surveys, interviews, and group brainstorming sessions. For purposes of the case study, six areas are identified:

1. Organizational Issues

   - Authority, responsibility, management
   - Personnel functions: who does what and why

- Operating policies, belief systems, and performance drivers
- Budget and actual costs

2. Accounts Payable and Cash Disbursements Functions

- Accounts payable processing
- Open payables control
- Vendor payment processing
- Cash disbursement processing
- Record keeping and analysis

3. Accounts Receivable Processing

- Credit policies: establishment and maintenance
- Sales order processing
- Billing procedures
- Open receivables control
- Collection procedures
- Customer statistics
- Record keeping and analysis

4. Payroll Processing

- Processing procedures
- Payroll statistics: types, frequency, number of personnel, cost, dollar amount
- Reports produced
- Personnel statistics
- Record keeping and analysis

5. General Ledger

- Chart of accounts
- Processing procedures

- Journal entry processing
- Reports produced
- Record keeping and analysis

6. Accounting, Financial, and Operational Reporting

- Reports produced
- Information lacking
- Use of reports
- Analysis and interpretation

FINANCIAL REPORTING

At the time of review of the business selected for study, the only financial reporting that was found consisted of a monthly balance sheet and income statement generated by the general ledger function. These statements, once the controller is sure of their accuracy, are distributed to all management personnel as strictly confidential over ten days after the end of the month. Most management personnel merely file these financial statements; some look at them, but very few understand them. The statements have no effect on their operations.

An example of these statements is shown below.

Balance Sheet
As of December 31

ASSETS	
Cash	$ 60
Accounts receivable	3,720
Inventory	5,360
Current Assets	9,140
Property, plant, & equipment	7,580
Accumulated depreciation	(2,160)
Net property, plant, & equipment	5,420
Other assets	840
TOTAL ASSETS	$15,400

Liabilities and Equity

Liabilities:	
Accounts payable	$ 1,960
Notes payable	200
Current: long-term debt	840
Other current liabilities	560
Current liabilities	$ 3,560
Long-term debt	7,680
Total Liabilities	11,240
Equity:	
Common stock	200
Additional paid-in-capital	200
Retained earnings	3,760
Stockholders' equity	4,160
TOTAL LIABILITIES AND EQUITY	$15,400

Income Statement
For year ending December 31
(000's omitted)

Net Sales	$12,500
Cost of Goods Sold:	
Material	2,260
Labor	3,260
Manufacturing Expenses	2,080
Total Cost of Goods Sold	7,600
Gross Profit	4,900
Selling expenses	1,120
General and administrative expenses	1,480
Total Operating Expenses	2,600
Net Profit	2,300
Provision for income taxes	640
NET INCOME	$1,660

These statements are distributed as shown, with no additional comments or explanation. Many of the other departments maintain their own internal reporting systems, as they cannot rely on the general ledger section to provide such information on a timely basis.

Quarterly, an outside accounting firm comes in to perform a review and prepare resulting financial statements for the company's lenders. These statements are ignored internally.

The general ledger section provides no explanations with its submission of these financial statements. Operations managers want to know how these numbers affect what their areas are accomplishing. They need to know the differences between financial and accounting data and operational data that they can use to improve their operations. Specifically, they need to understand the following differences:

- Sales are recorded when made (when the goods are shipped to the customer) and set up as an accounts receivable, with cash payment for a sale received at time of customer payment (typically 30 days or later).

- Expenses are incurred on a different timing schedule from cash receipts. For example, payroll, material, supplies, and other expenses are paid when due, but the payback from the customer sale will be some time (if at all) in the future (reflecting the time to complete delivery to the customer plus the collection period).

- Profits shown on the income statement are based on accrual accounting; that is, sales are recorded when made, not when receivables are collected, and expenses are recorded as incurred, not when they are paid from accounts payable.

- An increase in inventory is a cash outlay, but not an expense; an inventory reduction is an expense, but not a cash outlay. That means that an inventory reduction program will have a positive effect on cash flow but a negative impact on profits.

- Some expenses, such as depreciation and amortization, are recorded via accounting entries and do not represent cash outflows; similarly, prepaid items are expensed currently, but represent prior disbursements of cash.

- Expenditures for fixed assets (e.g., property, plant, and equipment) are paid for currently, but do not immediately appear on the income statement as expenses.

- Financial statements do not provide all of the necessary data needed to manage and operate effectively. For instance, operations management should know operating facts such as the real costs and profits generated by each customer and manufacturing order, the number of on-time quality deliveries, the amount of returned customer merchandise, and the amount and cost of scrap, rework, and rejects.

DEVELOPING THE OPERATIONAL REVIEW SURVEY FORM

One of the most important elements of the operational review is the survey form. The main purpose of a survey form is to organize large amounts of data into categories or areas that can be more easily compared. The questions on the survey form are developed by the review team and directed toward those areas that have been defined as most critical in the planning phase. The review team can use an initial survey form in the planning phase to gather general data and look for patterns in identifying critical areas. The survey form used in the field work phase should be more detailed as to the specific activities and results of identified critical areas.

The survey questions should be designed to elicit information the review team believes is significant. Each question should focus on one factor of an area to be measured. The questions should be designed to generate objective answers and data relative to the performance criteria in question, and to identify unique methods and best practices.

The survey form is developed and field tested by the operational review team. Each question is probed as to its objectivity, purpose, data to be provided, and closed endedness. Typically, a survey form is designed for each individual operational review, although questions from previous reviews can be used if they are appropriate to the current situation. A sample survey form related to the accounts payable function is shown below. A similar survey form is developed for each of the other accounting functions: accounts receivable, payroll, and general ledger.

Sample Operational Review Survey Form
The Accounts Payable Function

---

1. Organizational Issues
   a. How is this function organized? Is it hierarchical, vertical, integrated, or otherwise organized? Provide an organization chart showing positions and personnel.
   b. To whom does each activity within the function report? Title and name.
   c. Who manages each activity? Title and name.

    d. How many employees are included in each activity?

    e. What are the major accounts payable policies? (e.g., dollar limit for accounts payable) Provide documented policies and procedures.

    f. What are the total budget and actual allocations for this function?

    g. Do you have a functional job description for each position? Provide a copy of each one.

2. Accounts Payable Processing

    a. On what basis and what percentage of total payments do you pay vendors?
- Prepay at time of order
- Payment upon receipt
- Payment with invoice/receipt within discount terms
- Payment with invoice/receipt within 30 days
- Do not take discount
- Take discount anyway (beyond discount period, e.g., 10 days)

    b. How often do you process payables for payment?

    c. Do you make any exceptions between payment periods?

    d. Do you provide for off-line manual vendor payments?

    e. On average, what is the amount of new payables at any time? Number of payments? Total dollars?

    f. Is accounts payable processing part of an integrated computer system?

    g. What is the amount of annual payments? Number of payments? Total dollars?

3. Open Payables Control

    a. Are open payables part of an integrated computer system?

    b. How often do you process payments?

    c. Is there a policy to take vendor discounts? Within/at the discount period? Regardless of the discount period?

    d. On average, what is the amount of open payables? Number of vendor invoices? Total dollars?

    e. Are open payables accessible on an on-line basis? Only accessible by accounts payable personnel? By others? (describe)

4. Vendor Payment Processing

    a. Do you provide a prepayment listing of due bills prior to processing?
- On screen
- Listing only
- Both options

    b. Can an authorized individual select bills for payment?

- Manual
- On-line
- Additions
- Deletions
- Changes

c. Can an authorized individual determine the dollar amount for total payment? What is the basis for selection?

d. How often do you process checks for payment? Do you hold to that schedule? How many times did you go off that schedule last year?

e. Do you automatically combine vendor invoices into one payment?

f. Do you provide detail as to what invoices are being paid?

g. Do you reconcile vendor statements to individual invoices?

h. Do you ignore vendor statements and pay only by invoice?

i. Do you automatically net vendor debits against payments?

j. On average, what is the amount of vendor debits? Number of debits _____ Total Amount _____

k. Once selected for payment, are checks with payment detail automatically processed? Provide sample of check and detail memo.

l. What is your cost per payment?

m. What is your cost per processing cycle?

n. On average, how many payments do you process at one time?
   - Per process run
   - Per month
   - Annually

5. Cash Disbursement Processing

a. Are payments as processed automatically sent to the vendor? Electronic data transfer? Mail?

b. How often do you process cash disbursements?

c. On average, what are the number of checks written? By process _____ Monthly _____ Annual _____

d. Do you combine payments by vendor? On what basis?

e. On what basis do you process payment? Receipt of items? Invoice? Both? Other?

f. Do you use a remote bank location?

g. Do you use any methods to slow the receipt of the payment to the vendor? Describe.

h. What is your cost per check disbursement? What is your cost per disbursement cycle?

i. How many times have checks been processed late? In the last year? Sent out late?

    j. What percentage of checks have been reported as having errors upon receipt? How many hours are spent in correcting errors, and at what cost?

    k. Do you provide electronic data transfer (EDT) for vendor payments?

    l. Is timeliness of payment (e.g., EDT) considered a factor in vendor price negotiations?

6. Record Keeping and Analysis
   a. What records do you keep for each payment?
      - Purchase requisition
      - Purchase order
      - Receiver/bill of lading
      - Vendor invoice
      - Payment voucher
      - Check copy
      - Other
      - All computer maintained
   b. What type of analysis do you do relative to payments?
      - Payments by vendor: numbers and dollars
      - Returns by vendor
      - Billing errors
      - Processing errors
      - Other
   c. Are there other records/analysis that you keep/do? Describe.
   d. What report options do you provide?
      - Standard in software
      - Custom defined
      - User
   e. What software do you use for these functions?
   f. What computer hardware configuration do you use? Provide details.

7. Vendor Relations, Negotiations, Analysis
   a. What is the total number of vendors in your system?
   b. Are your vendors coded by type of commodity class?
   c. Can you provide a summary of vendors by commodity class? Commodity Class: _____ Number of Vendors _____
   d. How often do you negotiate with vendors? Each purchase, monthly, annually, other.
   e. How many vendors make up approximately 80 percent of your total purchases? Can you provide this information by commodity class?
   f. Do you use long-term contracts or blanket purchase orders to lock in price, quality, and on-time deliveries?

g. Do you integrate purchases of raw materials into your production schedule?
h. Do you maintain vendor analysis statistics? Do they include the following?
   - Total sales volume
   - Total sales volume by item
   - Quality data
   - Merchandise return data
   - On-time delivery data
   - Other
   Provide a sample report(s) of such statistics?
i. Are company individuals assigned contact responsibility for major vendors?
j. How often are long-term purchase contracts renegotiated?
k. Do you have an ongoing process for identification of potential vendors? Describe.
l. How many vendors have you added during the past year?
m. How many vendors have you deleted during the past year?

COMPILING THE DATA

When the survey forms have been returned by all employees (management and operations), the review team must review and analyze each one for inappropriate, misleading, or inadequate responses. This usually requires going back to the respondent for clarification, either by phone or in a personal visit. If possible, it is good practice to have one or more individuals assigned to each respondent. By effectively working together, they will be able to finalize all responses for each participant.

Once the review team is satisfied with the legitimacy of each of the participants' survey responses, the next step is to summarize these responses in one document for analysis purposes. The analysis is to help identify areas of operational deficiencies, performance gaps from desired results and basic business principles, and best practices among survey respondents in total and by individual area. Summarization can be done quite easily by the review team by recording each participant's responses directly on the questionnaire document itself.

The operational review team should then individually and collectively (normally, in a brainstorming session) identify areas for improvement, and summarize process deficiencies for those areas determined to be most critical, for presentation to management. The review team may decide to spend additional analysis time with specific functions and activities to ascertain the accuracy of survey responses. They may also decide to visit other companies (e.g., competitors or others in similar industries) to evaluate what others are doing and whether they operate under better practices.

A form summarizing the survey and possible process deficiencies, identified with an *, for the accounts payable function under review is shown below.

Sample Operational Review Survey Form
The Accounts Payable Function
Summary of Responses

---

1. Organizational Issues

a. How is this function organized? Is it hierarchical, vertical, integrated, or otherwise organized? Provide an organization chart showing positions and personnel.
Response: Hierarchical *
The organization chart for all accounting functions, including accounts payable, is shown as an attachment.

b. To whom does each activity within the function report? Title and name.
Response: Accounts Payable Manager (Ray Simms) reports to the Controller (Dave Behal). Accounts Payable Supervisor (Betty Grimes) reports to Ray Simms. All others (five accounts payable processors and two clerical personnel) report to Betty Grimes.

c. Who manages each activity? Title and name.
Response: Accounts payable function; Ray Simms, Accounts Payable Manager. Accounts payable processing activities; Betty Grimes, Accounts Payable Supervisor.

d. How many employees are in each activity?
Response: Manager – 1, Supervisor – 1, Processing – 5, Clerical – 2

e. What are the major accounts payable policies? (e.g., dollar limit for accounts payable)
Response: All vendor purchases for $50 or more are processed through the Purchasing Department. The Accounts Payable

Department is responsible for processing all vendor invoices for these purchases. * There are no documented policies or procedures.

f. What are the total budget and actual allocations for this function? *Response:* Budget: $346,000 Actual: $385,000 *

g. Do you have a functional job description for each position? Provide a copy of each one. *Response:* No

2. Accounts Payable Processing

a. On what basis and what percentage of total payments do you pay vendors?
    - Prepay at time of order *Response:* None
    - Payment upon receipt *Response:* None
    - Payment with invoice/receipt within discount terms *Response:* 30%
    - Payment with invoice/receipt within 30 days *Response:* 70% take discount
    - Do not take discount *Response:* None
    - Take discount anyway (beyond discount period, e.g., 10 days) *Response:* Generally

b. How often do you process payables for payment? *Response:* Twice a week *

c. Do you make any exceptions between payment periods? *Response:* Yes. 10 to 20% of all transactions *

d. Do you provide for off-line manual vendor payments? *Response:* Yes. About 3 to 5% of all transactions *

e. On average, what is the amount of new payables at any time? Number of payments? Total dollars? *Response:* Payments 800, total dollars $460,000 *

f. Is accounts payable processing part of an integrated computer system? *Response:* No *

g. What is the amount of annual payments? Number of payments? Total dollars?
    Response: Payments 26,000, total dollars $14,800,000 *

3. Open Payables Control

a. Are open payables part of an integrated computer system? *Response:* No

b. How often do you process payments? *Response:* Twice a week

c. Is there a policy to take vendor discounts? Within/at the discount period? Regardless of the discount period? *Response:* Yes

d. On average, what is the amount of open payables? Number of vendor invoices? Total Dollars? *Response:* Vendor invoices 1,400, total dollars $1,620,000 *

e. Are open payables accessible on an on-line basis? Only accounts payable personnel? Others? (describe) *Response:* No

4. Vendor Payment Processing

a. Do you provide a prepayment listing of due bills prior to processing?
  • On screen
  • Listing only
  • Both options
  Response: No *

b. Can an authorized individual select bills for payment?
  • Manual
  • On-line
  • Additions
  • Deletions
  • Changes
  Response: Manual only *

c. Can an authorized individual determine the dollar amount for total payment? What is basis for selection? *Response:* Yes/ dollars available for payment

d. How often do you process checks for payment? Do you hold to that schedule? How many times did you go off that schedule last year? *Response:* Twice a week/yes/never

e. Do you automatically combine vendor invoices into one payment? *Response:* No *

f. Do you provide detail as to what invoices are being paid? *Response:* No *

g. Do you reconcile vendor statements to individual invoices? *Response:* Yes *

h. Do you ignore vendor statements and pay only by invoice? *Response:* No *

i.   Do you automatically net vendor debits against payments?
Response: No *

j.   On average, what is the amount of vendor debits? Number of debits? Total Amount? *Response:* 140/$28,000+ *

k.   Once selected for payment, are checks with payment detail automatically processed? *Response:* No

l.   What is your cost per payment? *Response:* $48 *

m. What is your cost per processing cycle?
Response: $1,800+ twice a week *

n.   On average, how many payments do you process at one time?
- Per process run
- Per month
- Annually
Response: 350/2,800/34,000 *

5. Cash Disbursement Processing

a.   Are payments as processed automatically sent to the vendor? Electronic data transfer? Mail? *Response:* Mail only *

b.   How often do you process cash disbursements?
Response: Twice a week

c.   On average, what are the number of checks written?
By process _____ Monthly _____ Annual _____
Response: 350/2,800/34,000 *

d.   Do you combine payments by vendor? On what basis?
Response: No *

e.   On what basis do you process payment?
Receipt of items? Invoice? Both? Other? *Response:* Both

f.   Do you use a remote bank location? *Response:* No

g.   Do you use any methods to slow the receipt of the payment to the vendor? Describe. *Response:* No

h.   What is your cost per check disbursement? What is your cost per disbursement cycle? *Response:* $1.12/$392 *

i.   How many times have checks been processed late? In the last year? Sent out late?
Response: Times in last year 12, times late 12 *

j. What percentage of checks have been reported as having errors upon receipt? How many hours are spent in correcting errors, and at what cost? *Response:* 12%/180 hours/$3,600 *

k. Do you provide electronic data transfer (EDT) for vendor payments? *Response:* No *

l. Is timeliness of payment (e.g., EDT) considered a factor in vendor price negotiations? *Response:* No *

6. Record Keeping and Analysis

a. What records do you keep for each payment?
- Purchase requisition
- Purchase order
- Receiver/bill of lading
- Vendor invoice
- Payment voucher
- Check copy
- Other
- All computer maintained

Response: All, not computer maintained *

b. What type of analysis do you do relative to payments?
- Payments by vendor: numbers and dollars
- Returns by vendor
- Billing errors
- Processing errors
- Other

Response: None *

c. Are there other records/analysis that you keep/do? Describe. *Response:* None *

d. What report options do you provide?
- Standard in software
- Custom defined
- User

Response: Standard only *

e. What software do you use for these functions? *Response:* Low end *

f. What computer hardware configuration do you use? Provide details. *Response:* PC network with three stations

7. Vendor Relations, Negotiations, Analysis

a. What is the total number of vendors in your system? *Response:* 587 *

b. Are your vendors coded by type of commodity class?
Response: Yes

c. Can you provide a summary of vendors by commodity class?
Response: Yes

d. How often do you negotiate with vendors? Each purchase, monthly, annually, other. *Response:* By exception *

e. How many vendors make up approximately 80% of your total purchases?
Can you provide this information by commodity class?
Response: 128, cannot be provided by commodity class *

f. Do you use long-term contracts or blanket purchase orders to lock in price, quality, and on-time deliveries?
Response: Rarely *

g. Do you integrate purchases of raw materials into your production schedule? *Response:* No *

h. Do you maintain vendor analysis statistics? Do they include the following?
• Total sales volume
• Total sales volume by item
• Quality data
• Merchandise return data
• On-time delivery data
• Other
Provide a sample report(s) of such statistics?
Response: No *

i. Are company individuals assigned contact responsibility for major vendors? *Response:* No *

j. How often are long-term purchase contracts renegotiated?
Response: Rarely *

k. Do you have an ongoing process for identification of potential vendors? Describe. *Response:* No *

l. How many vendors have you added during the past year?
Response: 57 *

m. How many vendors have you deleted during the past year?
Response: 68 *

ANALYZING THE DATA

Data collected with the use of such survey forms is known as user-provided data. The operational review team uses these forms as a quick method of accumulating information about the function under review. The review team summarizes the data to identify patterns of bad practices, operational deficiencies, and areas for further review. The accumulation and analysis of such user-provided data often becomes the starting point for further field work. Thus, the survey is a good tool to bring immediate focus to those areas to be considered in the review.

The operational review team is aware that data reported via such a survey may be unclear and misleading as the result of any number of factors:

- Methods of data gathering

- Misunderstanding of terminology

- Attitude of person providing the data

- Incompleteness and accuracy of database

- Misunderstanding of data requested

Because of the possibility of data inaccuracy, the operational review team will usually analyze thoroughly the data provided prior to identifying critical areas for further review and operational deficiencies. As review team members may rely on the data provided by management and operations personnel in determining their conclusions about areas for further review, they must determine whether any data elements require further backup from the respondent as to methods of estimation, formulas used, and calculation routines. Normally, a range of results emerges, so that if one respondent's replies are off, it becomes readily apparent. This allows the review team to easily identify those items out of the range and to contact that respondent for further review and resubmission.

Based on an analysis of survey form results, the review team develops its work program to include those critical areas in the field work phase. Typically, the survey form procedure is supported by interviews with appropriate management and operations personnel, physical review and observations of actual operations, and review of documentation such as policies and procedures, organization charts, job descriptions, and workload statistics. This is the planning phase, the first phase of the operational review.

During the field work phase, the third phase, those areas identified as critical operational concerns or deficiencies are further investigated for the implementation of best practices in a program of continuous improvements. Among the tools that can be used for this purpose are systems flowcharts, layout flowcharts, detail interviews, trend analysis, benchmarking strategies, and cost principles.

ORGANIZATIONAL ISSUES

As identified in the survey form for the accounts payable function, the accounting function appears to be overstaffed. A review of all other functions within the accounting area supports this conclusion.

A full organization chart of the accounting function is shown below.

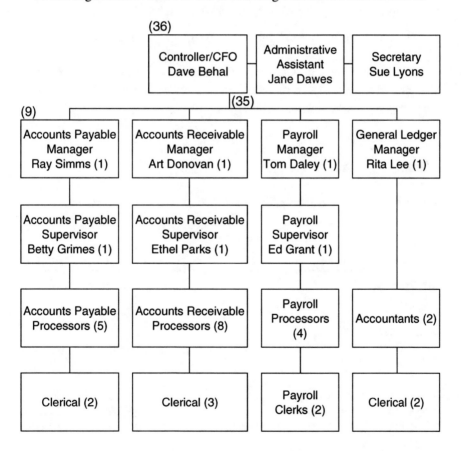

Among the concerns the review team could raise, based on an analysis of this chart, are:

- The need for 38 people to provide accounting functions of a primarily non–value-added character.

- The purpose of having a controller/chief financial officer (CFO), together with an administrative assistant and a secretary, to oversee basically repetitive accounting functions.

- The necessity for a manager for each of the accounting functions: accounts payable, accounts receivable, payroll, and general ledger.

- The need for supervisors, in addition to managers, for the accounts payable, accounts receivable, and payroll functions.

- The use of the number of operations personnel in each function

- The need for nine clerical personnel assigned to these functions

The company must look for ways to reduce costs in these areas, perform these accounting activities more efficiently, and produce results that enable the company to manage better and make more profitable decisions.

BUDGET ANALYSIS

A list of personnel with corresponding budget and actual costs for each of the accounting functions is.

	Budget	Actual
Controller/CFO	$ 82,000	$86,400
Administrative Assistant	26,000	28,200
Secretary	18,000	22,700
Total Personnel Costs	126,000	137,300
Other Costs	34,000	36,300
Total Controller Costs	160,000	173,600
Accounts Payable Manager	38,000	36,700
Accounts Payable Supervisor	28,000	24,300
Accounts Payable Processors (5 @ $18,000)	90,000	72,400

	Budget	Actual
Clerical support (2 @ $14,000)	28,000	22,600
Total Personnel Costs	184,000	156,000
Other Costs	12,000	8,400
Total Accounts Payable Costs	196,000	164,400
Accounts Receivable Manager	44,000	39,300
Accounts Receivable Supervisor	36,000	28,500
Accounts Receivable Processors (8 @ $22,000)	176,000	144,800
Clerical support (3 @ $16,000)	48,000	41,200
Total Personnel Costs	304,000	253,800
Other Costs	18,000	10,300
Total Accounts Receivable Costs	322,000	264,100
Payroll Manager	34,000	32,400
Payroll Supervisor	22,000	18,600
Payroll Processors (4 @ $16,000)	64,000	56,700
Payroll Clerks (2 @ $12,000)	24,000	20,800
Total Personnel Costs	144,000	128,500
Other Costs	10,800	8,200
Total Payroll Costs	154,800	136,700
General Ledger Manager	26,000	28,400
Accountants (2 @ $22,000)	44,000	46,800
Clerical support (2 @ $16,000)	32,000	36,300
Total Personnel Costs	102,000	111,500
Other Costs	6,000	8,400
Total General Ledger Costs	108,000	119,900
Summary of Costs		
Personnel Costs	**$860,000**	**$787,100**
Other Costs	**80,800**	**71,600**
Total Accounting Function Cost	**$940,800**	**$858,700**

As shown in this list, it is costing the company about $860,000 in actual dollars to provide accounting services of a non–value-added nature. It is apparent that this is too costly for a company with $12,500,000 in sales.

The accounting function costs equal about seven percent of sales, far too much for a company of this size. A quick benchmarking review of five other similar companies this size resulted in a range of accounting function costs of two to three percent of sales, which may also be too high.

An analysis of the accounting function budget breakdown, presents the operational review team with nine particular concerns:

1. The cost for a Controller/CFO, budgeted at $82,000 with an actual cost of $86,400. It appears that this person's function is merely to supervise mechanical accounting functions. Whatever additional expertise and advice that may be provided by this individual could probably be provided more adequately at less cost.

2. Total controller functional costs of $173,600. It would be quite surprising if the company is realizing sufficient value for these costs.

3. Controller function costs budgeted at $160,000 with actual costs of $173,600, an 8.5 percent increase over budget. It appears that the controller may be building an empire and using company funds indiscriminately for his own purposes.

4. Managers for each function at a total cost of $142,000 budgeted dollars ($136,800 in actual costs). This appears to be a superfluous cost, particularly for supervisors and processing personnel.

5. Supervisors for accounts payable, accounts receivable, and payroll at a budget cost of $86,000 (actual cost of $71,400). Again, is value provided by these individuals?

6. Processors and accountants for each of the functions. Are they merely mechanically processing accounting transactions, or are there any value-added activities?

7. Clerical support costs for each function. How many support personnel are really necessary, and what do they really contribute? Are they really doing the mechanical work, or do they merely duplicate the work that higher paid personnel should be doing?

8. Other costs of $80,800 budgeted, $71,600 actual. What are these costs? Are they necessary or just an invitation to spend money?

9. The aspect of accounts payable, accounts receivable, and payroll actual costs being less than budgeted dollars. Is the controller keeping costs down to look good (possibly holding off budget cuts), or are these the realistic costs? What should these costs be?

ANALYSIS OF FUNCTIONAL COSTS

Another important aspect of the operational review of the accounting functions is to analyze each activity of the function and determine its cost. The starting point is to review and analyze the function as it is presently being performed in order to identify those activities that result in added-on costs. This can be done through observation, interviews, consideration of workload statistics, and the development and analysis of systems flowcharts. This process will not only allow the review team to fully understand how the function operates, but will also identify areas for positive improvement and generate recommendations for such improvements. The goal of this analysis is to begin the review team's development of best practice recommendations so that each function can operate with the most economical and efficient systems possible.

For example, the review team may identify and develop costs for those activities which make up the accounts payable and accounts receivable functions as follows:

Accounts Payable

- Receive open purchase order (PO) copies from Purchasing Department
- File in open purchase order files: by vendor, by PO number
- Receive "receiving report" from Receiving
- Pull open purchase order from file and compare to receiving report

  If no invoice, hold in open receipts/no invoice file

  If invoice, pull from invoice/no receipt file

- Receive invoice from vendor
- Match invoice to open receipts

  If match, process for payment

  If no match, hold in invoice/no receipt file

- Process any invoice or receiving errors
- Enter payment data into computer system
- At time of payment, set up computer system for check preparation
- Mail checks to vendors

- File paid payable voucher
- Handle vendor inquiries

Accounts Receivable

- Receive billing information from Shipping Department: bill of lading, sales order, etc.
- Match to sales order copy in open sales file
- Prepare bill on computer system
- Verify accuracy of bill
- Mail bill to customer
- Receive payments from customers (usually checks in the mail)
- Match payment to amounts due in computer system
- Code bill as to allocation to open customer invoices
- Process payment into computer system
- Follow up on any discrepancies (e.g., wrong amount, improper discount taken)
- Expedite open customer invoices not paid within time terms (e.g., net/ 30days)
- Initiate collection procedures for overdue accounts
- File payment data by customer (e.g., check stub, copy of bill, sales order, etc.)
- Prepare cash receipts for bank deposit

  Prepare daily cash receipts report

  Prepare bank deposit
- Handle customer inquiries

As operational review team members identify each activity in the preceding list and determine its cost, they question whether the entire function is necessary (e.g., does it have to be purchased and paid for in this manner?) or each activity is necessary (e.g., is it necessary to have customer bills or can electronic data transfer be used?). The total costs for each activity (accounts payable and accounts receivable processing) are based on the methods presently used to process these transactions. There may be other processes that should be performed but are not because of the constraints of time, volume, or limited personnel. In addition, the cost to process an individual transaction may be undercalculated owing to the time pressures to complete each transaction (e.g., in a hurried, incomplete manner). Moreover, if the volume is somewhat reduced, the cost per transaction will probably increase if the corresponding costs of processing are not reduced as well.

An example of such activity costs for the accounts payable and accounts receivable functions and related activities is shown below.

Accounts Payable Activities And Costs
Labor Hour Cost: $16 Per Hour

Activity	Cost Element	Time	Cost
1. Receive purchase order (PO) from purchasing and file in open (PO) file	Labor	2 Min	$ .50
2. Receive "receiving report" from receiving, pull open (PO) from file, and compare hold in open receipts file	Labor	4 Min	$1.00
3. Receive invoice from vendor and match to open receipts or pull open PO and compare and hold as open invoice	Labor	6 Min	$ 1.60
4. Invoice/receiving errors	Labor	—	—
5. Computer data entry	Labor, Edp	3 Min	$ .80
6. Computer check prep checks	Labor, Edp	2 Min	$ .50
7. Mail checks	Labor, envel, postage	2 Min	$ .50
8. File paid payable	Labor	2 Min	$ .50
9. Meetings, phone, fax	Labor, phone	4 min	$1.00
Total Cost			$6.40

Number of payments processed per year: 26,000

Cost of processing annual payments: 26,000 × $6.40 = $166,400 (actual costs = $164,400)

Accounts Receivable Activities and Costs
Labor Hour Cost: $20 Per Hour

Activity	Cost Element	Time	Cost
1. Receive billing information from shipping department	Labor	2 min	$ .67
2. Match to sales order copy in open sales file	Labor	2 min	$ .67
3. Prepare bill on computer system	Labor	5 min	$1.67
4. Verify accuracy of bill	Labor	3 min	$1.00
5. Mail bill to customer	Labor, bill, env, postage	2 min	$ .67
6. Receive payments from customers	Labor	—	—
7. Match payment to amounts due in computer system	Labor	3 min	$1.00
8. Code bill as to allocation to open customer invoices	Labor	4 min	$1.33
9. Process payment into computer system	Labor	3 min	$1.00
10. Follow up on any discrepancies	Labor	—	—
11. Expedite open customer invoices	Labor, phone	1 min	$ .33
12. Initiate collection procedures	Labor	1 min	$ .33
13. File payment data by customer	Labor	1 min	$ .33
14. Prepare cash receipts for bank deposit	Labor	1 min	$ .33
15. Handle customer inquiries	Labor, phone	—	—
Total Cost			$9.00

Number of customer bills processed per year: 30,000+

Cost of processing annual customer bills: 30,000 × $9.00 = $270,000 (actual costs = $264,100)

Although the activities and costs shown above are rough estimates of the processing of accounts payable and accounts receivable, they also represent the expenditure of resources allocated to these two activities. Theoretically, it could be assumed that each vendor payment or customer bill that could be eliminated from processing would result in a $6.40 or a $9.00 savings to the company.

In reality it does not work that way. It may be difficult for the review team to find a sufficient number of vendor payments or customer bills that can be eliminated to provide a significant reduction in work effort, resulting in substantial cost savings. However, the costs of processing a vendor payment or a customer bill can be used in the company's internal cost system in convincing management that its costs are too high. These figures can also be used to calculate cost savings in the review team's ultimate recommendations.

The review team compares such costs and numbers of transactions to those of three comparable competitors with the following results:

Accounts Payable

Number of payments processed annually: Us = 26,000
#1 = 16,000 #2 = 18,000 #3 = 12,000

Amount of annual payments: Us = $4,800,000
#1 = $2,200,000 #2 = $3,300,000 #3= $2,800,000

Cost of accounts payable function: Us = $164,400
#1 = $128,000 #2 = $111,000 #3 = $84,000

Accounts Receivable

Number of customer bills processed annually: Us = 30,000
#1 = 14,000 #2 = 16,000 #3 = 8,600

Amount of annual customer bills: Us = $12,500,000
#1 = $15,600,000 #2 = $18,800,000 #3 = $22,500,000

Cost of accounts receivable function: Us = $264,1000
#1 = $187,000 #2 = $156,000 #3 = $68,000

As the above data show, the company under review handles the largest volume of accounts payable and receivable transactions at the greatest cost of all three competitors. As part of the operational review, the review team visits each of these other companies to determine their best practices in an effort to develop the best practice for the company.

ANALYSIS OF ACCOUNTING OPERATIONS

Accounts Payable

The accounts payable manager, Ray Simms, is responsible for making sure that the required work is done and vendor payments are made properly, with no overpayments individually or in total. The accounts payable supervisor, Betty Grimes, is responsible for ensuring that each day's detail work is accomplished. She is quite proud that the day's work is always completed before the staff leaves for the day, even if it means that nobody leaves until all the work is done. Three of the five accounts payable processors are responsible for processing vendor receipts and payments. Before a vendor invoice can be paid, each item on the invoice must be checked for proper budget approval, the proper accuracy of the receipt, and the correct billing by the vendor. All of these operations are duplications of computer processing.

The other two accounts payable processors spend most of their time dealing with vendors, primarily in adjusting debits to the vendor's bills for defective and returned merchandise. The two clerical personnel spend most of their time filing and refiling accounts payable data: open purchase orders, vendor receiving data, vendor invoices, and paid vouchers. The result of all of these operations is the payment of vendor invoices, with few value-added functions.

An analysis of accounts payable transactions using the present computer system for the current year disclosed the following:

Overall Data

Total number of payments:	26,000
Total amount of dollars:	$4,800,000
Cost to process a payment:	$6.40
Total cost of accounts payable:	$164,400
Average time to pay invoice:	22 days

Payment Statistics

Payment Amount	Number	Percent	Amount	Percent
Under $20	5,760	22.2%	$ 72,000	1.5%
Between $20 and $50	8,440	32.4%	306,000	6.4%
Between $50 and $100	6,680	25.7%	561,200	11.7%
Between $100 and $1,000	1,640	6.3%	1,033,200	21.5%
Over $1,000	3,480	13.4%	2,827,600	58.9%
Totals	**26,000**	**100.0%**	**$4,800,000**	**100.0%**

A further analysis of vendors and related payments disclosed the following:

Vendor name	Number	Percent	Amount	Percent
Peterboro, Inc.	4,628	17.8%	$ 816,000	17.0%
Roadway Company	4,030	15.5%	782,400	16.3%
Delilah Manufacturing	3,848	14.8%	753,600	15.7%
Delta Controls	3,614	13.9%	724,800	15.1%
Eager Specialties	3,432	13.2%	561,600	11.7%
North Facing	2,808	10.8%	412,800	8.6%
Totals	22,360	86.0%	$4,051,200	84.4%
Other Vendors	3,640	14.0%	748,800	15.6%
Totals—All Vendors	**26,000**	**100.0%**	**$4,800,000**	**100.0%**

Accounts Receivable

The Accounts Receivable Manager, Art Donovan, is responsible for ensuring that all accounts receivable activities are done properly: customer billing, collection efforts, posting to accounts receivable record, and cash deposits. The accounts receivable supervisor, Ethel Parks, is responsible for making certain that all customer bills are sent out on time (within three days of shipment), receipts are posted in a timely fashion (within two days of receipt), and that unpaid bills are followed up (after 60 days from the date of the invoice). Five of the eight accounts receivable processors are responsible for computer processing customer bills, setting up and maintaining the computer accounts receivable files, processing customer cash receipts, and submitting nonpayments (after 60 days) to the collections unit in the sales department.

The other three processors spend most of their time in dealing with the credit unit in the sales department, working with customers who return merchandise and obtaining the proper credits, and processing billing adjustments. Customer credit limits are established by the credit unit of the sales department and monitored by the accounts receivable section. When customers place orders that exceed the credit limit (outstanding bills plus current order), the accounts receivable unit notifies the credit unit for disposition. The normal recourse is that the credit unit increases the credit limit, making such credit policies almost useless. This has resulted in increasing the collection period from an average of 28 days to more than 48 days, with a corresponding increase in uncollectible receivables. As the amount of returned merchandise has increased, so has the amount of bills paid late and uncollectibles. Three clerical personnel are responsible for correspondence and filling/refiling activities.

An analysis of customer sales statistics and accounts receivable data disclosed the following:

- Number of customer bills processed annually: 30,000

- Cost of accounts receivable function: $264,1000

- Total sales for the year: $12,500,000

- Accounts receivable at the end of year: $ 3,270,000

- Average collection period: 48 days

- Billing terms: 1% ten days/30 days

Billing Statistics

Billing Amount	Number	Percent	Amount	Percent
Under $100	14,220	47.4%	$ 898,560	7.2%
Between $100 and $500	11,810	39.3%	2,869,830	22.9%
Between $500 and $1,000	2,300	7.7%	1,453,600	11.6%
Between $1,000 and $5,000	1,280	4.3%	3,143,680	25.1%
Between $5,000 and $10,000	180	.6%	1,138,320	9.2%
Over $10,000	210	.7%	2,996,010	24.0%
Totals	**30,000**	**100.0%**	**$12,500,000**	**100.0%**

Sales Statistics

Customer name	Number	Percent	Amount	Percent
Paul Brothers Company	5,460	18.2%	$2,412,500	19.3%
Apex Industries	4,890	16.3%	2,325,000	18.6%
Kontrol Manufacturing	4,410	14.7%	1,562,500	12.5%
Sandstone, Inc.	3,930	13.1%	1,075,000	8.6%
Textite Industries	2,880	9.6%	962,500	7.7%
Ace, Inc.	2,520	8.4%	1,300,000	10.4%
Totals	24,090	80.3%	9,638,303	77.1%
Other Customers	5,910	19.7%	2,861,697	22.9%
Total —All Customers	**30,000**	**100.0%**	**$12,500,000**	**100.0%**

Payroll

The payroll unit is responsible for the following functions:

- Processing biweekly payrolls
- Manufacturing operations—102 employees on an hourly basis
- Manufacturing supervision—26 employees on salary basis
- Office operations—72 employees on salary basis
- Sales personnel—12 employees on salary plus commission basis (paid at time of sale, regardless of when customer pays)
- Management payroll—8 employees on salary plus quarterly bonus

The payroll manager, Tom Daley, is responsible for making sure that all payrolls are accurately processed. He reviews and approves all payroll changes and payroll registers prior to payroll check processing. He is also responsible for the maintenance and processing of the management payroll. The payroll supervisor, Ed Grant, is responsible for ensuring that all daily operations are performed correctly because of the sensitivity of payroll. The four payroll processors are responsible for the following functions:

- Maintenance of computerized payroll and personnel records, including all additions, changes, and deletions. Ed Grant reviews and approves all such daily changes.
- Maintenance of off-line controls by type of payroll to ensure the integrity of each computerized payroll file.
- Review and reconciliation of manufacturing operations personnel labor distribution charges to manufacturing orders and non-chargeable time. This is done daily to ensure that these costs are recorded accurately on an ongoing basis.
- Reconciliation of all payrolls to off-line controls and review of computer processing as to its accuracy.
- Distribution of payroll checks on an individual basis. All employees are paid at the end of the same biweekly period.

- Maintenance of records and preparation of federal, state, and local payroll tax and related reporting (monthly, quarterly, semiannually, and annually).

- Maintenance of personnel records such as sick leave, vacation time, status and pay changes, and location changes.

The two payroll clerks are responsible for clerical duties such as correspondence, filing and refiling of payroll details and computer reports, and control of various forms.

An analysis of payroll processing disclosed the following data:

Payroll Type	Number of Employees	Annual Dollars	Average Pay Amount
Manufacturing:			
Manufacturing operations	102	$2,284,800	$22,400
Manufacturing supervision	26	975,200	37,500
Total Manufacturing	128	$3,260,000	
General and administrative:			
Accounting functions	38	$ 787,100	$20,700
All others	34	692,900	20,380
Total General and Administrative	72	$1,480,000	
Sales Department—salespeople	12	$ 620,000	$51,700
Management	8	$ 512,000	$64,000
Total—All Payrolls	220	$5,872,000	$23,488

General Ledger

The integrity of the general ledger, which includes a record for each account in the company's chart of accounts, is the responsibility of the General Ledger Manager, Rita Lee. She is also responsible for establishing and maintaining the company's budget system for manufacturing operations, as well as line item budgets for each of the nonmanufacturing support functions. Two accountants report to Rita. Although there are no standard assignments, the two accountants are responsible for doing whatever Rita requests, and the two clerical personnel aid Rita in whatever else needs to be done.

The company has an integrated computerized accounting system where each of the subsystems, such as accounts payable, accounts receivable, and payroll automatically update the general ledger. However, general ledger personnel also trace each entry into the computerized general ledger to ensure its accuracy. Rita Lee oversees the posting of all journal entries to the general ledger, manually preparing the journal entry and then tracing it into the general ledger after computer processing. She does not trust the computer producing automatic journal entries, even standard entries such as depreciation and allocation of prepaid expenses.

This unit is responsible for developing the annual budget and inputting it into the computer system. Its staff members are also responsible for ensuring that no expenses are incurred that would put any line item in an over-budget position. They do this by reviewing every purchase request against the budget prior to allowing the purchasing department to prepare a purchase order. If a line item total expense does exceed the budgeted line item, the general ledger unit will analyze the cause for such an excess and move the overage to a line item in which there is still money left. This laborious task is performed for each line item in the budget at the end of every month. If a department or unit needs additional budgeted dollars subsequent to the beginning of the year, it must request a budget change from the general ledger unit; such a change is rarely approved regardless of the need.

An example of the present static budget system monthly report for the company's two manufacturing divisions is shown below.

Manufacturing Budget Report
(000's omitted in dollar amounts)

	Division A			Division B		
	Budget	Actual	Variance	Budget	Actual	Variance
Units Produced	20,000	18,000	(2,000)	20,000	24,000	4,000
Sales	$ 1,000	$ 940	($ 60)	$ 1,000	$ 1,152	$ 152
Costs:						
Material	200	190	10	200	225	(25)
Direct Labor	140	130	10	140	160	(20)
Variable						
Overhead	135	125	10	135	158	(23)
Fixed						
Overhead	175	170	5	175	173	2
Total Costs	650	615	35	650	716	(66)
Gross Profit	$ 350	$ 325	($ 25)	$ 350	$ 436	$ 86

Effective cash flow management is also essential to the success of the company. Miscalculating the availability of cash when needed (e.g., to pay vendors or payroll) may cause severe internal or external crises. Cash flow management assists the company in avoiding such operational crises and takes advantage of operational opportunities by applying some basic principles. Remember that the company is continuously in the cash expansion and conversion business. The business cycle starts with a cash infusion (e.g., owner investment or customer payments) and eventually ends in a cash liquidation (e.g., employee or vendor payments). If the company is successful, its ending cash will exceed starting cash by a sufficient amount to more than cover expenses. The company should not be in the business of investing in accounts receivable or sales backlog, inasmuch as neither can be reinvested until it is converted to cash. The availability of cash may be the principal limiting factor in the growth of the business. The company's goal should be to accelerate the cash conversion process as much as possible.

Effective cash flow management maximizes cash generation for the company. This means generating positive cash flow by applying effective techniques for conserving cash (e.g., keeping expenses and costs to a minimum) and for collecting cash due to the company (e.g., customer sales) as soon as possible. For the company to survive, it must have cash when it is needed. At present, the company has no way of knowing when cash will be available. The company's expenses are exaggerated, accounts receivables are excessive, and the ability to pay vendors on a timely basis is questionable. Sufficient cash availability (cash in and cash out) is necessary for the company to grow and survive.

Presently, the company uses a basic cost accounting system that accumulates direct labor from employee records, direct material from purchases and inventory issues, and an allocation of overhead based on a percentage of direct labor hours and costs. There are many inaccuracies in labor reporting (e.g., allocating as much time as possible to customer orders and the least to nonchargeable time) and material reporting (e.g., charging scrap, rework, and rejects back to the customer). Such labor and material cost inefficiencies are merely passed on to the customer along with overhead allocation in economies, resulting in greatly overstated costs and corresponding prices, which has made it difficult for the company to maintain the existing customer base. It has become the high cost, last alternative for many of its customers. Rather than building a business from a sound base of existing customers, the company's sales staff is continually searching for new (often undesirable) customers. The company has to adopt a sound cost and pricing system to remain competitive and to survive. It should consider activity-based costing principles.

The costs that are accumulated to develop product costs do not all behave in the same manner. Some costs may vary in proportion to changes in volumes or activity (e.g., labor or machine hours), others may not change regardless of the volume (e.g., rent or maintenance), and still others vary with changes in volume but not proportionately (e.g., repairs or use of overtime). An effective analysis of such cost behavior should be used by the company for:

- Cost-volume-profit break-even analysis, to determine the impact on profits of such factors as product prices, product mix, activity volume, variable costs of products, and the fixed costs of the business (which should be continuously analyzed for reduction).

- Variance analysis and cost control, to allow the company to address the cause of variances and take corrective action so that each operation can be made the best and kept that way.

- Short-term decision making, such as make or buy decisions or the acceptance or rejection of a large special order.

- Appraisal and evaluation of managerial and operational performance, so that corrective action can be taken to prevent the same mistakes from happening again and again.

- Use of associated systems, such as flexible budgeting, activity-based costing, responsibility reporting, and profitability reporting by production order, process, and customer.

SPECIFIC RECOMMENDATIONS

The operational review team performs the following work steps in conducting the operational review:

- Observation of all accounting function activities.

- Development, analysis, and summary of survey forms for each accounting function.

- Interviews of all accounting management and operations personnel.

- Development and analysis of systems flowcharts for all accounting functions and activities.

- Development and analysis of data, as listed here, for each area of the accounting function.

- Contact with and visits to three representative competitors to determine similarities and differences and to identify best practices.

- Periodic meetings with accounting personnel to review, orally, findings and conclusions to determine their appropriateness.

Based on the preceding work steps, the operational review team develops recommendations by functional accounting area:

Accounts Payable

The following five recommendations were made for accounts payable:

1. Reduce the number of accounts payable payments through consideration of the following recommendations:

   - Eliminate all payments for $100 or less by establishing a direct cash payment system, such as department credit cards, direct cash system, or telephone orders, as a release from a total dollar commitment.

   - Reduce the number of payments for larger items by negotiating with major vendors on paying at the time of merchandise receipt, with the guarantee of on-time quality deliveries. Items to consider in such negotiations include long-term commitments with shorter-term releases, the ability to deliver on time at close to 100 percent quality (no returned items), the loss of a discount (at present mostly 1 percent for 10 days or an annual rate of 18.4 percent), and savings in accounts payable processing.

   - Solicit other vendors to become part of a similar payment system. The review team talked to the six major vendors, and they are all interested in developing such a pay on receipt system. Two of the company's competitors have already installed such systems.

     It is estimated that the company can reduce the number of accounts payable payments to be processed from the present level of 26,000 annually to fewer than 6,000.

2. Work with major (and other) vendors to educate them on how the company operates so that they can be directly plugged into the company's production control system, allowing for 100 percent on-time deliveries and quality of product.

3. Integrate the receipt of merchandise with the approval of the payment, which will eliminate the need for accounts payable personnel to review the same documentation. In effect, the receipt of the merchandise should trigger the processing of the payment.

4. Reduce the number of personnel assigned to the accounts payable function, once the aforementioned recommendations are in place, from the present level of nine to no more than two individuals. There is no need for a manager and a supervisor or accounts payable processors. The remaining processing can be accomplished through the use of two data base analyzers. This should result in an annual savings of more than $115,000, based on last year's actual costs of $164,400.

5. Integrate the above cost savings into product cost structures so that the company can effectively reduce its product costs and related pricing to become more competitive.

Accounts Receivable

Six recommendations were developed for accounts receivable:

1. Integrate the sales forecast system into the overall company plan so that manufacturing can produce to a greater level of real customer orders, ensuring a greater degree of quality on-time deliveries. This will allow the company to better negotiate with major customers on long-term commitments and increased overall sales.

2. Establish long-term contracts with each of the company's major customers, including the ability to receive payment via electronic data transfer at the time of shipping merchandise. This will require the company to guarantee 100 percent quality and on-time deliveries. If this can be accomplished, the company can negotiate such long-term contracts, locking in price, production and delivery schedules, and future payments for cash flow purposes. This will enable the company to better plan profit and cash flow projections.

3. Reduce the number of customer billings through the implementation of the following recommendations:

- Establish a direct cash payment system for items less than $500, using credit cards, direct cash payments, and similar vehicles.

- Implement a policy of payment upon shipment or receipt of merchandise for major customers, considering such factors as ability to make on-time quality deliveries, negotiated long-term contracts with adequate notice regarding delivery schedules so as to incorporate such deliveries into the production schedule, the loss of a 1 percent ten-day discount for the customer, and the ability of the customer to pay on this basis.

- Encourage other customers to accept either the direct cash or pay-on-receipt system. With better control over costs and pricing, the company should be able to lower prices overall to make these systems attractive to their customers. Three competitors are already implementing such systems into their operations.

  It is estimated that the company can reduce the number of customer bills from the present level of 30,000 annually to fewer than 4,000.

4. Establish effective credit policies so that each customer is sold only that amount of merchandise that it can adequately pay for within the company's payment systems. Such credit policies must be flexible so that each customer's sales can be maximized without risking long or no payment.

5. Reduce the number of personnel assigned to the accounts receivable function once the aforementioned recommendations are in place, from the present level of thirteen to no more than four individuals. There is no need for both a manager and a supervisor or accounts receivable processors. The remaining processing can be accomplished through the use of two data base analyzers, one customer service contact, and one credit and collections coordinator. This should result in an annual savings of more than $150,000, based on last year's actual costs of $264,100.

6. Integrate billing, accounts receivable, and collections into the overall company computer system so that only minimal off-line processing

is necessary. This will result in the use of two database analyzers rather than accounts receivable processors.

Payroll

The biweekly payrolls that are processed by the company do not incorporate any features that would be unexpected in standard payroll processing. It is presently costing the company more than $136,000 annually to process these payrolls. It is recommended that the company consider one of three proposals for an outside payroll servicer to take over these functions at an annual savings of at least $100,000. The operational review team has talked to the following payroll vendors and has found that their annual costs to support the company's 220-person payroll would be as follows:

- ABC Payroll: $35,000

- The Payroll Company: $28,000

- Your Payroll: $32,000

All of these vendors are substantial in the field, and all offer the features necessary to fit the company's circumstances:

- Uploading of payroll data from the company's computer systems.

- Integration of payroll processing with manufacturing labor distribution and the company's budget system.

- Processing of all salary payrolls on an exception basis; that is, no input required unless there has been a change.

- Processing and control of all payroll changes, with feedback and approval by the company, prior to payroll processing.

- Full maintenance of personnel-related data fields, such as vacation time accrued and taken, sick time, personal leave, and nonchargeable time.

- Confidentiality in processing all payrolls, including the management payroll.

- Downloading of data files and reports from the servicer's computer system to the company's as a standard, by request, or in combination.

- Preparation and submission of all payroll reports to regulatory and taxing authorities.

- Preparation of W-2's for each individual at the end of the year.

All five of the company's competitors that were visited by the operational review team presently handle their payrolls in this manner.

General Ledger

The company has an integrated computerized accounting system in which each of the subsystems automatically update the general ledger. It also allows for automatic posting of standard journal entries. There is little else that has to be entered into the general ledger. The company should allow the system to work as intended. Through the use of one data base analyzer, the company should be assured that the general ledger is accurate. With such up-to-date processing accuracy, the company should be able to prepare financial statements (via screen display or hard copy report) whenever it desires.

Within the company, functional disciplines (e.g., sales, manufacturing, marketing, purchasing, accounting, and computer processing) are interdependent. All of these functions must work together to successfully achieve organizational goals and objectives. The overall plans of the organization must be clearly communicated so that each functional area is aware of what needs to be done to ensure smooth integration with other areas and the entire company. Effective profit planning and budgeting are among the tools used to coordinate the organizational plans and the detailed activities of each of the disciplines. The budget, then, is a detailed plan depicting the manner in which monetary resources will be acquired and used over a period of time. The budget is the quantitative manifestation of the current year of the company's strategic plan. It is an integral part of the company's short-term operating plan.

The company's budget system, within the preceding definitions, can be initiated and maintained through the computer system. Revenue transactions can be automatically posted through the recording of sales transactions. These sales data can be compared with sales forecasts (by salesperson, customer, or product). Expense transactions can be automatically posted against the budget system, with suspect items flagged and automatic budget adjustments processed. The budget should be considered part of the company planning process and a continual process (not once a year) with attention to flexible budgeting concepts. In this manner, the plan can be continuously reviewed and updated along with the corresponding budget.

With the implementation of the preceding recommendations, the company will be able to eliminate the entire general ledger function, at an annual savings of $120,000. One of the previously mentioned data base analyzers will also be responsible for the general ledger data files.

ORGANIZATION RECOMMENDATIONS

The accounting functions are primarily working as if an integrated computerized accounting system is not in existence. Each function, although it inputs data into the computer system, works on a stand-alone basis. Many of the activities that characterize a manual accounting system (e.g., matching physical documents, checking for coding errors, verifying math calculations) are still being performed. In addition, for limited control advantages, the company processes almost all vendor payments, customer billings, and collections on a manually controlled basis. The operational review team's recommendations to reduce the amount of accounts payable and accounts receivable transactions, to outsource the payroll function, and to allow the computer system to predominantly maintain the general ledger should allow the company to realize personnel savings of $692,700 as follows:

- Eliminate the internal controller position and its related staff positions. For those functions, such as borrowing, investing, and capital expenditures, the company should engage the services of an external controller. Review team members have talked to three extremely competent individuals and their firms about assuming these duties and reviewing financial and operational activities on an ongoing basis. Each one of them would perform such services for a monthly fee of $3,000.

- Eliminate the manager and supervisor positions in each of the accounting functions. The company should embrace a policy of motivated self-discipline of their employees so that such positions are unnecessary for policing their employees' activities. In effect, each employee is responsible for his or her own results.

- Use the integrated computer system as it was intended, so that the company does not need to pay processors but can engage database analyzers and coordinators instead.

- Eliminate the clerical positions through the use of computerized routines that are based on electronic data rather than on paper documentation.

- Streamline all remaining systems so that procedures can be accomplished most economically, efficiently, and effectively, using computerized routines to the extent possible and eliminating all non–value-added activities.

- Dovetail all other company operations that would be affected by such changes so that the company achieves overall benefits.

- Identify by-product benefits and best practices that can be implemented within the remaining accounting activities and other related areas.

The effective implementation of the preceding recommendations will result in the following personnel requirements for the accounting functions:

• External controller at $3,000 per month	$ 36,000
• Outside payroll processor	35,000
• Database analyzers: for accounts payable, accounts receivable, general ledger, and reporting systems (two at $30,000 per year)	60,000
• Systems coordinator to provide interface with other internal departments and the outside payroll processor	25,000
Total Proposed Personnel Costs	$156,000
Present Personnel Costs	787,100
Proposed Personnel Savings	$631,100

In addition to the above proposed personnel savings, the company should not have to spend more than an additional $10,000 per year on other costs to support these activities. This represents an additional annual savings of $61,600, based on the current year's actual costs of $71,600.

In reviewing the organizational concerns within the accounting functions, the operational review team identified the following concerns to be addressed within the accounting area as well as all other areas of the company.

- The need for a high-priced individual at the vice president level (e.g., controller) for each function within the organization. This practice appears to be justified by the need to police and control those employees reporting to these persons. There is minimal value-added effort contributed by these individuals. For instance, the operational review team is recommending the replacement of the controller (but not necessary functions) with the use of an external controller service.

- The use of managers for each function who report directly to a person at the vice-president level. These individuals are responsible for overseeing the activities performed in their areas, but offer minimal value-added efforts. This appears to be an extension of the policing and control belief system. It is a costly practice.

- Individuals with the title "Supervisor," who appear to be responsible for accomplishing the daily activities but are really chief workers.

- The practice of adding individuals to the workforce rather than simplifying work systems so that fewer personnel are required. For instance, there are eight processors in the accounts receivable section, where no more than two (even with present work volumes) are needed for most of the month.

- The assignment of clerical personnel to each functional activity. Although a certain amount of clerical support is required for each activity, it is rare that such support constitutes a full-time job (once redundancies and unnecessary work steps are eliminated).

OTHER AREAS FOR REVIEW

The scope of this operational review is to review and analyze those functions and activities associated with the accounting division of the company. However, the review team finds that many of their observations, findings, conclusions, and recommendations have an impact on other functional areas of the company as well. Accordingly, they must bring these areas to the attention of management so that management can take the appropriate follow-up action as part of a quest for best practices in a program of continuous improvements. Examples of other such areas for review are grouped in four major categories:

1. The recommendation to reduce the number of accounts payable transactions includes the use of a direct cash payment system for small purchases and payment to vendors at the time of receipt for large, long-term contractual-type purchases. Such practices will require the company to address related activities in various ways:

   • Responsibility of each department and work unit to control its own budget and related expenditures using a direct cash system.

   • Reduction in the number of purchase requisitions and purchase orders. This will affect all departmental support staff as well as reduce Purchasing Department efforts.

   • Increased responsibility for Purchasing Department personnel to effectively negotiate with vendors, especially major vendors.

   • With the present high level of merchandise returned to vendors, the company must work more closely with its vendors to ensure close to 100 percent on-time, quality deliveries.

   • Manufacturing systems, such as production and inventory control, must be fine-tuned so that they can effectively accommodate just-in-time practices based on the reliability of vendors rather than on excessive internal quality controls.

   • Increased reliance on computer processing systems rather than elaborate manual control systems.

2. Accounts receivable recommendations that encompass payment upon receipt for small and low-ticket sales and payment upon receipt for large sales to major customers will require the company to consider the following areas as well:

   • Establishment of procedures and controls to accommodate a cash payment system for low-ticket items.

   • Effective negotiations with major customers to develop long-term contracts with guaranteed delivery dates at prices at which the company can improve its profit margins. This will require a full analysis of cost systems so that the company can produce the items at the lowest cost possible. Each customer contract should be considered a profit center.

- Integration of the sales function with company planning. Sales forecasts must be more realistic so that they can be relied on to plan production activities. Product should be produced for real customer orders rather than for inventory. The Sales Department should be guided by the company plan rather than by the desire to maximize compensation. Such changes may require a full operational review of the sales and manufacturing areas, as well as the company planning processes.

- Customer analysis to determine with which present customers to increase or decrease sales and which customers to terminate. In addition, there should be effective planning on which products to sell, in what quantity, and to whom. Part of such a plan should be the identification of prospective customers and how they can be approached.

- Increased attention to peripheral activities such as credit policies, collection procedures, factoring, and electronic data transfer.

- Increased discipline within the manufacturing area so the company can meet all of its customer commitments on an on-time, quality basis. Production schedule and control procedures must be integrated with customer requirements. The company has to remove itself from the inventory business and move back into the customer service and cash conversion businesses.

3. The change from an internal payroll department to an outside payroll processor necessitates that the company look at the following concerns:

- Accurate data discipline by all operating areas, as there will no longer be personnel in-house to correct payroll input errors, which never should have happened. Corrections can be made only on an after the fact basis.

- Investigating the effective use of such outsourcing concepts for other areas. For instance, the use of an external controller is recommended. Economies and efficiencies can be realized in other areas as well, including manufacturing operations (e.g., grinding and smoothing), sales (e.g., brokers and representatives), and engineering (e.g., per diem personnel as needed).

- Integration of outsiders into company operations, making them part of the organization even though they are not employees. The company must change its belief system that everything must be controlled internally with its own employees.

- Elimination of in-house activities and controls that will be taken over by the outside servicer, such as data controls, numeric reconciliations, and output verifications.

- The reduction and change in activities and related job positions, which allow greater efficiency at much less cost within the accounting functions, should be considered in an analysis of all other functions of the company.

4. Integration of the general ledger with computerized subsystems and the implementation of responsive financial and operating controls and reporting will impact on company operations in the following ways:

- Real-time information which will necessitate immediate action to address the cause of a problem rather than the symptoms. This will require self-motivated discipline by all employees and less reliance on managers (and fewer managers) within a working together atmosphere. Such a reporting system will assist the company in becoming a learning organization.

- The reality of a continuous planning and flexible budget system which will require quick responsiveness to changes and more effective management of each employee's responsibilities.

- Adoption of an effective cost accounting system according to activity-based costing principles will aid in reviewing all costs and activities in an effort to bring costs and related prices to the minimum possible. This will allow the company to become more competitive and build business on a core of satisfied customers.

- Use of effective cash flow management techniques will allow for pushing costs to their minimums (e.g., labor and material), collecting sales proceeds as soon as possible, and making payments as economically as possible.

- Employees will have the flexibility to go to the work, rather than waiting for the work to come to them. Each employee should be evaluated and rewarded based on results accomplished rather than a subjective system such as seniority or personal preference.

- There will be greater reliance on computer procedures rather than on manual controls, which should be implemented in all areas of the company.

CONCLUSION

Effective operational review procedures allow a company to identify its critical problem areas and opportunities for positive improvement—maximizing positive aspects of existing procedures and focusing the operational review on the most critical areas. Through coordinating activities of various areas, the operational review process achieves positive changes in these areas simultaneously. The process also allows such areas to work together in the analysis of present practices and the implementation of new systems and procedures. In this manner, all areas learn with less reinventing and change within the same time period.

The operational review can be a stand-alone project to identify critical problem areas and provide standardized improvements. It can also minimize the practice of reinventing good practices that already exist in another part of the organization or that have been unsuccessful. The operational review can also provide a comparison between the ways in which different people perform the same task in the same area, or a comparison of performance across different work units within the company. It can also provide the knowledge of operations that is essential to the success of the operational review.

In the review of the accounting function, a number of areas of potential improvement are identified to make the company operate more economically, efficiently, and effectively. The implementation of such improvements places the company in a better position for future growth and profitability and will enable the company to compete more effectively in the marketplace. Although there are many other aspects of the company's accounting practices that can be addressed for productivity or profit improvements, these materials contain effective examples of the types of conclusions and recommendations that can result from such an operational review. Because each company and each operational review is different, the findings, conclusions, and recommendations resulting from an operational review will also be unique to that particular company.

In this present atmosphere, with emphasis on customer service, quality, economies and efficiencies, and profit maximization, the operational review becomes not a one-time, stand-alone project, but an ongoing process of searching for best practices in a company program of continuous improvements. The application of operational review procedures is everyone's responsibility.

CHAPTER THREE

Work Program Phase

The operational review work program is written for the review of selected activities as determined in the planning phase. It becomes the bridge between the planning phase and the field work phase. The work program is a plan of action for conducting the operational review. The operational review team considers each significant area identified in the planning phase for further review, and develops specific work steps that they believe will most clearly demonstrate the extent and cause of the operational deficiency and lead to recommendations for improvement. The work program is as important to the operational reviewer as a map is to a navigator.

This chapter discusses the work program phase of the operational review. It is in phase that the operational reviewer focuses on the significant operational areas identified in the planning phase and develops specific work steps for further review and analysis. Through the performance of these work steps, in the field work phase, the reviewer determines the extent of any operational deficiencies and begins to develop operational review findings. In effect, as stated earlier, the work program phase is the bridge between the planning phase and the field work phase. The operational review work program is, therefore, the plan of action for conducting the operational review. However, it is initially written for the preliminary review of those selected activities as determined in the planning phase. Accordingly, it is subject to change based on actual findings during the field work phase.

The following four points are discussed in this chapter:

1. Benefits of the operational review work program.

2. Standards by which operational review work programs are developed.

3. Who develops the work program.

4. Work program development procedures.

In addition, a sample operational review work program and related work steps will be presented. By the end of this chapter, via the use of case study materials, an increased understanding of the development of an operational review work program for areas identified in the planning phase will have been obtained.

BENEFITS OF THE OPERATIONAL REVIEW WORK PROGRAM

A well-constructed operational review work program is essential to conducting the operational review in an efficient and effective manner. Operational review work programs are the key to successful operational reviews as they provide benefits such as:

- A systematic plan for the work to be performed in the operational review that can be communicated to all operational review staff.

- A systematic basis for assigning work to review staff members according to their specialized skills, technical competencies, and type of task.

- A means by which operational review supervisors and other reviewers can compare performance with approved plans, review standards, and requirements.

- Assistance in training inexperienced staff members and acquainting them with the scope, objectives, and work steps of the operational review.

- The basis for a summary record of work actually performed in the operational review.

- Aid in familiarizing successive review groups with the nature of the work performed in the present operational review.

Although these written work programs are essential to efficient and effective management of an operational review assignment, they should never be used simply as a checklist of work steps to perform in a way that stifles individual reviewer initiative, imagination, and resourcefulness in achieving the desired objectives. Remember that the operational review work program is written for the preliminary review of selected activities as determined in the planning phase, but is subject to change based on what is actually found in the field work phase of the review.

> ### The Work Program
> ### Is the Key to a Successful
> ### Operational Review

OPERATIONAL REVIEW WORK PROGRAM STANDARDS

The operational review work program is really a plan for the review work steps that the reviewer believes will achieve the best results. Once the actual results are determined, the reviewer may want to change the plan. For instance, in conducting a review work step the perceived deficiency may not really be significant. In this case, the reviewer would curtail this work step and any others associated with it. On the other hand, if it is determined that a particular area is really more significant than expected, then the work program should be increased by additional work steps.

The operational review work program is developed for the specific circumstances of the organization or department under review. Therefore, each operational review work program is a unique entity. This being the case, the operational review work program is normally developed for one-time use. Unlike financial audits, operational reviews have no previous year's work papers to refer to. Although there may be previous operational reviews available for reference, keep in mind that each situation is unique and the use of borrowed work steps should be minimized and used only in those cases where they are appropriate.

In preparing the operational review work program, the reviewer should consider certain standards, such as:

- The operational review work program should be tailor-made to fit the specific operational review assignment's type of organization, personnel involved, systems and procedures in effect, degree of sophistication, and so on.

- Each work step should clearly set forth the work to be done and the reason for doing it. Including a clear explanation of the reasons for each work step is helpful because:

  - The staff member carrying out the work must know why the work step is being done. With this information, the reviewer can be expected to do a much better job than if asked to perform a work step without sufficient background.

  - It minimizes the inclusion of unnecessary work steps. Sometimes the inability to cite a good reason for doing something leads the work program writer to the conclusion that the work step is not really needed.

  - It makes possible a more intelligent review of the work program for advance approval and post review of work performed.

- The work program should be flexible and permit application of initiative in deviating from prescribed procedures. As the work program is really a plan based on the work steps that the operational review team believes will achieve the best results, once the actual results are determined, the reviewers may want to change the plan.

- The work program should specifically provide for the development of individual findings. In this respect, it should help to:

  - Determine why the results and conditions found are as they are, not just how they are. In effect, performance is analyzed, not simply reported.

  - Direct attention to evidential matter in support of conclusions.

  - Evaluate performance and evidence in comparison with relevant standards and norms of performance. Note that relevance is a judgment factor dependent on the experience, imagination, and common sense of the operational reviewer.

The Work Program
Fits the Situation

WHO DEVELOPS THE WORK PROGRAM

There is no good reason that the review manager has to be solely responsible for the development of the work program. In fact, the more input into review program development, the better the finished product. As a general rule, all members of the operational review team should be involved in developing the work program, particularly those staff members who were involved in the planning phase. In addition, others may be considered to provide input into the work program development process, such as:

- Operational review staff members who have some expertise in the area under review or have participated in a similar review in the past

- Client personnel who work in the area being reviewed, who have some special input to provide (Be sure that such client personnel maintain their objectivity)

- Outside consultants or experts who have special expertise in the area being reviewed or in the operational review process

- Personnel from other similar organizations or functions who may be able to offer another perspective

The same personnel can also be used in the field work phase, development of findings and recommendations, and reporting phase of the operational review. In fact, normally, the greater the mix of personnel involved in the operational review, the greater the potential for positive results. Involving user personnel to the extent possible usually ensures a greater likelihood of the acceptance of recommendations. Often, the use of outside assistance enhances the quality of the operational review, while allowing for the use of operational review personnel in the areas where they are most familiar. However, be aware that outside consultants can be costly, so use them judiciously.

Although the use of the team approach is recommended for the optimum development of the operational review work program, it can be more costly and time consuming than having one or two operational review team members develop the program. Moreover, it is not always cost effective to use the team approach, particularly when there are a number of different areas or locations involved. Many times, the approach to be taken depends on the size of the review and the total of budgeted operational review hours.

> *The Greater the Input,*
> *the Greater the Work Program*

WORK PROGRAM WORK STEPS

After deciding on the makeup of the operational review program team, the next step is to develop the work steps to be performed for each area identified as significant in the planning phase. Although each operational review work program is unique, this does not prevent the reviewers from using specific work steps from previously completed operational reviews, but they must be careful to use them only if they meet the requirements of the present operational review. Otherwise, entirely new work steps need to be developed. To help in developing these work steps, the reviewer needs to be aware of some of the following 17 common field work techniques:

1. Review of existing documentation, such as policy and procedures manuals

2. Preparation of organization charts and related functional job descriptions

3. Analysis of personnel policies and procedures related to hiring, orientation, training, evaluation, promotion, and firing

4. Analysis of organizational policies and related systems and procedures, both administrative and operational

5. Interviews with management and operations personnel

6. Flowchart preparation
   - Systems flowcharts, showing the processes of a functional area
   - Layout flow diagrams, showing the physical layout of a work area and its related work flow

7. Ratio, change, and trend analysis

8. Questionnaires, for use by the reviewer or client's personnel

9. Surveys, by phone or in written form, for customers, vendors, and so on to respond to

10. Questions within the review work program

11. Review of transactions, in which the different types of normal and abnormal transactions are considered

12. Review of operations, by techniques such as observation, work measurement, time studies, work performance forms or logs, and so on

13. Forms analysis

14. Analysis of results

15. Review and analysis of management information system and related reports

16. Compliance reviews; as to compliance with laws, regulations, policies, procedures, goals, objectives, and so forth

17. Use of computer processing; using computer auditing "through the computer" techniques or review and analysis of computer-produced information

These field work techniques should be used, of course, only where they are appropriate. To determine which techniques to use in operational reviews, use this rule: Whatever work step works best in the situation, use it. There is no reason a reviewer cannot use specific review techniques used on different operational reviews in the past. In fact, this should be encouraged, as it is usually easier and ensures a greater degree of success to use tried and true techniques rather than untried innovative approaches. However, this is not meant to discourage creative and innovative approaches to operational review work steps, as quite often such approaches are necessary to fit a specific situation and yield the greatest results in improved operations. The goal is to identify those specific review techniques that most closely fit the situation and have the best possibility of providing operational benefits.

> ### *The Best Work Step*
> ### *for the Situation*
> ### *Is the One that Works*

WORK PROGRAM DEVELOPMENT PROCEDURES

In the development of the operational review work program, the review team must keep in mind the following four procedural steps:

1. Identification of the critical operational areas and their related control and risk areas. These risk areas usually relate to the inability to achieve the operational areas' goals and objectives.

2. Development of key questions and work steps to validate and quantify the perceived risk areas. For instance, for the purchasing function, the reviewer might question procedures relative to purchase specification changes, price changes, competitive bidding, and vendor relations and analysis.

3. Identification of the work steps needed to provide answers to the perceived risk areas and key questions. This entails matching the field work tasks mentioned above and others appropriate to the risk area in question. Work steps could include observations, flowcharts, interviews, and so on.

4. Development of review work plans for each area to be reviewed; including personnel assignments, time schedules, and review budgets.

As an example of using these steps to develop the review program, consider the purchase requisitioning procedure. The identified control and risk areas include the possibility of not ordering needed materials and services, ordering materials or services that should not be ordered, or ordering more materials than are needed. The objective of the work steps might then be to ascertain that only those materials or services that are needed are properly and promptly ordered. The six work steps that could help the reviewer meet the objective may include:

1. Selecting a number of operating departments or units where the reviewers would interview and review with department management and operations personnel the way their purchase requisitions are controlled and processed;

2. Identifying the need for selected materials, equipment, or services for approved purposes, plans, or programs;

3. Determining authority for purchase requisition approvals, including purpose and budgetary requirements within the operating department;

4. Analyzing the establishment of purchase lead times and their integration with departmental plans and activities;

5. Flowcharting the purchase requisition process to determine that there are adequate controls and processing procedures to ensure the accurate recording of all purchase requisitions and the subsequent processing by the purchasing function; and

6. Reviewing and analyzing purchase specification and quality control procedures to ensure that the right items are being ordered at the most economical prices.

> ### The Work Step Relates
> ### to Controls and Risks

SAMPLE WORK PROGRAM: PURCHASING FOUNDATION

A more complete sample operational review work program for the purchasing function that provides examples of many of these work step techniques is shown in Exhibit 3.1. Note that the sections of the work program and the corresponding areas within each section should relate back to the areas for further review as identified in the planning phase. For demonstration purposes, a number of different areas are presented for review, each of which could have been identified as significant in the planning phase. However, in the conduct of a typical operational review, the number of areas to be reviewed would be based on the establishment of priorities related to their significance and criticalness to overall operations and the amount of review budget time allocated to that particular operational review. In Exhibit 3.1, four operational areas were selected for review:

1. Company policy and organization, including organizational status of the Purchasing Department, responsibility for purchasing, authorization for purchasing, and decentralized purchasing.

2. Purchasing Department operations, including department procedures, department forms, physical facilities, value analysis program, and collateral operations.

3. Review of purchase transactions, including selection of transactions to include various types of transactions that the reviewer has identified as possible areas of deficiency, and examination of purchase transactions selected.

4. Records and reports—management information and controls being reported, as well as those that should be, but are not being reported.

EXHIBIT 3.1   Operational Review Work Program: Purchasing Function

---

I.   COMPANY POLICY AND ORGANIZATION

A.   *Organizational Status of Purchasing Department*
   1.   Secure or prepare an organization chart of the Purchasing Department with descriptions of each work unit's specific functions. Determine to whom the head of the Purchasing Department reports. Perform analytical work to determine whether such reporting is proper or whether it results in operational concerns and problems. Analyze each work unit's functions to determine whether they are appropriate and proper Purchasing Department functions.
   2.   Document the duties and responsibilities of each Purchasing Department employee. Obtain copies of existing job descriptions, and validate through interviewing each employee and related supervisor. Observe actual work being performed. Determine necessity of all duties and responsibilities.
B.   *Responsibility for Purchasing*
   1.   Obtain or prepare company policy on purchasing functions and activities. Determine that the responsibility of the Purchasing Department is clearly defined and understood by Purchasing Department personnel and other non-purchasing employees. Ascertain whether the Purchasing Department staff has knowledge of conflicting purchasing responsibility assumed by other departments. Document any principal procurement activities for which the Purchasing Department has no responsibility or limited responsibility.

EXHIBIT 3.1   (*Continued*)

2. Obtain or prepare policy covering other departments' relations with vendors as to contacts or discussions with sales personnel or correspondence. Analyze such activities within selected operating departments to determine the extent of such vendor relations. Select a number of heavily used and critical vendors to survey as to their relations with the Purchasing Department and other departmental personnel. Use both telephone survey and written response survey techniques.

C. *Authorization for Purchasing*

1. Obtain copy or document policies as to:
   - Approval of purchases by departments requiring material.
   - Approval limits as to types of purchases and amounts.
   - Capital expenditures.
   - Budget approval prior to commitment

2. Analyze procedures through the review of selected transactions where the final cost of an order exceeds the amount originally estimated on the purchase order:
   - Where limit of approval of original signer is not exceeded by final cost.
   - Where limit of approval of original signer is exceeded.

3. Analyze procedures through the review of selected transactions where changes are made in the quantity or specifications of the original purchase requisition.

D. *Decentralized Purchasing*

1. Determine company policies and procedures on purchases made by decentralized operating units, through petty cash, etc. as to:
   - Limits of authority
   - Reporting responsibility
   - Review or control by central Purchasing Department

2. Select a number of such decentralized operating units for review. Analyze their operations as to compliance with existing company policies related to decentralized purchasing.

   Note: The purpose of this portion of the review is to learn of the policies and general conditions under which the Purchasing Department operates. The sources of information will usually be the head of the Purchasing Department, other Purchasing Department staff, and company manuals.

   Where policies are lacking or indefinite, there may be weakness in control, duplicating fields of responsibility, or other deficiency that will be evidenced in the course of the review. Also evidenced will be variations between policy and actual operations.

EXHIBIT 3.1 *(Continued)*

II. PURCHASING DEPARTMENT OPERATIONS

A. *Department Procedures*
1. Obtain or prepare a copy of the Purchasing Department operating procedures.
2. Prepare flowcharts of the major purchasing operations, such as the handling of requisitions, processing of purchase orders, control over open purchases, receipt of merchandise, and vendor payment procedures.
3. Review procedures related to bidding by vendors:
    • Dollar amounts of orders on which bidding is required.
    • Requests for bids.
    • Form of bids (sealed, oral, etc.).
    • Summarization of bids and selection of vendors.
B. *Department Forms*
    Obtain a copy of each specialized form used by the Purchasing Department. These should be studied so that the purpose and usage is thoroughly understood. Areas to be considered include:
    • Purchase order form clear and complete, so that the vendor understands all terms and conditions.
    • Protection of blank purchase order forms.
    • Routing of copies of purchase order forms.
    • Necessity of each copy of the form.
    • Forms designed for efficient and simple completion.
    • Use of specialized forms to eliminate repetitive processing such as:
        • Traveling requisitions: for repetitive orders of the same item.
        • Blanket purchase orders for repetitive purchases from the same vendor.
    Note: It is common to find overelaborate routines relating to the preparation of purchasing forms, particularly the purchase order. The result is the unnecessary duplication of files in various departments.
C. *Physical Facilities*
    Prepare a layout flow diagram of the Purchasing Department showing its layout and general facilities, with particular attention to:
    • Work flow efficiencies and inefficiencies
    • Arrangements for reception of and interviews with salespeople
    • Office layout for effective/ineffective operations
D. *Value Analysis Program*
1. Review the Purchasing Department's value analysis program, including:

EXHIBIT 3.1 *(Continued)*

- Determination that price revisions covering changes in materials and methods are negotiated with vendors.
- Review of market trends, particularly on long-term contracts and contracts containing escalation clauses.

Note: In a value analysis program, the Purchasing Department works with vendors and with affected company departments (such as engineering and production) in the analysis of specifications, consumption, and requirements. Through such analysis and cooperative effort, it is possible to make savings through redesign, change in specifications, purchase in more economical quantities, or manufacture by the company itself.

E. *Collateral Operations*
1. Determine and describe all operations performed in the Purchasing Department that are not directly concerned with placing orders and follow-up for delivery. For example, the Purchasing Department may be assigned responsibility for such operations as:
    - Reporting on quantity, quality, and timeliness of received materials
    - Authorization of payments to vendors
    - Sale of scrap
    - Purchases for employees

In the review of the collateral operations of the Purchasing Department, the reviewer will have a twofold concern: first, the effect that the inclusion of these operations under the responsibility of the Purchasing Department will have, as far as internal control is concerned; second, the review of the assigned collateral operations.

Because of the many variables, it is not possible to specify any definite program for the review of specific collateral responsibilities of the Purchasing Department. The reviewer must shape his or her study to cover each situation, and it may develop that a supplementary inter-departmental survey of a particular field should be made.

III. REVIEW OF PURCHASE TRANSACTIONS

A. *Selection of Transactions*
Examine files covering all purchase orders placed over a period of XX months. From these, select, for detailed examination, orders that include some of each of the following:
- Purchases made by each buyer.
- Requisitions by each major operating department.
- A number of Rush and Confirming Delivery orders.

EXHIBIT 3.1 *(Continued)*

- Single orders divided between several suppliers.
- Orders in which purchase is not made from lowest bidder.
- Orders in which final specifications or quantities are revised from the original requisition.
- Orders in which freight is allowed.
- Orders for capital equipment.
- Orders in which price is not specified, or that include some variable pricing arrangement.
- Orders providing for trade-in allowances.
- Orders in which substantial overshipment is made and accepted.
- Blanket or continuing orders, in which a number of deliveries are made over a period.
- Orders in which specification of item, quantity, or price is not definite.
- Orders placed under long-term purchase contracts.

Note: The selection of an adequate sample of orders is of utmost importance. The objective is to set aside for detailed examination a group of purchase orders that will adequately represent both the normal and the abnormal. There must be enough of the normal for the reviewer to verify general policies and procedures and reveal situations that may call for more extensive examination.

B. *Examination of Purchase Transactions Selected*

The examination of each type of purchase transaction selected should be completed in enough detail, through examination of all supporting records, to enable the reviewer to acquire sufficient knowledge as to how each of the operations, from origination and approval of requisition to the completion of the order, was handled. The reviewer must be constantly concerned with what was done and why; to achieve satisfaction that each order was placed and handled in the best interests of the company.

Through this examination the reviewer may become aware of situations, in the Purchasing Department or in other departments of the company, that require further study. The objectives are (1) through verification, to provide the basis for appraisal of current policies and procedures and (2) to give a basis for constructive recommendation. The following list is intended only as a sample of questions that will occupy the reviewer's attention and may be the subject for further inquiry:

- Where an order was divided among several vendors, what was the reason?

EXHIBIT 3.1 (*Continued*)

- On Confirming Orders, did some operating department really assume the purchasing function?
- If orders are placed for such items as memberships, just what is gained by clearing these through purchasing routines?
- Are there any indications of favoritism to vendors?
- Where changes are made from original specifications in a requisition or order, are these adequately approved and brought to the attention of those who should be concerned?
- How are allowances and adjustments handled and approved?
- Are transportation allowances verified?
- If price is omitted from an order, why?
- If an order calls for services or materials on a cost plus or other basis indefinite as to exact amount, how are final charges verified?
- Does the employee approving a requisition appear to have adequate information to enable intelligent approval?
- How are trade-in arrangements determined and approved? (It is often possible to secure more for replaced equipment from outside sale than from trade-in.)
- How completely do possible sources of supply seem to be covered?
- Are F.O.B. points and routings shown and followed?
- Does it appear that effort is made to ship by most economical methods? Is the traffic department consulted regarding routes and methods?
- How were long-term contracts negotiated?
- What consideration is given to the tax status of materials: sales and use taxes, excise taxes, and so on.?

IV. RECORDS AND REPORTS

The various records that are used in current operations will have been reviewed and appraised in the study of departmental procedures. This will include such records as those showing sources of supply and numerical listings of purchase orders placed.

Beyond these will be a variety of records and reports that are not required in the normal flow of work but are maintained to provide information considered valuable for administrative response. Examples of this type of record or report are:

- Records of orders placed with each vendor.
- Records of orders placed by each buyer, showing number of orders and total value.
- Reports of future commitments.

EXHIBIT 3.1 (*Continued*)

- Reports of departmental operations to management.
- Reports of commodity price trends to operating departments.
- Reports that have been rendered to management covering special savings or other accomplishments.

The examination and appraisal of records and reports has two objectives:

A. First should come verification of the accuracy of the records of statements that are maintained or reported. This should be done on a test basis. For example, if a saving was claimed, there should be a test to be sure that the claimed saving was actually realized.

B. After verification of the general accuracy, the second step is appraisal of the value to the department or executive using or receiving the record or report. In this appraisal, the reviewer should ascertain the answers to such questions as:

- Is each record really used?
- Does each report serve a useful purpose?
- Does each report give a complete and accurate picture?
- Are reports incomplete, so that important factors are not brought to management's attention?

The answers to these and other questions that arise will require discussions with those who prepare the records and reports and with those who receive and use them.

OPERATIONAL REVIEW ENGAGEMENT BUDGET

At this point, the operational review team has finalized the initial work program by identifying the specific work steps and techniques to use for the significant operational areas selected for review. Now the amount of time necessary to complete each work step must be determined to arrive at an overall engagement budget. For those work steps and techniques that have been used on previous operational reviews, there is some experience upon which to base budget estimates. However, for new work steps or techniques, best professional judgment will have to be used in arriving at budgeted hours.

Keep in mind that an operational review budget needs to be flexible and is subject to change. Such flexibility in budgeting is necessary because of the greater possibilities of budget changes resulting from activities performed in the field work phase—either requiring additional time for areas warranting more attention or less time for areas found to be less critical than expected.

For instance, additional field work may be needed when the area under review requires more analysis to identify findings and recommendations for operational improvements; or additional significant operational deficiencies may be identified that were not included in the initial work program scope, which require additional budget hours or reallocation of existing budget hours. An area under review may not yield significant review findings to the extent originally expected. If that happens, the reviewer should stop operational review efforts and reallocate any hours remaining in the budget to other work steps.

Sample operational review budgets for the work program presented in Exhibit 3.1 are shown for the planning phase in Exhibit 3.2 and for the field work phases in Exhibit 3.3. These budgets are prepared prior to the actual work and are best estimates, subject to change.

The operational review budgets shown in Exhibits 3.2 and 3.3 are for a relatively large review of a purchasing function. They are presented as examples of work programs for both the planning phase and the field work and reporting phases. The scope, extent, and number of hours needed to perform a specific operational review in a given situation would, of course, need to be scaled downward or upward as appropriate.

The estimated budget hours shown in the work program examples are intended only as representations. They are not meant to imply or relate to actual hours required. The planning phase normally takes a substantial amount of time as compared with the field work phase—in the example, 226 hours as compared with 630 hours, or approximately one-third.

It is important to understand the significance of the planning phase activities and not to look for budget shortcuts. A well-defined and performed planning phase not only helps to focus correctly on the right operational activities to review during the field work phase, but it also reduces unnecessary field work steps. Both of these work programs are front-end estimates regarding the necessary work steps and budget hours required. These are subject to change, based on actual conditions found as a result of the performance of the work steps themselves. Accordingly, the work program could be changed dramatically upward or downward.

EXHIBIT 3.2 Operational Review Budget: Purchasing Function, Planning Phase

PLANNING PHASE

	Hrs	Dates	Staff
1. *Goals and Objectives*			
a. *Review legislative and internal materials* that define general goals and objectives	6	3-1/2	Mary
b. *Planning systems and procedures*			
• Document with narrative and/or flowchart	12	3-1/2	Bill
• Determine planning: long-term and short-term	4	3-3	Bill
• Review present plans: goals and objectives	4	3-3/4	Bill
• Review detail plans and reporting systems	6 / 32	3-4/5	Bill
2. *Budgets*			
a. Review budget process, as related to plans	3	3-8	Bill
b. Review budget justification procedures	2	3-8	Bill
c. Analyze budget reporting procedures:	6	3-8	Bill
• Budget versus actual		to	
• Flexible budgeting		3-10	
• Monitoring and controls	11		
3. *Organization Chart and Procedures Manual*			
a. Obtain copy or prepare organization chart and analyze	6	3-10/11	Betty
b. Obtain copy of procedures manuals and review	8 / 14	3-11/3-16	Betty
4. *Flowcharts*			
a. Familiarize with Purchasing Department procedures	4	3-8	Mike
b. Prepare general systems flowcharts of major systems and procedures	16	3-8/3-10	Mike
c. Analyze flowcharts	8 / 28	3-10/11	Mike

EXHIBIT 3.2 (*Continued*)

	Hrs	Dates	Staff
5. *Reports*			
a. Obtain copies of management/ operating reports	2	3-1/2	Mary/Cliff
b. Discuss reports with appropriate personnel and write up description of each report	10	3-2/3-4	Mary/Cliff
c. Review and analyze reports	6	3-4/5	Mary/Cliff
	18		
6. *Personnel*			
a. Obtain current job descriptions and operating reports	4	3-8	Jane/Roy
b. Review personnel folder; compare background to job description	6	3-8/9	Jane/Roy
c. Analyze personnel functions: • Experience and training requirements • Determination of number of staff required • Formal or informal staff training • Employee evaluation procedures	8	3-10/11	Jane/Roy
d. Prepare summary of positions and compare with: • Organization charts • Budgets • Job descriptions	6	3-11/12	Jane
e. Observe employees at work	5	3-9/10	Jane/Roy
f. Review employee statistics: • Turnover rate • Sick leave • Lateness • Overtime	4	3-11/12	Jane
	33		
7. *Facilities*			
a. Observe work layout and working conditions	4	3-15	Mike
b. Prepare and analyze work layout flow diagram	4	3-15/16	Mike

EXHIBIT 3.2   (*Continued*)

	Hrs	Dates	Staff
c. Review use of equipment	2	3-16	Mike
d. Analyze general operating procedures	2	3-16	Mike
e. Review fixed assets used in operations	4	3-15	Jane
	16		
8. *Review of Planning Phase Results*	10	3-17/19	Betty
Total Planning Phase Work Steps	162		
9. *Preparation of Planning Phase Work Program*	24	2-23/24	Betty/Cliff
10. *Ongoing Review Management*	40		Betty/Cliff
Grand Total Budget	226		

The review team must be flexible about shifting work steps to be performed, as well as the assigning of review personnel, estimated budget hours, and scheduled start and completion times. This requires the exercise of proper and adequate management control over the operational review engagement, together with sufficient reporting from operational review staff to provide timely identification of any work scope changes. For the greatest effectiveness in conducting and controlling the work program, there must be cohesive team effort between operational review management, staff, and client personnel.

ASSIGNMENT OF STAFF

Once the work program has been developed and work steps have been identified, the next step in the work program phase is to assign appropriate staff personnel to conduct each work step. In most projects, this is a fairly simple matter, as there is a great interchangeability between staff members in their ability to perform required work steps. In addition, many of the work steps are repetitions of other similar projects and even from the same project performed in previous years. This is not so in an operational review. First, some of the required work steps for a particular operational review may be one-time activities being performed for the first time and possibly

EXHIBIT 3.3 Sample Operational Review Budget: Purchasing Function, Field Work Phase

FIELD WORK PHASE

	Hrs	Dates	Staff
1. *Company Policy and Organization*			
a. Organization Status of Purchasing Department			
• Organization chart and analysis	20	3-25/30	Bill
• Employees' duties and responsibilities	30	3-26/4-7	Bill
b. Responsibility for Purchasing			
• Purchasing functions and activities	8	4-12/20	Bill
• Relations with vendors	12	4-15/20	Bill
c. Authorization for Purchasing			
• Approval of purchases	4	3-22/23	Jane
• Procedures: final cost exceeds PO amount	3	3-23	Jane
• Procedures: quantity or spec changes	3	3-23	Jane
d. Decentralized Purchasing			
• Policies and procedures	6	3-25/26	Joe
• Review of decentralized operating units	14	3-29/31	Joe
Total Company Policy Organization	100		
2. *Purchasing Department Operations*			
a. Department Procedures			
• Purchasing Department operating procedures	8	3-29/30	Mike
• Flowcharts: purchase requisitions and orders	32	3-30/4-6	Mike
• Bidding by vendors procedure	10	4-5/4-6	Mike
b. Department Forms	20	3-31/4-5	Mary
c. Physical Facilities	12	3-29/3-30	Roy
d. Value Analysis Program	8	3-25/3-26	Cliff
e. Collateral Operations	16	3-29/4-1	Jane
Total Purchasing Department operations	106		

EXHIBIT 3.3   (*Continued*)

	Hrs	Dates	Staff
3. *Review of Purchase Transactions*			
a. Selection of Transactions	20	4-7/12	Joe/Beth
b. Examination of Purchase Transactions	30	4-13/20	Joe/Beth
Total Review of Purchase Transactions	50		
4. *Records and Reports*			
a. Verification of Accuracy of the Records	12	4-20/22	Jane
b. Appraisal of Value to the Department	22	4-23/29	Jane
Total Records and Reports	34		
5. *Review of Field Work Results*	60	4-28/5-7	Betty/Cliff
Total Field Work Phase Work Steps	350		
6. *Development of Findings*	80	5-10/19	Betty/Bill Jane/Mary Cliff/Roy
7. *Oral Reporting*			
a. Preparation for Meetings	8	4-9,30	Betty/Cliff
b. Meetings with Client Personnel	12	5-20/21	Betty/Cliff
8. *Written Report: Draft and Final*	40	5-24/6-2	Betty, Bill, and Cliff
Total Work Program Work Steps	490		
9. *Preparation of Work Program*	40	3-17/19	All
10. *Ongoing Review Management*	100	Ongoing	Betty and Cliff
Grant Total Budget	630		

not again. Second, certain work steps may require specific specialized skills, such as analytical ability, communications skills, knowledge of specific systems and procedures, perceptual ability, organizational and personnel structure skills, and specific technical abilities.

Accordingly, it is extremely important in the performance of an operational review to match the skills and abilities needed with staff members' expertise in performing a particular work step. Theoretically, the closer the match between the skills needed for a particular work step and the skills possessed by the staff member doing the work, the greater the results. In reality, there is not always the luxury of having sufficient staff to assign to optimize such a matching of skills. Normally, an effort is made to optimize such skills matching based on staff personnel available, while dealing with the constraint of having to perform work steps requiring similar skills within the same time frame. The critical task of assigning the right staff members to the right work steps often becomes a case of making the best of the situation.

> ### *Assign the Right Staff*
> ### *to the Right Task*

OPERATIONAL REVIEW MANAGEMENT

The initial consideration in assigning staff to the operational review is review management. Where possible, it is always best to share such management responsibilities between the operational review staff and the client's operational personnel. The operational review staff manager should be clearly responsible for the technical content and timely completion of the operational review work steps, while the client's staff person should be responsible for ensuring the cooperation of departmental management and operational personnel, as well as providing liaison, coordination, and integration between operational personnel and the operational review staff. The specific individuals selected to manage the operational review are extremely critical to its ultimate success. They should be selected most carefully, considering such attributes as:

- Past performance on operational reviews

- Knowledge and experience relative to the area being reviewed

- Ability to effectively manage for results

- Ability to recognize operational deficiencies, identify the causes, and recommend realistic positive improvements

- Communication skills with operational review staff members, client management and operations personnel, and organizational decision makers

- Expertise or understanding in required technical skills such as interviewing, flowcharting, and so on

- Ability to work with the operational review team and client personnel

- Flexibility as to changes in identified critical areas, work steps, and staff assignments

- Persuasiveness required to convince client management to implement developed recommendations

- Organizational skills to keep the various pieces of the operational review together in a cohesive and understandable framework

> *Operational Review Management—*
> *Internal and External—*
> *Ensures Successful Results*

The managers assigned to the operational review (Betty White of the operational review staff and Cliff Chambers, the purchasing supervisor from the client's operations in our case study of the Example Company) would then be responsible for assigning the staff to work on the operational review. In most instances, the starting point is to determine which review team staff members, client personnel, and outside technical assistance are available for assignment during the time required to conduct the operational review.

The process then becomes one of scheduling the best fit between work steps and personnel attributes. For example, the review staff available to perform the operational review of the Example Company purchasing function are Joe Super, Senior Reviewer; Jane Plath, Junior Reviewer; Beth Herman, a new reviewer; and Bill Brown, Review Supervisor. Client personnel available to be assigned to this operational review include Roy David, a Buyer II; and Mary George, the Standard Specifications Unit Supervisor. In addition, Mike Clark, an outside consultant is available to provide assistance. Descriptions of each of these individuals and their availability are shown in Exhibit 3.4.

Based on these sketches of available personnel, the review managers, Betty White and Cliff Chambers, must assign the appropriate staff to each proposed operational review program work step. The preparation of the planning phase work program would most likely be done by the operational

EXHIBIT 3.4   Operational Review, Descriptions of Personnel Available: The Example Company

1. Joe Super, Operational Review Senior who has reviewed the purchasing function's operations and internal controls in the past and is known for his ability to get along with client management and operations personnel.
   Availability: March 22 to April 30.
2. Jane Plath, a Heavy Operational Review Junior who is well-respected for her ability to perform technical assignments in an orderly and timely manner.
   Availability: immediately through duration of review as her schedule allows.
3. Beth Herman, a recent addition to the operational review staff who has proven to be conscientious and a hard worker but requires direct supervision.
   Availability: April 5 to May 20 on limited basis per schedule.
4. Bill Brown, an Operational Review Supervisor, with past experience and special expertise in the areas of planning and budget systems.
   Availability: As needed on limited basis, with exception of possible one day schedule conflicts.
5. Roy David, a Buyer II in the Purchasing Department, with more than 15 years' experience with the organization, eight of them in the Purchasing Department. He is extremely knowledgeable about the purchasing functions, particularly purchasing policies and procedures.
   Availability: Up to two days per week for the duration of the operational review.
6. Mary George, the Standard Specifications Unit Supervisor, who has worked in all of the Purchasing Department's functions during her 18 years with the organization.
   Availability: Up to two days per week for the duration of the operational review, but normally not the same two days as Roy David is assigned to the operational review.
7. Mike Clark, an outside consultant who has worked with the review organization before in the performance of other operational reviews. His special areas of expertise include systems and procedures, flowcharting, facilities layout and work flow, and data processing.
   Availability: As needed with exception of other client commitments.

review managers with additional assistance as requested (e.g., other review team staff, client personnel, outside consultants), while the field work review program would be prepared by all concerned. Many times the field work program must be submitted to management prior to the start of the operational review. However, in most instances it will be changed as a result of the planning phase. The preparation and submission of field work review programs prior to the completion of the planning phase is particularly difficult to achieve with any degree of accuracy. It is good practice to request that management wait until completion of the planning phase. This is even more critical for outside consultants, as they may be forced to provide budgets and fees before they are aware of the scope of the work.

Review management would then assign the work steps of the planning phase and field work phase, based on the personnel available. It is good practice to document the operational review team on an organization chart, showing reporting relationships and time availability, similar to that shown in Exhibit 3.5.

To help review managers assign staff to work steps based on time availability, they could use a review program calendar, as illustrated in Exhibit 3.6, showing the available work days.

Once staff assignments are made for the work steps, the planned dates for completion and the staff assigned to each work step are noted on the review budget. See Exhibits 3.2 and 3.3; note that assignments have been based on personnel capabilities and time availability.

OPERATIONAL REVIEW SCHEDULE CONTROL

The operational review, including the planning, field work, and reporting phases of the purchasing function, is scheduled to be performed during the 14-week period of March 1 through June 2. The planning phase is scheduled for the three-week period of March 1 through March 19; the field work phase is scheduled for the seven-week period of March 22 through May 7; and the development of findings and reporting phase is scheduled for the four-week period of May 10 through June 2.

The performance of the operational review is not always a continuum, owing to staff scheduling conflicts, unavailability of needed client personnel, and so on. The review program calendar (Exhibit 3.6) shows total elapsed time and does not necessarily imply that operational review work steps will be continually performed. Another tool that could be used in operational

EXHIBIT 3.5 Operational Review: Purchasing Function Project Team Organization Chart

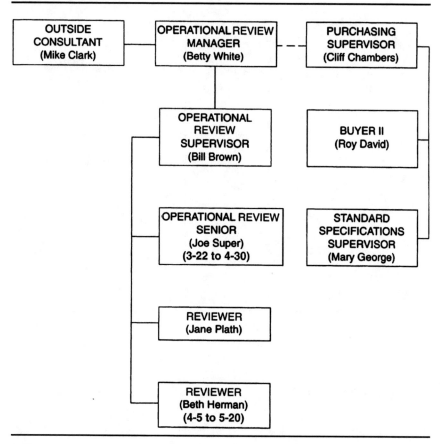

review staff scheduling is a Gantt chart, which graphically depicts the major work steps, their scheduled time frames and personnel assignments, and the interrelationships between work steps. Examples of Gantt charts for both the planning and field work phases are shown in the workbook.

If Gantt charts are used, the completion of the chart with scheduled dates and personnel assignments allows review management the ease of filling in the columns for scheduled dates and staff assigned on the operational review budget forms (Exhibits 3.2 and 3.3). These two tools then act as effective scheduling control documents.

EXHIBIT 3.6   Operational Review: Purchasing Function Work Program Calendar

	M	T	W	TH	F	
MARCH	1	2	3	4	5	
	8	9	10	11	12	PLANNING
	15	16	17	18	19	PHASE
	22	23	24	25	26	
	29	30	31			
APRIL				1	X̶	
	5	6	7	8	9	FIELD WORK
	12	13	14	15	16	PHASE
	19	20	21	22	23	
	26	27	28	29	30	
MAY	3	4	5	6	7	DEVELOPMENT
	10	11	12	13	14	OF FINDINGS
	17	18	19	20	21	AND
	24	25	26	27	28	REPORTING PHASE
	3̶0̶	31	1	2		

ENGAGEMENT CONTROL

Before starting the actual operational review, the engagement manager should prepare some form of engagement control tool. These tools include:

- Planning Phase Budget Hours Control, by personnel and time period
- Planning Phase Budget Control, by task and personnel
- Field Work Phase Budget Hours Control, by personnel and time period
- Field Work Phase Budget Control, by task and personnel

Any or all of these forms may be used for control purposes in conducting the operational review, or original forms can be designed.

EXAMPLE COMPANY WORK PROGRAM PHASE

Consider again the Example Company to see how the work program phase might work for the operational review of its purchasing function. Four operational areas were identified in the planning phase for further review:

1. Organization concerns, including the function and authority of the Purchasing Department and personnel, and the function and necessity of specific job classifications.

2. Purchasing Department responsibility for processing regular purchase orders and processing outside the central Purchasing Department.

3. Purchase order processing procedures, including purchase requisitions, purchase order processing, open purchase order control and work flow.

4. Purchase order preparation costs, including the cost to process a purchase order, its relationship to the amount of the actual purchase, such as under $50, $50 to $100, and $100 to $200; and the annual cost to process such small purchases.

Suggested work steps are shown for the completed work program in Exhibit 3.7.

WORK PROGRAM TO FIELD WORK PHASE

These operational review work steps will be followed up in the next chapter on the field work phase, but remember, not all work steps developed in the work program phase result in the development of significant operational review findings. However, because the reviewer does not know which work steps will provide the most significant findings, all work steps in a work plan must be followed through. The Example Company work program will be followed through in the field work phase, and identified findings will be developed and reported in succeeding chapters.

The Work Program
Is the Plan
for the Field Work Phase

EXHIBIT 3.7   Purchasing Function, Operational Review Work Program:
The Example Company

I.   *Organization*
A.   *Function and Authority of Purchasing Department*
    1.   Obtain copy or prepare organization chart of the Purchasing
         Department. Determine to whom the head of the Purchasing
         Department reports.
    2.   Document the functions of each of the Purchasing Department's
         units to ascertain appropriateness and whether they are proper
         Purchasing Department functions.
B.   *Function and Necessity of Specific Job Classifications*
    1.   Document the duties and responsibilities of the following job
         classifications, by obtaining copies of existing job descriptions
         and validation via interviewing and work observation.
         • Purchasing Supervisor
         • Buyers I and II
         • Clerk Supervisor
         • Clerical Supervisor
         • Clerk Typist
         • Standard Specifications Unit
            • Standard Specifications Supervisor
            • Procurement Technician
            • Management Trainee
            • Clerk Stenographer
            • Clerk
    2.   Observe the actual work being performed and determine the
         necessity of all duties and responsibilities.

II.   *Purchasing Department Responsibility*
A.   *Processing of Regular Purchase Orders*
    1.   Obtain or prepare copy of Purchasing Department systems and
         procedures.
    2.   Interview and observe work of Purchasing Department personnel
         responsible for purchase order processing to validate accuracy
         of systems and procedures.
    3.   Prepare flowchart of the purchase order processing procedures,
         including related purchasing operations such as purchase
         requisitioning, preparation and placing of purchase orders, open
         purchase order control, and receipt of merchandise.
    4.   Calculate the cost of processing a purchase order, considering
         such things as:

EXHIBIT 3.7 (*Continued*)

- Direct cost of operating the Purchasing Department
- Indirect costs related to the purchasing function
- Number of actual purchase orders processed

5. Analyze purchase orders processed, using purchase order reports provided by the data processing department.
   - Purchase orders processed by departmental source
   - Purchase order register by month in purchase order number sequence
   - Purchase register by month, showing purchases by department and type (account number)

6. Stratify the number and amount of actual purchases as to:
   - Under $50.00
   - $50.00 to $100.00
   - $100.00 $200.00, and so on

   Obtain a copy of the year-to-date purchase order detail data file maintained in data processing for the previous year. Develop and run computer audit program to analyze data file and print out results for above.

7. Calculate the annual cost to process small purchases, using the present cost of processing a purchase order as calculated in work step 4 above, and the number of small purchases as determined in work step 6 above.

B. *Decentralized Purchasing*

1. Obtain copy or prepare policies and procedures relative to purchases made outside the central Purchasing Department, such as:
   - Emergency purchases
   - Direct purchases
   - Petty cash purchases

2. Select a number of such decentralized operating units for review. Analyze their operations as to compliance to existing company policies relative to decentralized purchasing.

III. Purchasing Operations and Work Flow

A. Prepare a layout flow diagram of the Purchasing Department, depicting the personnel and work flow within the department. Analyze the flow diagram to identify any possible inefficiencies.

B. Interview appropriate Purchasing Department personnel and observe related work flow to determine the extent and cause of identified operating deficiencies.

CHAPTER FOUR

Field Work Phase

The operational review work done in the planning phase should produce indications of possible management weaknesses or significant operational areas for improvement in a particular area or activity. However, more information is usually needed to determine that there definitely is a management or operational weakness. The work program, then, is the plan for conducting the operational review work steps in the field work phase. In this phase, additional information is gathered relative to management and operational controls and activities to identify those areas in which time and effort should be spent on an in-depth examination. The work program steps are performed, and, as a result, areas are identified in which to develop specific findings to present to management.

If the operational review team decides to proceed with an in-depth development of a finding, the information gathered in the field work phase provides a basis from which to proceed. Besides providing an understanding of particular inefficiencies within the organization or department being reviewed, field work also helps the review team to understand the departmental organization and how it functions. Such an understanding is usually necessary in the event that additional information is needed in the development of the finding.

> *Field Work Steps*
> *Identify Areas for Findings*

This chapter discusses the field work phase of an operational review in which work steps are performed, as defined in the work program phase. The operational review team makes a determination, based on the performance and results of these work steps, as to whether those areas of possible weaknesses identified in the planning phase are worth going into in greater detail. If they are, any additional analytical work is done to fully develop the finding for presentation to management. There may be additional critical areas discovered that require further analytical work. This chapter also reviews some of the procedures and techniques that can be used by the operational review team in conducting the field work phase.

This chapter will address four main topics:

1. Increase understanding of the purpose of the field work phase in an operational review.

2. Present various techniques that can be used in the field work phase.

3. Increase knowledge of how to use information gained in the field work phase in the further development of review findings.

4. Describe field work phase documentation and operational review work file contents.

FIELD WORK CONSIDERATIONS AND TASKS

Based on the critical areas identified in the planning phase and the work steps designed in the work program phase, the following two items are considered in the field work phase:

1. Whether the reviewee's policies, and the related procedures and practices actually followed, are in compliance with basic authorities, statutes, and legislative intent

2. Whether the system of operating procedures and management controls effectively results in activities being carried out as desired by top management in an efficient and economical manner

Four general tasks that would be performed to assist in reaching the correct conclusions include the following:

1. Fact-finding or verification, for example, are management procedures being followed?

2. Evaluation, for example, analyzing deviations from procedures and determining whether the cause is the policy or procedure itself, or other factors.

3. Review of findings, for example, meeting occasionally with the review supervisor and other members of the review team to get a better understanding of matters requiring interpretation.

4. Recommendations as to the areas having sufficient significance to warrant a more detailed examination directed toward the development of an operational review finding.

Operational review recommendations resulting from effective field work are based on the reviewer's determination as to the adequacy and effectiveness of management and operations.

> *Effective Field Work*
> *Results in Effective*
> *Findings and Recommendations*

FACTORS IN REACHING CONCLUSIONS

In reaching conclusions in the field work phase, the operational reviewer must consider 13 specific factors, which include:

1. Management's use of standards or goals for judging accomplishment, productivity, efficiency, or utilization of goods or services. For example, the reviewer may observe the use of net profit only, as a measure, as opposed to evaluating controllable results such as units shipped, goods returned, quality control, and so on.

2. Lack of clarity in written instructions, which may result in misunderstandings, inconsistent applications, or unacceptable deviations.

3. Capability of personnel to perform their assignments. For instance, the reviewer may observe individuals who are unable to complete their assignments, such as indicated by a backlog of unprocessed purchase orders.

4. Failure to accept responsibility. There may be persons who do not do what is expected of them in their functional job descriptions, such as preparing periodic reports.

5. Failure to properly control operations and activities. There may be a work unit in which some individuals are overloaded and others are underloaded.

6. Duplication of efforts within departments and across departmental lines. An example is account code checking by the purchase requisitioner, by purchasing department personnel, and by accounting department personnel.

7. Improper or wasteful use of financial resources. An example may be the presence of data processing equipment and procedures, while the operations they could perform are still being performing manually.

8. Cumbersome or extravagant organizational patterns, such as an overburdened hierarchy with multilevels of supervisors and managers or an excessive number of staff personnel.

9. Ineffective or wasteful use of employees. For example, the use of administrative assistants or staff personnel to perform functions that could and should be performed by the person to whom they report.

10. Work backlogs that are inappropriate to the activity. For instance, the reviewer may find incompletely processed purchase orders, more than six months old, owing to an individual's processing the easy purchase orders first.

11. Necessity for, and effectiveness of, various operating and service units in relation to the costs of maintaining them. For example, the reviewer may discover a purchasing specifications unit that was established at the outset of the company but is, for the most part, no longer used, as there are very few changes made to purchase specifications.

12. Relevance and validity of criteria used to judge effectiveness in achieving operating results. An example may be an oversupply of inventory,

caused by the inability to change reorder points and reorder quantities for slow moving items, or an undersupply of items selling much faster than they can be placed in inventory.

13. Appropriateness of methods used to evaluate effectiveness of achieving results. For example, the reviewer may observe insufficient reporting that does not relate the performance of activities to the achievement of results.

---

*The Reviewer
Must Consider
All Aspects of the Operation*

FIELD WORK TECHNIQUES

Many different field work techniques are used in the field work phase, depending on the particular circumstances of an engagement. However, the best tools are common sense and analytical ability. It is not necessary for the reviewer to have mastered all the various technical tools before beginning an operational review, but the reviewer should be able to analyze problems logically, and, in many cases, this is the only tool needed.

The review team should also be aware of the various management and operational techniques that have been used effectively in the past or are currently in vogue, such as:

- Total quality management (TQM)

- Participative management

- Benchmarking strategies

- Restructuring, reengineering, and reinventing

- Principle-centered leadership

- Learning organizations

- Revision of mental models

- Spirituality in the workplace

- Activity-based costing/management (ABC/ABM)

- Strategic, long-term, short-term, and detail planning

- Flexible budgeting

- Systems theory

- Complexity theory (complex adaptive systems)

> *Field Work Techniques*
> *Are All-Inclusive*

SPECIFIC FIELD WORK TECHNIQUES

The reviewer can use various methods to gather the necessary information to identify weaknesses in management and operational systems. The reviewer follows the adage: Whatever works, use it. However, certain tools and techniques are used consistently from one operational review to another.

Some of the more common techniques were mentioned in Chapter 3 relative to developing work program work steps. These work steps, using these tools and techniques, are carried out in the field work phase. Often, however, further work steps are added in the field work phase. It is to the operational reviewer's advantage to be familiar with as many of these techniques as possible. The more effective the technique, the more effective the review results. Moreover, to be able to use a specific technique, the reviewer needs to be familiar with it. These field work techniques and others are documented again in Exhibit 4.1.

> *Whatever Works,*
> *Use It*

One or more of these techniques may be used in each work step assignment. The techniques used will depend on the particular circumstances encountered and the objectives established for each work step. Therefore, there are no hard-and-fast rules as to the work to be done or the techniques to be used in the field work phase. The most effective approach is to indi-

EXHIBIT 4.1   Field Work Phase: Field Work Techniques

1. Review of existing documentation, such as policy and procedures manuals.
2. Preparation of organization charts and related functional job descriptions.
3. Analysis of policies, systems, and procedures.
4. Interviews with management and operations personnel.
5. Flowcharting preparation:
    • Systems flowcharts, showing process of functional areas
    • Layout flow diagram, showing physical layout of a work area and its related work flow.
6. Ratio, change, and trend analysis.
7. Questionnaires for reviewer or client personnel use.
8. Surveys, by phone or in written form, for customers, vendors, and so on to respond to.
9. Questions within the operational review work program.
10. Review of transactions, in which the different types of normal and abnormal transactions are considered.
11. Review of operations by such techniques as observations, work measurement, time studies, and work performance forms or logs.
12. Forms analysis.
13. Analysis of results.
14. Review and analysis of management information systems and related reports.
15. Compliance reviews as to compliance with laws, policies, procedures, goals and objectives, detail plans, and so forth.
16. Use of data processing; using "through the computer" techniques or analysis of computer-produced information.

vidualize the field work steps and related techniques to meet the needs of the particular situation. The operational reviewer's expertise is to know under what circumstances which technique should be applied to achieve desired results.

Although many tools and techniques can be used in the field work phase, a number are used consistently. The operational reviewer should be most aware of these techniques, which include:

• Interviewing

• Systems flowchart

- Layout flowchart
- Ratio, change, and trend analysis

Interviewing

As previously mentioned, interviews in the planning phase are generally limited to management, along with some interviewing of operations personnel. In the field work phase, however, interviews are not limited to management, but primarily include those employees who actually do the work, in order to determine what is going on and why. Exhibit 4.2 provides some notes relative to the operational review interview.

The purpose of the operational review interview is to correlate practice and theory; to gather facts, opinions, and ideas, and to establish a positive image of the reviewers in the minds of the client's personnel. To conduct a successful interview, there must be adequate preparation. The reviewer should learn as much as possible about the operation through policies and procedures manuals, organization charts and functional job descriptions, internal and external reports, prior review reports and working papers, and technical journals. It is the reviewers' responsibility to do their homework prior to the interview, and not spend interview time asking questions to which they already know the answers.

INTERVIEW AGENDA AND WHOM TO INTERVIEW. As part of the reviewer's interview preparation, an interview agenda is prepared; which includes the major areas to be covered and the basic questions to be answered. The agenda is used as the reviewer's guideline, not to share the details with the interviewee, but only the general areas to be covered. However, the reviewer should be prepared to deviate from the agenda as required by answers obtained in the actual interview. The questions to be asked depend on who is being interviewed. For example, if the interviewee is decision management, the reviewer would gather information relative to policies and objectives. If operating management, including department managers, supervisors, and the like, is being interviewed, the reviewer might cover such things as work flow, interdepartmental relationships, present problems, and future improvements. If operating personnel, the people responsible for a specific job, are being interviewed, the reviewer might ask about the specific work flow and related systems and procedures.

EXHIBIT 4.2   Operational Review Interview Notes

I.   *Importance of the Operational Review Interview*
A.   Correlates practice and theory.
B.   Gathers facts, opinions, and ideas.
C.   Establishes the reviewer's image in the mind of the client.

II.   *Preparing for the Interview*
A.   Learn something about the organization through:
   1.   Policies and procedures
   2.   Operating manuals
   3.   Organization charts and functional job descriptions
   4.   Legislation: laws, charters, and ordinances
   5.   Reports: internal and external
   6.   Prior review reports
   7.   Working papers
   8.   Technical journals
B.   Prepare an interview agenda.
   1.   Write out basic questions.
   2.   Review and rephrase questions.
   3.   Organize and consolidate questions.
C.   How and what the reviewer asks depends on whom he or she is talking to.
   1.   Decision Management: Aim at gathering information about policy and objectives.
     a. Do:
       • Ask about policy.
       • Ask about goals and objectives.
       • Encourage free exchange of ideas.
       • Sell yourself and the review team.
       • Concentrate on the big picture.
     b. Don't:
       • Use technical terminology.
       • Get involved in great detail.
       • Inject yourself in the middle of a story; let the interviewee talk.
       • Interrupt.
       • Criticize the operation.
   2.   Operating Management: Including department managers, supervisors, and the like. Some of the areas to be covered with this group are work flow, present problems, relationship to other departments, and future improvements.

EXHIBIT 4.2 (*Continued*)

   a. Do:
- Evaluate work flow.
- Document functions of departmental personnel.
- Sell yourself.
- Anticipate reluctance.
- Plan ahead and be prepared to discuss operations.
- Observe operations while you talk.

   b. Don't:
- Use technical terminology.
- Inject your ideas in the middle of a story; rather, direct the conversation.
- Be reluctant to stimulate the interviewee to action.
- Ignore the day-to-day problems.
- Gloss over interdepartmental relationships.

3. Operating Personnel: These include people responsible for a specific job.

   a. Do:
- Have a list of questions.
- Know the general work flow.
- Be friendly and complimentary.
- Sell yourself.
- Concentrate on the areas of responsibility of the interviewee.

   b. Don't:
- Use technical terminology.
- Use words that can allow the interviewee to draw the wrong inference.
- Criticize the operations or personnel.
- Try to overpower the interviewee.
- Allow the interview to deteriorate into a complaint session.

D. Remember, never go into the interview cold and unprepared; do your homework before the interview.

III. *Scheduling the Interview*

A. Make advance arrangements.
   1. Time and place; interviewee's work area most desirable.
   2. Probable duration of meeting; limit to an hour or less.

B. Arrange favorable hours and days.
   1. Avoid hours immediately before or after lunch.
   2. Avoid late Friday afternoon, day before or after a holiday or vacation.

EXHIBIT 4.2 (*Continued*)

　　　3. If possible, try for early morning, shortly after workday begins, or mid-afternoon.
　C. Share the agenda and request materials.
　　　1. Indicate generally the subject of the meeting.
　　　2. Request materials: sample forms, statements, and so on.
　D. Keep interview generally one-on-one, with no supervisors or supervisees present.

IV. *Opening the Interview*
　A. Be punctual; it helps your image.
　B. Put the person at ease, but control the amount of small talk.
　C. State clearly the purpose of the interview.
　D. Assure the interviewee you will protect his or her anonymity.

V. *Conducting the Interview*
　A. Be open, objective, and reasonable.
　B. Convey to the other person that the review is a matter of joint concern.
　C. Use your agenda to direct the interview and prevent undue subject wandering.

VI. *Questioning the Interviewee*
　A. Ask questions that require more than yes or no answers.
　B. Seek the other person's analysis of causes and effects; statements of things that are of concern to the interviewee.
　C. Do not ask loaded questions:
　　　1. Those that indicate you have already assumed an answer.
　　　2. Those that indicate what you would like to hear.

VII. *Note Taking*
　A. Never record complete minutes.
　　　1. Adversely affects other person.
　　　2. Not conducive to good listening; hence, you may not be able to separate material from immaterial items.

VIII. *Effective Listening*
　A. Ask the person to repeat or restate if you do not understand.
　B. Ask for concrete examples if language is general or vague.
　C. Summarize or rephrase in order to encourage elaboration.

EXHIBIT 4.2   (*Continued*)

D.   Ask the interviewee what he or she would do to correct or improve conditions.
E.   Allow periods of silence in which to think.
F.   Don't:
- Debate or waste time in disagreeing over any point, no matter how important.
- Be sarcastic.
- Jump to conclusions.
- Contradict a person in front of others.
- Quote other people you have interviewed; the interviewee will not trust you to keep his or her responses confidential.

IX.   *Closing the Interview*
A.   Stick to the time schedule even if you have not finished your agenda; simply arrange for another meeting.
B.   If the other person wishes to extend the interview, then do so; but let this be his or her option, not yours.
C.   Before leaving, summarize the major facts obtained in the interview.
D.   Thank the interviewee for his or her time.
E.   Leave the door open for further questions or information.

X.   *Recording the Interview*
A.   Review, organize, and record your notes as soon as possible after the interview; at least on the same day.
B.   Write out enough, so that conclusions are reasonably self-explanatory.
C.   Send a copy of your notes to the interviewee for his or her review and agreement, where appropriate.

The interview agenda is used by the reviewer as a guideline to ensure that each agenda item is adequately covered in the interview. If the reviewer needs to deviate from the agenda into unforeseen but more important areas as a result of the interviewee's responses, the reviewer makes sure the agenda items are covered in this or a subsequent interview.

SCHEDULING THE INTERVIEW.   Another significant issue is the proper scheduling of the interview. It is the reviewer's responsibility to make advance arrangements as to the time and place, at the convenience of the interviewee. It is usually best to meet at the interviewee's work area so that the person being interviewed is most at ease and the reviewer can observe ongoing operations during the interview.

There should be agreement on the length of time the interview will take. A good rule is to limit the interview to an hour or less. In scheduling the interview, the reviewer should arrange for the most favorable hours and days. If possible, the interview should be conducted in the early morning, shortly after the beginning of the workday; or in the mid-afternoon, sometime between an hour after lunch and an hour before quitting. Try to avoid immediately before or after lunch, first thing Monday morning, late Friday afternoon, and the day before or after a holiday or vacation.

SETTING UP THE INTERVIEW.   When setting up the interview, the reviewer should indicate what the general agenda is to be, but should not share the actual agenda with the interviewee. If the reviewer would like the interviewee to provide specific materials either before or at the time of the interview, the reviewer should ask for them at this time so that the interviewee has sufficient time to make them available, either prior to or at the time of the interview. The reviewer should not wait until the time of the interview to request such materials. It should also be made clear to the interviewee that the interview should include just that individual and the reviewer. This ensures confidentiality and helps the interviewee to feel free to speak, which might not happen in the presence of supervisors or supervisees. This also ensures getting more honest and correct information from both parties. It is also a good idea not to bring anyone else along, which only increases anxiety. A one-to-one interview can thus be more productive than an attempt to save time by talking to more than one person at a time.

STARTING THE INTERVIEW.   It is the reviewer's responsibility to be punctual and to arrive at the interview site a little before the scheduled start time. While it might be inconsiderate of the interviewee to arrive late or to keep the reviewer waiting, remember that it is the reviewer's goal to get information from the other person during work time, and therefore, sometimes the reviewer will be inconvenienced. In addition, being on time helps to enhance the reviewer's professional image and create a favorable impression. From the outset, the interviewee should be put at ease. An effective icebreaker or small talk can be helpful, but the reviewer should control the amount of time used for this purpose. An effective transition can be used to state clearly the purpose and general agenda of the interview. The reviewer should assure the interviewee that his or her anonymity will be protected and confidentiality respected.

When conducting the interview, the reviewer should be open, objective, and reasonable. The interviewee should be assured that the operational review is a matter of joint concern and that the reviewer's role is to help improve operations and make the job easier. The basic agenda is used to direct the interview, prevent unnecessary wandering, and ensure that all agenda items are covered. The interviewee should not have a copy of the actual agenda. This keeps the reviewer from being constricted by a written agenda and able to pursue more significant areas of concern that may arise.

QUESTIONING PROCEDURES.   When asking questions, the reviewer should stay away from yes or no questions, as they limit the amount of information to be obtained. Rather, the reviewer should ask questions that require the interviewee to analyze causes and effects, state matters of concern, and give opinions. The reviewer should never ask loaded questions, those indicating that an answer is already assumed, or those that indicate what the reviewer would like to hear, for instance, "Your systems are really lousy, aren't they?"

NOTE TAKING.   While conducting the interview, the reviewer should not take full notes or minutes as the interviewee is talking. Such note taking may adversely affect the other person, and no one wants to look at the top of another person's head. Moreover, such note taking is not conducive to good listening; it can cause the reviewer to be unable to separate material items from those having little impact. A good practice is to take abbreviated notes to trigger subsequent recall, including the recording of facts, source references, rough diagrams, quick flowcharts, key words, and so on.

EFFECTIVE LISTENING.   Since the purpose of the reviewer is to gather information and learn more, it is important to be an effective listener and to get accurate facts and statements. People learn by listening, not by talking. A good technique to increase the effectiveness of listening skills is to ask the interviewee to repeat or restate items that are not completely understood. However, this technique should not be overused, as it may turn off the interviewee. Nor should the reviewer ask the interviewee to repeat something that can be found out easily elsewhere. Another good listening technique is to ask for concrete examples if the person's language is too general or vague. However, the reviewer must be sure these are not areas that should have been known before the interview. Other techniques that can be used include summarizing or rephrasing what the interviewee has stated in order to encourage elaboration, or asking how the interviewee would correct or improve conditions.

During the interview, it is good practice to allow periods of silence in which to think. It is not the reviewer's responsibility to fill in the silent awkward periods. Often, the interviewee needs these silent periods to gather thoughts. It is also important not to antagonize the interviewee by debating a point, making sarcastic comments, jumping to conclusions, or contradicting him or her the interviewee, particularly in front of others. Moreover, the reviewer should never quote from past interviews with others, as this might get others in trouble, while the present interviewee will not trust the interviewer to keep his or her responses confidential.

CLOSING THE INTERVIEW. When closing the interview, the reviewer must make sure to stay within the one-hour time agreement, even if the interview agenda is not finished. In this case, another interview can be arranged. However, if the interview can be completed in a short time, say within 10 minutes, and if the other person wishes to extend the interview, the reviewer can do so, but allowing the decision to be the interviewee's.

At the close of the interview, the reviewer summarizes the major areas covered and the facts obtained to assure their completeness and accuracy. Then the reviewer sincerely thanks the interviewee for his or her time, and asks cordially whether the person may be contacted again should there be additional questions or further information needed.

NOTE RECORDING. After the interview, the reviewer should review, organize, and record the notes taken as soon as possible, at least on the same day to ensure the accuracy of interview records. In recording interview notes, the reviewer must be sure to write out sufficient details so that conclusions are reasonably self-explanatory. A good practice, where appropriate, is to send a copy of the interview notes to the interviewee for review and agreement. This ensures accuracy and completeness while the interview is still fresh in his or her mind and provides more accurate data on which to base conclusions.

SAMPLE INTERVIEW. A sample interview between an operational reviewer and a department manager is shown in the workbook. To reinforce the materials covered on effective interviewing techniques, review and analyze the interview presentation and document any good or bad points identified. When a point is identified, try to think of how it affects the interview and later relations with the interviewee and the department. Some comments are provided in the workbook directly after the sample interview.

Systems Flowchart

Another technique that is widely used in the field work phase is systems flowcharting. Its purpose is to document general and specific procedures to help the reviewer understand operations and activities. Flowcharts show the work that is actually being performed, who is doing it, and how it is done. Flowcharting provides far more satisfactory results than reviewing operating manuals and documentation, because the reviewer gains a better and more accurate understanding of operating activities. In addition, the process of flowcharting, which requires obtaining and documenting an understanding of operating systems, helps stimulate the reviewer's interest, enthusiasm, and imagination, resulting in a more realistic identification of weaknesses.

The systems flowchart is a graphic representation of the sequence of operations in a process. It is especially useful in showing where documents, equipment, reference materials, files, and new paperwork are introduced into the process. It documents what work is performed and how. It provides information relative to how operations are actually carried out, the necessity or usefulness of the work steps included in processing the transactions, and the effectiveness of the controls provided in the process.

The systems flowchart also helps the reviewer to identify the system's inefficiencies such as:

- Unnecessary handling

- Inefficient routing

- Unused information on documents or records

- Inadequate planning or delegation

- Inadequate instruction

- Insufficient or excessive equipment

- Poor use of data processing facilities

- Poorly planned reports

- Inadequate or improper scheduling

If the detailed operating procedures demonstrated in the systems flow-chart do not represent recommended procedures but, rather, procedures that the reviewer might uncover in an operational review, the reviewer's focus should not be on these detailed procedures, but on how the flowchart is structured, to identify strengths and weaknesses in the operations by classifying procedures by departments and relating their flow across departmental lines. The reviewer should question each step in the process as to the following:

• *Necessity.* Can the step be eliminated? Can the entire process be eliminated? Is the step a value-added or non–value-added process?

• *Economy.* Is the step being performed in the most economical manner?

• *Efficiency.* Is the method of performing the step the most efficient?

• *Effectiveness.* Does the step provide for desired results? Are desired results necessary?

The systems flowchart is also the starting point for documenting systems and processes as part of an internal and external benchmarking study to identify inefficient processes leading toward recommended best practices in a program of continuous improvement. In addition, as process steps are identified, they can begin to be assigned costs as part of an overall activity-based costing or management system by product or service, customer, and function Such costs enable the reviewer to quantify the costs of inefficiencies in the development of a review finding and recommendation.

Although it is important that the reviewer know how to prepare such systems flowcharts, it is equally important to know how to analyze them.

Layout Flowchart

A layout flowchart is a schematic diagram of the existing or proposed physical arrangement of a work area with the addition of the flow lines of the principal work performed there. This type of chart is used to document the existing layout and paths of movement of people, paperwork, or materials. The layout flowchart also enables the reviewer to disclose the following 10 inefficiencies in the system, such as:

1. Unnecessary functions or work steps

2. Unnecessary handling or inefficient routing of certain documents

3. Inadequate planning or delegation of work

4. Inadequate instruction to employees

5. Insufficient or excessive office equipment and computers

6. Poor use of computer processing capabilities

7. Poorly planned information system and reports

8. Bad work scheduling

9. Inefficient work area layout

10. Unnecessary personnel

In addition, the layout flowchart also enables the reviewer to identify certain potential personnel roadblocks to economical, efficient, and effective operations. Among these are:

- *Isolates*—individuals or work units that appear to be unconnected to the rest of the work area

- *Controllers*—individuals whose major function appears to be controlling or overseeing the work of others without any appreciable value added

- *Dispatchers*—individuals or work units whose main purpose is to receive work from one work unit or individual and pass it to another work unit or individual without appreciably adding to the work.

In addition, the reviewer should be aware of hierarchical pyramids, in which there is a reporting relationship either upward or downward, and in which the individuals appear to be mainly reviewing and/or redoing the work that was passed to them prior to passing it further up or down the pyramid. Most organizational pyramids are constructed so that each higher level can police and control the lower level, while often providing no other benefits than to ensure that the lower levels do their work. If these hierarchical levels can be eliminated, it can greatly reduce the cost of operations without sacrificing results; in fact, results are often increased. What is really needed is to motivate each worker's self-disciplined work behavior; in effect, to make the worker responsible for results.

An example of a layout or flow diagram is shown in the workbook. The solid lines between numbered blocks represent direct reporting relationships and the dotted lines represent indirect relationships. Inefficiencies or potential personnel roadblocks are shown in the workbook directly after the layout flow diagram.

Ratio, Change, and Trend Analysis

Ratio, change, and trend analysis is another technique used in the field work phase to strengthen and supplement other operational review tools and procedures. Using this technique, the reviewer critically examines, interprets, and explains relationships between sets of operating and financial data at a given point in time by comparing them over a number of periods. Ratios have no intrinsic significance; they are primarily useful in highlighting significant changes and relationships. They do not, in and of themselves, form a basis for reaching informed decisions.

Ratio, change, and trend analysis may be used for a variety of purposes. For example, investors may be interested in financial strength, creditors in solvency, or management in performance and deviation from what was planned or considered normal. Within the scope of the operational review, the reviewer uses ratio, change, and trend analysis to identify managerial and operational problems and trouble areas.

The identification and analysis of a problem situation is the initial step in developing an effective solution. Ratio, change, and trend analysis helps the reviewer to detect problem areas for further analysis. The reviewer should consider for ratio, change, or trend analysis those areas in which most significant change has occurred and those of greatest vulnerability. In applying these techniques, the goal is to determine and measure changes and interrelationships in data, and then to examine critically and evaluate the changes revealed and their significance.

In using ratio, change, and trend analysis, the reviewer considers each situation individually and develops the ratios to use accordingly. There are two prime sources of reference to be used in applying this technique:

1. Comparison with historical internal data and budget data

2. Comparison with external data, such as industry statistics, functional standards, and work performance standards

In using internal data, it is important to make sure that such data are accurate and collected and reported properly. It must also be determine that such data are recorded on a consistent basis from period to period. When using budget data, the reviewer must determine that budgets are constructed in relationship to organizational and departmental plans and that actual data are not just compared with budgets, but that actual and budget numbers are what they should be from the standpoint of economy, efficiency, and effectiveness.

For external data to be used effectively, they should be objective and independent, derived from similar and comparable operations, and if current, reflect experience during a comparable period with similar common economic factors and conditions. In using such external data, no two organizations are exactly the same even within the same company structure. Accordingly, the reviewer uses external comparisons as a yardstick or indicator, not as a finite measure. These results can indicate possible trouble spots and further field work to be performed.

Incidentally, ratios are but one tool available to the reviewer to determine changes. Others that can be used are indexes, percentages, relationships, variable budgets, correlation analysis, and so on. These tools are often used in conjunction with one another.

The development of ratio, change, and trend analysis as related to a review finding is not an end in itself. Such analysis must be evaluated, integrated, and interpreted as one factor in the development of an operational review finding. Typically, more analysis and field work are required to develop the full dimensions of the finding. The results of ratio, change, and trend analysis provide a measure of significance.

There are two situations in our operational review of the Example Company where we found the use of ratio, change, and trend analysis helpful in the measurement of changes and their significance.

The first situation relates to the apparent use of petty cash funds to circumvent the policy that all purchases over $50 be processed by the central purchasing department.

The second situation relates to the present status of inventory, where a relatively large number of zero usage items and increased usage items were found from one year to the next.

FIELD WORK: EXAMPLE COMPANY

Chapter 3 illustrated an operational review work program for the Example Company's purchasing function. As part of the operational review of the Example Company, the following three areas were defined for performance in the field work phase:

1. Organization
   - Function and authority of the Purchasing Department
   - Function and necessity of specific job classifications
2. Purchasing Department Responsibility
   - Processing of regular purchase orders
   - Decentralized purchasing
3. Purchasing Operations and Work Flow

Some of these work steps have already been accomplished through previously considered techniques such as:

- Obtaining or preparing a copy of the organization chart
- Determining authority for purchasing: policies and procedures manual
- Determining functions of each work unit: for example, work observation
- Interviewing: for example, determining job duties and responsibilities
- Obtaining or preparing copy of systems and procedures
- Determining purchase order processing procedures: for example, using systems flowchart
    - Decentralized purchasing: for example, reviews of petty cash procedures
    - Determining work flow: for example, using layout flow diagram

Additional work steps that need to be accomplished to complete the work program include.

- Function and authority
- Cost to process a purchase order
- Sample of small purchases

Function and Authority

One objective of the work program for the Example Company was to determine the specific functions, responsibilities, and authority of each personnel position. Therefore, the reviewer desires to document the duties and responsibilities of the following job classifications:

- Purchasing Supervisor
- Buyers I and II
- Clerk Supervisor
- Clerical Supervisor
- Clerk Typist
- Standard Specifications Unit
  - Standard Specifications Supervisor
  - Procurement Technician
  - Management Trainee
  - Clerk Stenographer
  - Clerk

The reviewer has obtained copies of existing job descriptions (which were found to be quite sketchy and inaccurate) and has attempted to validate them through interviewing and direct work observation. To assist in these efforts, a Job Responsibilities Questionnaire was developed for each employee to fill out and return to the reviewers. Such a questionnaire is used to help accumulate a large amount of information in a relatively short period of time and to obtain relevant nonthreatening data from each employee to substantiate actual duties and responsibilities.

The reviewer then analyzes the data to identify problem areas, intra- and interdepartmental patterns, indications of organization-wide personnel related issues, and so on.

Cost to Process a Purchase Order

The work program for the Example Company's Purchasing Department defined work steps to determine the cost to process a purchase order, considering such elements as the direct cost of operating the purchasing department, indirect costs related to the purchasing function, and the number of actual purchase orders processed. The data required to calculate the cost of processing a purchase order are shown below with the completed calculation.

Data: Cost to process a purchase order: The Example Company	
Number of Regular Purchase Orders	18,100
Purchasing Department:	
Payroll	$384,587
Elements directly associated with purchase order preparation	
Other Direct Costs	243,264
Other costs directly associated with purchase order preparation	
Indirect Costs	95,059
Allocated to purchase order preparation on basis of percentage that above payroll costs relate to total purchasing department payroll	
Fringe Benefits: Estimate (percentage of payroll)	28%
Other Expenditures: Allocated to Purchasing	101,000
Other company costs that can be directly attributable to purchase order preparation	

Calculation: Cost to process a purchase order	
Purchasing Department	
Payroll Costs	$384,587
Other Direct Costs	243,264
Indirect Costs	95,059
Fringe Benefits (28% X $384,587)	107,684
Other Expenditures: Allocated to Purchasing	101,000
Total Preparation Cost for Functions Directly Associated with Purchase Order Preparation	$931,594

Cost to Process a Single Purchase Order =
Total Cost (approximate) / Annual Number of Purchase Orders
$931,594 / 18,100 = $51 Per Purchase Order

Sample of Small Purchases

Another work program work step was to analyze the purchase order volume for small purchases: under $50, $50 to $100, and $100 to $200. Remember, in the planning phase it was determined that many small purchases were being processed by the purchasing department and many small purchases were circumventing central purchasing procedures. In addition, the cost to process a purchase had not been updated in many years. The objective of this work step is to determine the impact of processing of small purchases on the purchasing department.

The results of an analysis of a selected sample of purchase orders showing small purchases are shown below. These results will be used in the next chapter to develop a review finding related to small purchases and the corresponding cost to process a purchase order.

Sample of purchase orders: Purchase order volume of small purchases				
	Volume		Dollar Value	
	Number	% Total Sample	Amount	% Total Sample
Purchase Orders Process for:				
Under $50	17	2.9	460.74	.03
$50 to $100	43	7.4	3,173.03	.20
$100 to $200	76	13.2	16,022.55	1.00
Total $200 and under	136	23.5	19,656.32	1.23
Over $200	442	76.5	1,574,395.93	98.77
TOTAL	578	100.0	1,594,052.25	100.00

Total dollar value of purchases for the year was $48,158,617. The above distribution was arrived at by taking samples of two groups of purchase orders, consisting of approximately 300 each (actually 578 in total due to canceled orders). The first sample was chosen randomly, using tables of random numbers. Purchase orders in this first sample group were dated March and April. A second group of approximately 300 purchase orders was chosen from a later month, November, to be examined for their distributions of $0 to $200 and over $200.

OTHER TECHNIQUES

The operational reviewer can use many other tools and techniques in the field work phase, depending on the situation and the objective of the work step, too many to cover in this book. However, two significant techniques of which the reviewer should be aware are tests of transactions, and reviewing performance versus plans.

Tests of Transactions

The operational reviewer, in testing transactions, examines the procedures actually applied to specific transactions or items, from beginning to end. The transactions selected for review should represent the operations involved. The character or type of transactions selected is more important than the number of transactions selected. Operational review tests of transactions should be limited in the number of transactions used, but must be representative of actual transactions processed.

In addition to the information provided in flowcharting, the test of transactions provides the reviewer with information relative to the results of transactions in terms of management's objectives, specific requirements, and common sense practices. The operational review work program given in Exhibit 3.1 shows a selection of transactions and examination of transactions selected as sample work program steps.

Performance versus Plans

A review of performance versus plans allows the reviewer to examine existing plans that relate to the area being reviewed and the methods operations management follows, to compare actual performance with the plans. This technique can provide direct insight into the ability of management to effectively plan for the organization, as well as the relative strength and effectiveness of management control. This is a good technique to use in most operational reviews, to help analyze management controls over operations, primarily to help ascertain how management personnel themselves determine whether plans, policies, and procedures are being followed, and whether they are effective and efficient.

In many organizations that come under operational review, no effective planning procedures exist whatsoever. These organizations are typified by seat-of-the-pants and crisis management, which attempts to operate without adequate short-term detail plans and, in many instances, without a budget. Those organizations do have budgets often use it as a constraining and punitive tool, rather than as part of a helpful system. In these instances, this practice not only constitutes a review finding, but also makes it incumbent upon the reviewer to help management develop an effective planning and budgeting system. This is often one of the first steps of the operational review, as the definition of planning goals and objectives are necessary to effectively evaluate the results of operations.

WORK PAPERS

During the course of the operational review, various procedures are followed which are aimed at ascertaining what was found, what was measured against, what was the effect, why did it happen, and what does the reviewer recommend. To carry out this program in a systematic fashion, to have a record of what was done, and to accumulate the data, the reviewer must prepare work papers. These are the principal records of the work actually performed to substantiate the operational review report. Therefore, the review work papers must be complete and self-explanatory. They are the tangible means of measuring the operational review team's professional skill.

Information obtained on an assignment is of little or no continuing value if it is accumulated only mentally by staff members. To minimize errors and omissions, information given orally must be recorded in the work papers as soon as possible.

Work papers serve as the basis on which operational review work programs and reports are prepared and as a connecting link between work done and the report. Work papers provide systematic evidence of how review responsibilities in specific assignments were carried out. Any questions that may arise concerning the operational review must be answered by reference to the work papers. As a result, any omission of information may have serious consequences.

Use of Work Papers

Work papers are used in the following eight ways:

1. As the repository of the information obtained

2. To identify and support problems, events, or actions occurring during the engagement, findings, meetings, and the like

3. To give support to discussions with operating personnel

4. To provide support for the report

5. As a line of defense when facts, conclusions, and recommendations are challenged

6. As a basis for supervisory review; to provide evidence that work was performed according to the work program and consistent with reviewer's understanding of what was to be done

7. As a basis for appraising a reviewer's technical ability, skill, and working habits

8. As background and reference for subsequent review

Work Paper Identification

Each work paper supporting the operational review must be properly identified. A completed work paper should contain the following seven items:

1. Title

   A complete title consists of:

   - Department or unit number, entered in the upper left-hand corner of the work paper.

   - Department or unit name, entered in the center of the paper on the first line.

   - A description of the work paper, entered in the center of the paper on the second line. (The third line may also be used.)

   - The period covered in the work paper, entered in the center of the paper on the third line. (The fourth line may also be used.)

2. Reference index number entered in the center of the paper, last line.

3. Initials of the preparer and date prepared.

4. Initials of the reviewer and date reviewed.

5. Source (person, computer output, book, periodical, etc.) of information.

6. Indication of the review or verification of material received from the department or unit being reviewed.

7. Names of all persons present at conferences or discussions.

Sample Table of Contents

The following 18 sections should be included in the current operational review work paper files:

1. Work paper index

2. Work program

3. Review checklist

4. Time control

5. Engagement status reports

6. Supervision notes

7. Correspondence (both in and out)

8. Minutes of meetings

9. Planning papers

10. Fact finding: statement of condition

11. Fact finding: establishment of criteria

12. Analysis and conclusions

13. Development of recommendations: alternatives

14. Development of recommendations: final

15. Presentation outline: oral reporting

16. Written report: draft

17. Written report: final copy

18. Bulk material

EVIDENCE

The operational reviewer is also responsible for accumulating sufficient competent and relevant evidence to support opinions, conclusions, and recommendations.

Types of Evidence

The types of evidence that should be considered in the operational review include:

- Physical—Observations, photographs, slides, and so on
- Testimonial—Interviews, personal statements, and so on
- Documentary—Letters, contracts, grants, records, and so on
- Analytical—An analysis of information

Attributes of Evidence

The three basic attributes of evidence are:

1. Sufficiency—Presence of enough factual, adequate, and convincing material to lead a prudent person to the same conclusion as the reviewers. This is a judgmental decision.

2. Competence—Is the evidence reliable and the best obtainable through the use of reasonable review methods?

3. Relevance—The evidence must provide a logical relationship to the issue at hand.

Evidence in the Work Papers

To reflect the basic attributes of evidence, the work papers that generally constitute the evidence must be complete and accurate. They must express the intended message clearly, so that reviewers and report writers can understand it. They must have a purpose, and must explain the nature and the scope of the work done and the preparer's conclusions. It is important that work papers be concise, and they should be legible, neat, and restricted to matters that are material and useful, with reference to the objectives established for the review.

IDENTIFYING ITEMS FOR FINDING DEVELOPMENT

Those items identified as significant in the field work phase are further developed as operational review findings in the next phase. Before proceeding to Chapter 5, review the field work phase materials and the field work phase case study materials for the Joe Sorry Company in the workbook.

Case Study: Mercy College, A College Business Office

The operational review process is a tried and true method to evaluate the economy, efficiency, and effectiveness of an organization's operations and results. The process works in a similar fashion whether the entity is a large national or international corporation, a closely held or family-owned small business, a service provider or professional practice, an educational institution, a not-for-profit service provider, or some other type of organization. For each of these entities, the operational reviewer must gain a thorough understanding of the entity's operations, identify operational weaknesses, and recommend best practices that help move the organization forward.

This case study describes an operational review for an institution of higher learning, a small liberal arts college named Mercy College. As in the operational review of any entity, the operational review team must acquire operational knowledge about mission and vision, desired directions, long- and short-term plans, strategic issues, methods of operation, functional requirements, planning and budgeting systems, operating systems and methods, reporting systems, overall desired results as well as functional results, reasons for existence, basic business principles, existing mental models and belief systems, best practices, and areas for improvement.

An institution of higher learning is considered a not-for-profit organization that is established for educational purposes. Although such an entity is not permitted to make a profit, it is in existence to survive and provide the services for which it is established, for example, to provide optimum educational opportunities for its students in the most economical, efficient, and effective manner possible. Should the entity's revenues exceed expenditures for an operating period, the difference or excess (i.e., profit for a business, accumulated reserves or net assets for an educational institution) is allowed to be carried forward to succeeding periods to be used in future operations. In addition, such institutions are permitted to build up endowment funds, and the investment income from such funds can be used for operating costs in succeeding periods. It is the rare educational institution today that can operate and survive solely on student tuition and charges. Such entities must maximize all revenue sources and at the same time minimize all expenditures (academic and support services) not only to survive but also to grow and prosper. The institution is then in the business of providing educational-related services most economically, efficiently, and effectively while increasing net assets or reserves for each operating period.

This case study focuses on the manner in which such an educational institution can operate most economically, efficiently, and effectively within the guidelines and constraints of being a not-for-profit entity. One of the dynamics affecting educational institutions today is the public perception that some of these organizations are being managed and operated by ineffective and incompetent personnel, systems, and procedures. The public (particularly those attending such institutions) has witnessed a steady increase in tuition and other fees with little recognition of comparable increases in services. In fact, in many of these institutions, charges have increased while services have decreased. Educational institution management has been struggling under this scenario to function more economically, efficiently, and effectively. The past solution of merely increasing tuition and other charges is not as readily available, particularly with increasing competition from both other private and publicly supported institutions.

Some of these educational institutions have resorted to creative revenue raising measures, such as increased contribution demands from members of the board of trustees; use of the college president as a major fund raiser to the detriment of other operations; elaborate fund-raising events; special (sometimes nuisance) student fees, such as institutional, general, laboratory, parking, dorm maintenance, student services, and the like; business enterprises such as student stores, snack shops, college identifier merchandise, program advertising, room and dorm rentals; and so on. Thus, college management may not be any worse than it was in the past; rather, it may be more that the situation has changed but management is still trying to manage in the same old manner.

In addition, competition among educational institutions, both private and public, for students and personnel has resulted in increased costs. At the same time, many potential contributors (e.g., government, foundations, corporate, private, and alumni) are wary of contributing to an ever increasing upward cost spiral when they do not see an increase in services. Such contributors also become weary after receiving multiple requests for additional contributions for both general and specific purposes. There is also a perception among many that too large a percentage of real dollars are being spent for administration and other personnel rather than going to direct student services.

In today's multifaceted and multidisciplined economic environment, educational institution management must place a greater emphasis on increasing results and maximizing the delivery of services with fewer resources by evaluating the economy, efficiency, and effectiveness of the organization's operations. The operational review is the tool used to perform such an evaluation of operations. The purpose of this case study is to present operational review principles as they relate to such an entity as well as give the fundamentals for conducting an operational review in this type of environment. Educational institutions must be evaluated with regard to what works in the present environment (e.g., present best practices from all disciplines) but also have the vision to question past models that no longer work and industry specific systems and procedures that are no longer effective. In addition, all sources of best practices must be investigated, both internal and external (i.e., other institutions as well as other types of entities), in the institution's program of continuous improvements. Remember, the best system and procedure is the one that works. The source of best practices is less important.

It is important to understand that an educational institution is a business just like any other entity, private and public. Its mission is to provide desired educational services to its student body and its community. If it can do this successfully, in an economic, efficient, and effective manner, it will survive and prosper. It is the task of the operational review team to assist college management in making this happen. As one example, support functions can be redefined or minimized using forward thinking. They can be eliminated outright or performed by others (e.g., outsiders, faculty, academic departments, and students), or processing can be reduced, manual operations lessened, reliance on computer processing and controls increased, and so on.

The area selected for review in this case study is Mercy College's business office. The business office function is normally considered a support and non–value-added activity. Although business office activities are necessary to students, faculty, and staff, these activities constitute a cost center. Accordingly, they must be analyzed with regard to their necessity, redundancy, possible elimination, unnecessary cost, method of providing services, and so on. The goal is to satisfy only necessary business office requirements, in the most economical and efficient ways. The smaller the number of dollars allocated to such non–value-added functions means any cost savings can be reallocated to other necessary activities within the organization in its quest to become the most economical, efficient, and effective it can be. Furthermore, the operational review must consider the constraints under which an educational institution operates and issues with which the institution must deal. These issues include academic freedom, separation of academic services from other support services, provision of services to students, maintaining a uniqueness in service delivery, competition from other private and public educational institutions, governmental funding compliance, laws and regulations, required student record keeping, student service-oriented systems and procedures (e.g., student registration, billing, grading, record keeping, and reporting), and the costs of providing services versus the benefits provided to the institution or its students.

Although the business office is normally considered a non–value-added activity at a college, it must be considered a support function to both students, faculty, and staff. Typically, such small colleges cannot afford to pay salaries at the same levels as private companies within their geographic areas. However, the necessary services of a business office may be even more critical at a college. At the same time, the college is attempting to perform its required business office functions with the smallest number of personnel at the least costs. It is within this environment and these constraints that we conduct the operational review of these activities.

SCOPE OF REVIEW

We met with the President of Mercy College, Dr. Lynn Anderson, and the Comptroller, Dan O'Hara, to discuss the areas to be included in the operational review of the college's business office operations. It was determined that the following areas should be included in the review:

College Overview

- Mission of the college and whether the business office is assisting in meeting the mission and supports activities directed toward addressing the mission.
- Direction of the college—that is, its strategic plan—and the role of the business office, including:
  - Academic programs: expansion and contraction
  - Personnel: academic and support
  - Student body and services: areas such as in/out of state, under-graduate and graduate programs, continuing education, and so on
  - Use of facilities
- Short-term plan: goals and objectives, priorities, and resource allocation.
  - Revenue resources
  - Academic programs
  - Other programs: conference, extension, and so on.
  - Competition: lure for students
  - Tuition charges and cost containment

Comptroller's Function

- Review of comptrollers function: expectations, activities, and results
- Review of business office functions: necessary/unnecessary, performance gaps, and results
- Identification of purpose and analysis of performance related to purpose

Planning and Budgeting

- Review, analysis, and description of present planning system
- Review, analysis, and description of present budget system: revenues and expenses
- Pros and cons of present systems

Systems and Methods

- General: areas such as organization structure, management, and systems constraints

- Payroll: present procedures and analysis of in-house versus outside servicer

- Accounts payable: purchasing, vendor relations, receiving, posting, and payment procedures

- Accounts receivable: student and other receivable procedures

- Computer processing versus manual information processing and reporting

- Use of personnel and systems in place

- Performance gaps and where to go from here

Based on the agreed-upon scope of the operational review, we prepared the following confirming letter to inform the President of Mercy College of those areas that would be covered in the operational review of the business office and our estimated fees.

Mercy College Confirming Letter

Dr. Lynn Anderson, President
Mercy College
College Boulevard
College, XX 99999

Dear Dr. Anderson:

It was a pleasure meeting with you and the college's Comptroller, Mr. Dan O'Hara on April 7, 20XX, to discuss how Reider Associates might perform an operational review of your business office operations directed toward making such operations the most economical, efficient, and effective. As you requested, I am documenting our discussion and understanding as to performing such an operational review of the college's business office operations.

BACKGROUND

Mercy College has been in existence for more than 100 years. The college has always enjoyed a well-deserved national reputation for a quality liberal arts program. The college has graduated many well-known alumni in the fields of politics, literature, the arts, and the social services. However, it has not been able to accumulate sufficient endowment funds to lessen the impact of receding enrollments, stagnant tuition, and increasing costs. Many of its small liberal arts college competitors have had to greatly curtail or change their operations or go out of existence. Mercy College has been able to remain in existence and support its mission thus far. However, the Board of Trustees believes something needs to be done to continue the college's viability. Accordingly, you have requested that Reider Associates perform an operational review of the college's business office operations to determine how the college can operate within its mission in the most economical, efficient, and effective manner possible. We mutually agreed that we would begin with business office operations because you believe that this area is less threatened by and more receptive to positive changes than are other areas such as academics and administration.

SCOPE OF REVIEW

Such an operational review of the Business Office functions and activities will be accomplished as follows:

1. Interview and discussion with the Comptroller, Dan O'Hara, to go over the ground rules of the review and obtain his perspective as to business office operations.
2. Interviews and review of functions with all business office personnel: Assistant Controller, Business Operations Manager, Payroll Technician, Accounts Payable Coordinator, Restricted Funds Accountant, Accounting Technician, Accounts Receivable/Purchasing Coordinator, Cashier, and Business Office Secretary.
3. Meeting with the Comptroller and you to go over our major findings and conclusions and to decide which areas to include in your program for change and in the final report.
4. Letter type of report addressed to you, with a copy to the Comptroller, that would document our findings and conclusions, together with our recommendations, for your further use and follow-up. I would also be available to meet with you and/or the Comptroller and others to discuss the contents of the report. As we discussed, you can follow up on all or some of these recommendations. Should you decide to implement any

of the recommended operational improvements, I would be pleased to provide any required consultative assistance in these efforts.

ESTIMATE OF TIME AND COSTS

We estimate that our time participation should encompass no more than five working days for the review, another day for the oral report and meeting, and another two days for the preparation and review of the final written report. Based on such time estimates, our fees for performing this operational review should be between $16,000 and $20,000. In addition, we would expect to be reimbursed for all out-of-pocket expenses, such as for travel, lodging, subsistence, and the like.

We appreciate the opportunity to provide such important consultative services to Mercy College and look forward to working with you and your business office personnel. Should you have any further questions or require any additional information, please let me know.

Sincerely yours,

Rob Reider, President
REIDER ASSOCIATES

MISSION AND STATEMENT OF PURPOSE

Mercy College's mission is to be a well-respected private liberal arts college distinguished by educational excellence in a culturally diversified and student-centered environment. The college's academic emphasis is in the liberal arts and as such the college is dedicated to a strong core curriculum rooted in the humanities and liberal arts. Therefore, the college is invested in providing unique personal and professional enrichment opportunities for its students. Mercy College remains committed to the educational tradition of its founders, which is realized through the following attributes of its educational programs:

- Sound teaching and diligent advising in a highly personal environment

- Program delivery directed toward opportunities for lifelong learning

- Flexible programs and scheduling modes to meet the diverse educational needs of all its students

- Sensitivity to the educational and intellectual needs of its diversity of students

- Explicit attention to ethical questions and values in all programs and activities

- Strong dedication to the education of those who are less advantaged, whether it be economically, socially, intellectually, or physically

- An appreciation of multicultural diversity and expression

- A focus on producing graduates who are valuable local, national, and world citizens

BUSINESS OFFICE ORGANIZATIONAL STRUCTURE

Mercy College's business office organizational chart is shown below.

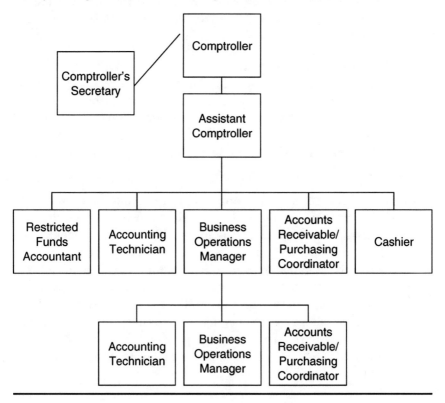

Mercy College Business Office Organizational Chart

Our review and analysis of this organizational chart identified the following 10 questions for further review:

1. What are the functions and scope of the Comptroller's position? Is this primarily a reporting position to the President and Board of Trustees and/or is it a day-to-day management position that directs operations of the entire business office? What is the relationship between the Comptroller and the Assistant Comptroller, and are both positions necessary? Is there a need for a separate secretary to the Comptroller, particularly in light of the existence of another secretary reporting to the Business Operations Manager?

2. What is the purpose of an Assistant Comptroller as well as a Comptroller? It appears that the Assistant Comptroller reports to the Comptroller, while the remainder of business office personnel report to the Assistant Comptroller. Is this the most economical and efficient manner to manage ongoing business office operations?

3. What is the role of the Business Operations Manager? It appears that this individual is responsible for supervising payroll and accounts payable operations, while those performing other business office activities, such as Restricted Funds Accountant, Accounts Receivable/Purchasing Coordinator, and Cashier, report directly to the Assistant Comptroller? In this scenario, is the Business Operations Manager position necessary?

4. Is the Payroll Technician position a full-time or a part-time position? What is needed to coordinate the processing of payroll? Typically, college personnel are on annual contracts with a standard amount paid each payroll period, typically every two weeks. In addition, most employee benefits and other payroll deductions are standardized. Accordingly, payroll processing normally does not need extensive ongoing support. In most instances, payroll processing is done off-site by a third-party contractor. An individual at the college is needed to control the accurate processing of each payroll, but such an individual does not have to be a full-time employee or devote his or her total time to payroll. How does this work at Mercy College?

5. What is the function of the Accounts Payable Coordinator? Is this individual responsible for all payments made by the college? Is the volume of transactions too little or too much for one person? Does the college have an exorbitant number and amount of accounts payable transactions, or are individuals within the college bypassing the accounts payable function? Can one person effectively process and control the college's entire payment processes?

6. Why is there a secretary who reports formally to the Business Operations Manager and informally to the Assistant Comptroller? This sets up a conflict not only between multiple bosses but also about which boss's work takes priority. What are the needs for secretarial support for the business office, both with this secretary and the one reporting directly to the Comptroller?

7. What are the activities of the Restricted Funds Accountant? What are the time and work requirements needed to provide accounting and controls over such funds? Is there an adequate workload to justify a full-time person or more work than one person can appropriately handle alone?

8. What is the purpose for an additional employee with the title Accounting Technician? What does this person do? Do they provide value or non–value-added services? Is this strictly an additional individual who is required because of business office inefficiencies, in turn allowing other personnel to do less? Is the college paying for this position in lieu of implementing more efficient and effective operating procedures?

9. What are the activities assigned to the Accounts Receivable/ Purchasing Coordinator position? How much in accounts receivable can the college have where the majority of students pay tuition (or arrange for payment) in advance? What else could be considered accounts receivable and why would it be necessary to assign such responsibility to a separate individual? What is meant by Purchasing Coordinator, and what activities are conducted by this individual?

10. What are the responsibilities and functions of the Cashier? Does this one person collect all of the cash received by the college? How are such cash collections controlled, and what is the volume of such cash

receipts? Is this a full-time function, and if so, how is this function handled in the absence of the Cashier?

FUNCTIONAL REVIEW

Each of the functions represented on the business office's organizational chart was reviewed and analyzed with the following facts and conclusions noted:

Management Positions

The college's business office operations are managed by a:

- Comptroller and Comptroller's Secretary
- Assistant Comptroller
- Business Operations Manager

This appears to be a top-heavy management team to oversee typical business office operations of payroll, accounts payable, restricted funds, accounts receivable, cash receipts, and general ledger updating. This has resulted in confusion and misunderstanding between these three positions as well as with operations personnel reporting to them. There is the dilemma of having multiple bosses as well as the employee's concerns regarding whom they should go to for direction.

The college's President and the Board of Trustees have made the Comptroller their exclusive source for operating data and special reports. This had made the Comptroller unavailable to properly manage and oversee business office operations. The previous Comptroller has been made an Assistant Comptroller, with delegated responsibility over business office operations. However, this individual has abdicated such responsibilities and works on special projects with her door closed. This has necessitated the hiring of a Business Operations Manager to oversee daily operations. This employee has formally been assigned responsibility over the Payroll Technician, the Accounts Payable Coordinator, and the Business Office Secretary; but because of the laxity of the Assistant Comptroller, the Business Operations Manager has had to take over responsibility for restricted funds accounting, purchasing, accounts receivable, cash receipts (Cashier function), and the functions of the Accounting Technician. This has resulted in a personal and professional conflict between the Assistant Comptroller and the Business Operations Manager.

Our comments, findings, and conclusions for each of these business office management positions are as follows:

COMPTROLLER.   The present Comptroller has been in this position for more than three years, with primary responsibilities as follows:

• Acting as liaison to the President and the Board of Trustees by providing financial and cost data relative to college operations mainly in the form of special requests and reports.

• Handling budgeting procedures including preparation of procedures as well as ongoing control on a monthly basis. As part of monthly control procedures, the Comptroller prepares budget change authorizations between line items to ensure that each reporting department's budget stays within overall expense totals. Staff salaries and fringe benefit costs as well as revenues are not budgeted by departmental entity. In effect, the present budget system encompasses only operating expenses, such as materials and supplies, copying costs, travel, and the like. An inordinate amount of time and control is spent on such a minimal budget approach. The budget is not part of an overall college planning system. There is really no planning system in effect.

• Preparing ongoing reports, such as financial reports (Statement of Financial Position, Statement of Operations, and Statement of Cash Flows) on a monthly basis.

• Acting as liaison with the outside accountants and auditors who are responsible for the Audit of an Institution of Higher Education in accordance with the Office of Management and Budget Circular A-133.

• Attending and participating in various committee and staff meetings within the college. We analyzed such meetings and determined that the Comptroller spends an average of 25 hours per week related to more than 15 such meetings. This consumes not only a major part of the Comptroller's time but also the time of others attending such meetings. This could be a prevalent problem area throughout the college.

- Overseeing the business office, including all functions and activities reporting to this position. With the present Comptroller's demand for other services as noted above, he has minimal time for such overseeing responsibilities. Accordingly, such oversight has been neglected.

COMPTROLLER'S SECRETARY.　The duties and responsibilities of the Comptroller's Secretary are:

- Maintaining the Comptroller's calendar and schedule of appointments. This appears to be a normal assignment of all secretaries at the college, possibly a costly procedure.

- Handling all incoming and outgoing correspondence within the college and from the outside that relates to the Comptroller. Typically, the Comptroller dictates or writes out all outgoing correspondence for the Secretary to compose using word processing software on a microcomputer. It should be noted that the Comptroller has a microcomputer system (newer and better than the Secretary's) but was found to use it on only a limited basis. The overall distribution and use of such microcomputer systems should be reviewed for the entire college.

- Picking up, sorting, and distributing all incoming mail for the Comptroller and other functions of the business office. The Secretary opens all mail, sorts it by individual or work unit, date stamps the mail, and distributes it to the appropriate parties.

- Controlling accounts receivable checks, primarily from students, for distribution to the Accounts Receivable/ Purchasing Coordinator. There is no return payment form, envelope, or separate mailing address provided with student statements to uniquely identify such receipts from all the other mail. This requires the Secretary to make sure that she captures all such checks in the mail. There is no system in place to control all checks distributed to the Accounts Receivable/ Purchasing Coordinator.

  The Accounts Receivable/Purchasing Coordinator identifies each check received, records the receipt to the computerized accounts receivable system, and then submits the checks back to the Secretary, who records each check (now with full accounts receivable data) on a check log. A copy of the log and the checks are then routed back to the Accounts Receivable/Purchasing Coordinator, who ultimately sends the checks to the Cashier. The Secretary files her copy of the check log but sees no purpose in such filing. The entire procedure for handling accounts receivable receipts needs to be further analyzed.

- Coordinating all committee meetings for the Comptroller, and taking minutes and transcribing them for a number of these meetings. In addition, she is responsible for scheduling the meeting rooms, arranging for refreshments, and setting up the rooms. There appears to be a number of areas in which functions are duplicated or another person is employed to do what someone else already employed could do for him or herself. This is a college-wide concern.

  It appears that the Secretary spends as much time as the Comptroller in committee and staff meetings and considerable more time in transcribing, copying, and distributing minutes as well as setting up meetings and calling committee and staff members.

- Attending other committee meetings as a member herself, such as the staff advisory council, and the staff support committee (as chairperson). Attendance at committee meetings seems to be another time consumer prevalent within the college.

- Preparing the monthly budget reports for each department within the college. She also reduces each report to 8 ½ by 11 inches from the original 11-by-14-inch size and places them in confidential envelopes. In addition, she distributes each budget report to the department, most often by hand because of the confidentiality of the reports.

- Annually distributing and coordinating departmental budget proposals, as well as providing controls to ensure that each department submits its budget properly and on time.

- Preparing the monthly financial report to the Board of Trustees. This includes a cover letter from the Comptroller (prepared by the Secretary but signed by the Comptroller), and a series of management reports and a cash flow statement that the secretary updates on her computer system. There are 30 to 35 members of the Board of Trustees, of which 17 are members of the finance committee.

- Preparing all correspondence for the Comptroller and other business office personnel (as necessary) and answers the Comptroller's phone (and the business office phone when necessary).

ASSISTANT COMPTROLLER. The present Assistant Comptroller has been in that position for the past two years. She was the college's Comptroller prior to this move. The presence of both a Comptroller and an Assistant Comptroller (who was the previous Comptroller) is causing considerable conflict and mistrust between the two individuals.

The Assistant Comptroller's position, which was created so that the present individual could assist the Comptroller, involves the following functions:

- Managing and supervising of the accounts receivable, accounts payable, and payroll positions; operating funds accounting; restricted, endowment, agency, and plant funds accounting; and preparing monthly financial statements (using a computer spreadsheet). The Assistant Comptroller also reviews biweekly reports from each staff member reporting to her and then submits a summarized report to the Comptroller. We noted very little direct supervision of these staff members.

- Scheduling of business office personnel as to time, functions, and activities.

- Participating in special accounting and financial projects as assigned by the Comptroller. There are also numerous instances in which the college's President or members of the Board of Trustees assign the Assistant Comptroller such special projects. This only tends to increase the tension between the Comptroller and the Assistant Comptroller.

- Handling insurance issues, such as claims, coverage, and the acquisition and changes to insurance coverage. The Assistant Comptroller maintains the insurance schedule and prepares the monthly journal entry into the general ledger.

- At one point, assisting in the budget process; but the Comptroller took her off this task.

- Participating in the purchasing and accounts payable process. For instance, she reviews all purchase requisitions and approves the same for all requisitions under $500 (those totaling more than $500 need the Comptroller's approval), and reviews and approves for payment those items on the bimonthly payment pre-list prior to payment.

- Conducting periodic staff meetings for those personnel reporting to her. These staff meetings are not presently being held. The last one was held more than eight months ago.

- Scheduling and coordinating materials, forms, and spreadsheets that are needed from business office staff by the outside accountants for the annual audit.

BUSINESS OPERATIONS MANAGER. The Business Operations Manager's position was added after the Assistant Comptroller's position to ensure that day-to-day activities were successfully completed. This position was made responsible for overseeing daily operations such as accounts payable, accounts receivable, cash receipts, and payroll. The Business Operations Manager, as well as accounts receivable and cash receipts, reports directly to the Assistant Comptroller. There appears to be great confusion between the Assistant Comptroller and the Business Operations Manager with regard to which one is responsible for what, what each one's role really is, and who makes what decisions. Some of the assigned responsibilities of the Business Operations Manager include the following:

- In general, overseeing the daily business operations of the business office, including all aspects of accounting functions, and maintaining and producing monthly financial statements for the college. The Business Operations Manager also assists the Comptroller in preparing and providing special request financial and accounting-related projects.

- Preparing monthly financial reports for the general operating fund, which are given to the Assistant Comptroller, who in turn gives them to the Comptroller with a cover letter.

- Preparing monthly financial statements through keyboard entry using a computerized spreadsheet application, because the computerized accounting system does not automatically provide such statements.

- Direct overseeing the accounts payable and payroll operations. In addition, the Business Operations Manager indirectly oversees the accounts receivable and cash receipts functions because the Assistant Comptroller who is assigned these responsibilities is not performing them. The Business Operations Manager also assists or acts as the Cashier when necessary.

- Manually comparing purchase requisitions from all areas of the college with the computerized budget reports because the computer system does not automatically check for budget availability. This is done on the 15th and 30th of every month, which results in no budget availability checking for interim encumbrance and payment transactions.

- Processing monthly actual versus budget reports for each department and entity within the college for distribution by the Comptroller. These reports should be produced by the computer system automatically, but the present accounting software does not allow for this.

- Processing budget amendments and changes, which are mainly end of the month line item changes (e.g., moving an over budget amount from materials and supplies to an under budget line item such as instructional supplies). The authority for these changes is from the Comptroller, who makes these changes each month together with three other staff personnel (usually the Business Operations Manager, the Comptroller's Secretary, and one other operations person) from the business office. This is not effective budgetary control but rather merely the movement of amounts between line items. The only result is to see clearly that the departmental budget as a whole is still within total approved budget dollars. The entire planning and budget process needs to be analyzed in detail.

- Assisting the Accounts Payable Coordinator in processing check requests (for items that do not have to be on purchase orders) by reviewing for proper account approval, signature authorizations, back up documentation, and so forth. These check request amounts are not checked against the budget for the availability of funds. The Business Operations Manager also assists in accounts payable vendor reconciliation, that is, reconciling individual vendor open invoices to the vendor's monthly statements, which is unnecessary with proper systems and procedures.

- Preparing monthly journal entries, such as payroll (12 pages of them must be entered because the outside payroll processor does not provide computerized journal entry data); plant, restricted, and endowment funds (as computer system does not provide for automatic posting); and accounts receivable collection fees (due to the lack of automatic posting). All of these journal entries could easily be posted automatically via the computer system.

- Handling insurance claims relative to the college's liability insurance. This entails the filing of the claims with the insurance carrier and follow-up to ensure proper claims payments.

- Reconciling accounts receivable details (mainly student accounts) to the computerized general ledger records monthly. For nonstudent accounts receivable, the Business Operations Manager prepares the bills using a computer spreadsheet application and records the receivable and subsequent payment to the general ledger computer system.

- Posting and controlling the computerized accounting system, for example, closing the subledgers such as cash receipts (daily), accounts payable (twice per month), and accounts receivable (monthly) and simultaneous updating to the general ledger. Although some of these tasks might ultimately be performed by others in the business office, the main responsibility for their completion rests with the Business Operations Manager.

CONCLUSION—MANAGEMENT POSITIONS. The Comptroller appears to be overworked and stretched into many insignificant areas, resulting in ineffective delivery of normally expected Comptroller services. The Comptroller's secretary and the Assistant Comptroller, rather than effectively assisting the Comptroller, seem to be overwhelmed with unnecessary detail on their own. In addition, the personal conflict between the Comptroller and the Assistant Comptroller does not lead to effective teamwork. Crisis management seems to be the primary force, which results in unnecessary shuffling around and rescheduling rather than taking the time to become more efficient and fix the causes of the crises rather than the blame.

The Assistant Comptroller and the Business Operations Manager suffer from unclear delegation of responsibilities, meaning neither knows what each should really be doing. The entire area of Comptroller, Assistant Comptroller, and Business Operations Manager needs to be analyzed in further detail to determine whether all three of these individuals are necessary. It appears that with the reduction and elimination of many of the unnecessary and redundant activities performed by these three individuals, a single individual in the Comptroller's role is all that is necessary.

Business Office Staff Positions

The business office is responsible for conducting typical college accounting functions, such as:

- Payroll processing and record keeping for all faculty and nonfaculty positions
- Accounts payable processing and vendor payments

- General operating fund accounting updating and reported (done by the Business Operations Manager, as described above)

- Maintenance of budgetary records and monthly actual versus budget reporting (done by the Business Operations Manager, as described above)

- Nongeneral operating fund accounting and reporting—restricted, plant, endowment, and enterprise funds

- Purchase processing and vendor contacts using properly approved purchase requisitions from all operating departments to prepare purchase orders for vendors

- Accounts receivable primarily for students accounts receivable but also other accounts receivable such as room rentals, equipment rentals, asset sales, and so on

- Cash receipts—all college cash received, either over the counter or through the mail

These functions are handled by the following personnel:

- Payroll Technician

- Accounts Payable Coordinator

- Business Office Secretary

- Restricted Funds Accountant

- Accounting Technician

- Accounts Receivable/Purchasing Coordinator

- Cashier

Although each of these functions is performed by one individual, most of the individuals in these positions have too much to do as a result of the limitations of the present computer system, which requires the individual to perform redundant and duplicate manual functions. Some of these individuals do not have full-time work to do at all times; but because of the lack of cross-training, they cannot effectively assist one another. As a result, some of these functions are overwhelmed with workload while other functions are waiting for work. Accordingly, there is an uneven distribution of work without effective backup, which under present conditions cannot be remedied. Overall accounting responsibilities need to be analyzed with an eye toward the need for management as well as the effective distribution of work so that the least number of personnel are needed to effectively accomplish all that is required. In addition, the present computer system capabilities need to be reviewed to determine not only what can be done to make the system more efficient in its present condition (and eliminate the unnecessary manual duplications of work) but also what needs to be done in the future with different and enhanced software.

The duties and responsibilities of these individuals are:

PAYROLL TECHNICIAN.   The payroll had been processed in-house for many years using the college's minicomputer system with an in-house maintained payroll software system. Around three years ago, because of many problems with the payroll software, the college decided to have the payroll processed by an outside processor. The Payroll Technician who had been responsible for maintaining the in-house system was retained as the interface between the college and the outside payroll processor. This position was reduced from a full-time 40 hours per week to a part-time 20 hours per week. However, we found that many of the same functions and activities were still being duplicated and the college was not making the most effective use of the outside processor and the data records and files that the outside processor maintained for the college.

The present functions of the payroll technician are:

- Biweekly payroll processing for full-time contract faculty (on 9-, 10-, 11-, or 12-month contracts), part-time teaching agreements (adjunct faculty), full-time salaried support staff, hourly paid staff with overtime, and work study students. Full-time faculty and support staff are paid on an exception basis; that is, the Payroll Technician only needs to input changes; otherwise, each individual, once established in the payroll system, is paid based on the data existing in the payroll master file. Data for part-time teachers are manually fed into the payroll system based on when the teacher is to be paid according to each teaching agreement, as this type of pay is not included by the outside processor. For hourly support staff, hours for each employee need to be recorded onto a payroll turnaround form for subsequent input by the payroll processor. Work study student hours worked need to be transferred from approved time cards onto another turnaround form by source of funds (e.g., college funds, financial aid, and federal grants).

- Processing of payroll action records from the Personnel Department for such things as position and pay changes, benefit changes, and withholding changes. Each of these changes is recorded onto another turnaround document, with the Payroll Technician maintaining control over and reconciling the records, ensuring that such changes are properly processed into the computer system.

- Payroll reconcilement to the results of payroll processing by the outside processor. The Payroll Technician receives from the payroll processor for each biweekly payroll the actual payroll checks (which go to the cashier for distribution and/or pickup) and the following reports:

  - Tax Liability Report—showing the amounts paid to the various federal and state taxing authorities

  - Payroll check journal—by department and by employee in alphabetical order, kept for reference

  - Departmental analysis—showing employee pay history, not using

  - Employee labor analysis—showing by department each employee's pay record for the period by account number, instruction, and support. This report is used by the Business Operations Manager as the basis for the manually prepared payroll journal entry.

  - Payroll Deduction Register—becomes the basis for making payments for such things as credit union contributions, gifts to Mercy College, contributions to United Way, and medical plans

  - Retirement report—used to enter and post entries on-line to a separately maintained retirement database

- Upkeep of separately maintained in-house payroll system (remnants of the original payroll system) for payroll masters, deductions, and vacation and sick leave. This is a duplication of information maintained by the outside payroll processor. In addition, a salary budget schedule is maintained using a computerized spreadsheet.

- Special project processing. The Payroll Technician is called on to participate in many of the special requests coming from the President of the College, the Board of Trustees, and the Comptroller. As a result, this part-time individual gets behind in the regular payroll processing work.

The duties presently performed by the Payroll Technician should be analyzed with a view toward which ones (if not all) can be accomplished more effectively by the outside payroll processor. Almost all the Payroll Technician's present functions and activities can be provided by the outside processor. The Payroll Technician should be data terminal and modem connected to the payroll processor so that data can be automatically inputted into the payroll system and resultant information and reports automatically updated into the general ledger and provided to the college in data file format.

ACCOUNTS PAYABLE COORDINATOR. The Accounts Payable Coordinator is responsible for the receipt of all purchase requisitions from all departments, instructional and other, and the subsequent conversion to purchase orders for those requisitions properly prepared and approved. There is no dollar limit on the amount for which a department must submit a purchase order, other than minor amounts (of less than $10), which can be processed as petty cash or a check request. This individual also processes vendor invoices for payment against the open purchase order file. These functions are performed as follows:

- The Accounts Payable Coordinator receives all purchase requisitions from instructional and support departments and reviews each requisition to make sure that it is properly prepared with regard to items being requested, account coding, and proper requisitioner and approver. Any additional data necessary to prepare a purchase order, such as vendor number and name, specific pricing and terms, vendor item numbers, and special conditions, is recorded on the requisition. The purchase requisitions are then routed to the Business Office Secretary, who prepares the purchase order on a typewriter (the computer system is not used). The purchase requisitions and purchase orders are then routed to the Business Operations Manager for a manual check against the computer budget system (electronic spreadsheet) for proper account number and budget availability. The encumbrance of the open purchase commitment is not posted in the budget data base.

- The Business Office Secretary signs the purchase order for the college and then distributes the copies of the three-part purchase requisition and the five-part purchase order as follows:

- Purchase requisition: #1 to department, #2 to Accounts Payable Co-ordinator, and #3 by the Business Office Secretary for daily control and reconcilement.

- Purchase order: #1 White—mailed directly to vendor
  #2 Green—filed numerically for the month by the Secretary
  #3 Yellow—stapled to requisition and sent to accounts payable
  #4 Pink—to ordering department as receiving copy
  #5 Goldenrod—to ordering department as file copy

- The purchase requisitions and purchase orders are then sent back to the Accounts Payable Coordinator, who files them alphabetically by vendor in an open purchase order file awaiting receipt of items ordered and a vendor invoice.

- Because there is no central receiving station for items purchased, when the Accounts Payable Coordinator receives the vendor invoice (from the Comptroller's Secretary when she opens the mail) she must match it with the receiving copy of the purchase order sent to her by the ordering department. For more than 40 percent of all receipts, the ordering department is not submitting receiving copies. Thus, the Accounts Payable Coordinator must spend considerable time tracing such receipts back to the ordering department. Presently, receipt authorization comes from many different individuals and is a slow, frustrating, and time-consuming process. This noncontrollable practice over receipts also delays vendor payments. Mercy College is not known as a good customer, with the result that many vendors refuse to deal with the college or raise prices to compensate for the lengthy time it takes to receive payment.

- The college does not make partial payments for partial receipts but requires the full receipt prior to payment processing. There is also no real purchasing function other then the preparation of purchase orders. The Accounts Payable Coordinator does not negotiate with vendors for open or blanket purchase commitments or for price negotiating. The ordering department usually specifies the vendor.

- The Accounts Payable Coordinator processes the receipt for payment as follows:

- Match vendor invoice and purchase order receiving copy from the ordering department to the open purchase order in the file.

- Record on the purchase order receiving copy the vendor invoice number, present date, and amount to be paid (if there is a large difference from original purchase order, approval for payment is obtained from the ordering department).

- Enters accounts payable into the computer system: vendor and payment information all payments entered as net 30 days (term discounts are ignored). The accounts payable packet (vendor invoice and purchase order copies) is filed by vendor name as a closed purchase

- At payment time on the 1st and 15th of the month, runs a pre-list accounts payable computer for payment approval by the Comptroller. For those items approved for payment, a three-part check and a two-part check register is computer produced.

The three-part check is distributed as follows:

- #1 Original—mailed to the vendor with a copy of the vendor invoice

- #2 Yellow copy—matched to closed purchase order and filed alphabetically

- #3 Pink copy—filed in numerical sequence

The two-part check register is distributed as follows:

- #1 goes to the Comptroller

- #2 is filed in accounts payable for future reference

The college is processing more than 1,000 checks per month for separate vendor invoices, because college policy is not to pay from a vendor statement of combined invoices. Vendor checks for up to $500 are signed by the Comptroller; vendor checks for more than $500 are signed by the Comptroller and the President or one of the two Vice Presidents.

BUSINESS OFFICE SECRETARY. As with every other department in the college, both instructional and support, a secretary is assigned to the department head as well as to the staff. Thus, the business office has an assigned secretary. Because she is present, she is used for various functions, secretarial as well as helping others in the department. For example, she

- Acts as telephone receptionist for the business office, answering calls from vendors, students, and college staff members. The college does not have a voice mail answering-type service, so each department must use one of their personnel (usually the secretary) as a telephone receptionist.

- Does word processing using microcomputer software to prepare memos for the other business office personnel, especially the Assistant Comptroller (who uses the secretary as her own personal secretary).

- Types (on a typewriter) purchase orders from purchase requisitions received from the Accounts Payable Coordinator. She looks up the vendor code from the alphabetic name using a computerized vendor data file that she updates and controls. She obtains purchase approval from the Assistant Comptroller, signs the purchase order on behalf of the business office, and then distributes the five copies of the purchase order. She totals the purchase order amounts using an adding machine and verifies that the total agrees with the total of all purchase requisitions.

- Enters each purchase order into the computer system: purchase order number, vendor code, issue date, line number, fund to be charged, account number, description, and amount committed. The computer system provides the total amount inputted for reconciliation to the manually produced control totals. There appears to be no reason why the present computer system cannot produce the purchase order, post it to the open purchase order file, check the budget for funds availability, encumber the amount and purchase order against the budget account, and provide adequate control totals. These features should certainly be provided with modifications and updates, as well as replacement, to the college's accounting software.

- Sorts mail as received from the Comptroller's Secretary:
  - Opens and date stamps each item received

- Sorts and distributes to other business office staff:
  - Vendor invoices and statements to accounts payable
  - Letters and memos to other staff personnel
  - Purchase requisitions to accounts payable

- Processes accounts payable checks by:

  - Matching checks to purchase order—attaches the yellow copy of the check to closed purchase order and files them alphabetically by vendor name

  - Filing the pink copy of the check in check number sequence

  - Mailing the vendor check out to the vendor, after signing by the Comptroller

- Performs the cashier's function as a backup when necessary. It is difficult for the Secretary to act infrequently as the Cashier, which results in errors and mistakes, poor customer (student) service, and the need for backup for regularly assigned secretarial functions.

RESTRICTED FUNDS ACCOUNTANT.   The Restricted Funds Accountant is responsible for maintaining and controlling the accounting records for:

- Restricted funds

- Endowment funds

- Loan funds (student loans)

- Agency or enterprise funds

Comments and observations made as a result of our review of this function are:

- Entries posted to these accounts come primarily from the biweekly payroll and the twice monthly (15th and 30th) accounts payable payments.

- Restricted funds include federal grants (such as multicultural, academic development, upward bound, and financial aid), which require monthly reporting for draw downs, and private gifts with restricted use and purposes, which require internal quarterly reporting to the Comptroller.

- The college has no overall indirect cost allocation plan, meaning indirect cost rates must be set within each federal grant agreement. Such an overall indirect cost allocation plan should increase the amount of federal grants accruing directly to the college.

- Endowment funds—restricted and unrestricted—require a quarterly report to the Board of Trustees. The assets in this fund are managed by an outside financial institution. Restricted endowment funds, primarily scholarships, are not being properly maintained and controlled with regard to the specific purpose of the restriction. This could make the college vulnerable to using such funds for an improper purpose, which could result in unnecessary lawsuits.

- Loan funds, which include loans by private lenders and a federal revolving loan fund, require record keeping regarding outstanding loans as well as payments to the revolving fund (so as to make new loans). An annual loan report is made to the President and the Board of Trustees, and to the federal departments involved.

- With regard to agency or enterprise funds, for which the business office acts as the custodian and maintains the accounting records, there are twelve such funds, which require the writing of checks and the monthly reconcilement of accounts. There is no official reporting on these accounts.

- The bulk of the activity for these accounts takes place twice a month, with additional work required at the end of the month. This job does not produce a consistent daily workload. This allows the Restricted Funds Accountant a lot more free time than other business office staff, resulting in animosity from the other staff. The individual presently in this position refuses to assist other staff members and tries to look as though he is busy all the time.

ACCOUNTING TECHNICIAN. The Accounting Technician position was created by the Assistant Comptroller to assist her in the development and preparation of special reports and projects. In many instances, the Accounting Technician is doing what would be expected of the Assistant Comptroller. It is questionable whether this position is really needed. To justify this position, this individual also does the following:

- Daily review of cash receipts:

  - Accounting for each receipt by receipt number and voided receipts

  - Verifying the correct account number for each cash receipt

- Reconciling each cash receipt to the Cashier's manually prepared cash sheet

- Verifying accounting transactions back to detail support, such as purchase requisitions, purchase orders, receiving documentation, vendor invoices, and so forth

- Sending adjustment requests to Cashier and following up

- Closing out cash receipts and tracing them to bank deposit

- Maintenance of daily cash balances on a manual log showing beginning balance, cash receipts, cash disbursements, and ending balance (beginning balance for next day). Cash receipts are posted daily; cash disbursements (accounts payable) are posted on the 15th and 30th of the month.

- Monthly reconcilement of cash accounts to bank statements (three bank accounts).

- Preparation of a weekly cash flow report using a computerized spreadsheet application. The report shows a weekly comparison of receipts and disbursements. The value of this report is questionable, particularly given the time required to prepare it and the issue of its usefulness.

- Responsibility for performing payroll preparation backup when necessary. Although assigned this responsibility, this individual has never had to perform this function.

- Assisting in various activities, such as budget maintenance, research requests (budget and otherwise), and special projects as assigned by the Assistant Comptroller and less often by the Comptroller.

ACCOUNTS RECEIVABLE/PURCHASING COORDINATOR. Mercy College charges students for tuition, student fees, room and board, and miscellaneous charges, such as laboratory fees, dormitory fines, parking fees, and bookstore charges. For those students who do not pay their tuition in advance, payment terms need to be approved of at the time of registration. In addition, the college is not automatically billing for room and board charges. Payment arrangements for these charges and others need to be made at the time of student registration. It is the responsibility of the Accounts Receivable/Purchasing Coordinator to ensure that such payment arrangements are properly authorized at the time of student registration and prior to the student's attending any classes or moving into the dormitories.

As part of the registration process, all students must have their payment method approved of by the Accounts Receivable/Purchasing Coordinator. As each student meets with the Accounts Receivable/Purchasing Coordinator, the following steps are followed:

- The Accounts Receivable/Purchasing Coordinator accesses the student file by student number to ascertain whether the student is undergraduate traditional, graduate, or nontraditional. Each student type has a different charge per credit hour, with undergraduate traditional the highest ($250), graduate next ($175), and nontraditional the least costly ($140). There are more nontraditional students (1,800) and graduate students (1,650) than undergraduate traditional (1,300).

- Students bring their registration form and financial aid voucher (if applicable) with them when they meet with the Accounts Receivable/Purchasing Coordinator. The Accounts Receivable/Purchasing Coordinator checks the financial aid voucher against a computer-produced financial aid register because the computer is not set up to allow for on-line access. Tuition and fees as shown on the registration form (and calculated by the Registrar's office) are rechecked against the computerized student record.

- The total amount due from the student (total charges less financial aid, grants, and loans) is then recalculated. The student may pay the total amount due at this time with a three percent discount. The student takes the paperwork prepared by the Accounts Receivable/Purchasing Coordinator and pays the bill directly to the Cashier. The student then returns to the Accounts Receivable/Purchasing Coordinator, who records the approved payment on the computerized student record. If the student is not able to pay at the time of registration, the total (or part) of the amount due can be financed on a ten month payment plan with an outside financial institution, which charges a $40 application fee. The college sends out statements each month and collects the monthly payments. The college then remits monthly receipts to the outside financial institution.

- An accounts receivable data record is set up for each student who owes a balance to the college. Tuition and fee charges are automatically set up, but the Accounts Receivable/Purchasing Coordinator needs to manually input all room and board charges (and other miscellaneous charges). The computer system is then used to input payments against the student record as well as any adjustments, such as refunds and under or overcharges.

The computer system also produces periodic reports, such as a student account record analysis, an accounts receivable status report, and an accounts receivable aging report.

- The Accounts Receivable/Purchasing Coordinator uses computer system reporting and analysis to control nonpayments for follow-up. If a student is late in payment (say 30 days), the procedure is to telephone the student to come in and make full or partial payment (with arrangements for the remainder). If payment is not made, a letter is sent to the student and the student's parents (if applicable). If payment is still not received, another telephone call is made to the student informing him or her that the account will be turned over to a collection agency. There is presently more than $500,000 outstanding with the collection agency, with many of these students still attending classes. The options available to the college for non-payment are to withhold transcripts, prohibit further registration, and withhold grades. Due to lack of coordination between administrative and academic departments, such courses of action are rarely used.

- The Purchasing part of this Accounts Receivable/Purchasing Coordinator position is really a misnomer as this individual's only role in the purchasing function is to maintain and make available to other staff members catalogs for such things as business office furniture and equipment, office supplies, and stationery items. There is no central purchasing function at the college. Each college employee is really on their own as to what to order. Very rarely are the catalogs maintained by the Accounts Receivable/Purchasing Coordinator used by other employees.

The review and analysis of the Accounts Receivable/Purchasing Coordinator revealed the following operational concerns for consideration:

- The student registration process is inefficient and ineffective. It is based on students taking their paperwork from one administrative office to another (i.e., Registrar, Financial Aid, Accounts Receivable, and Cashier) rather than a centralized process. The main reason for this is that the present computer system is not designed to integrate all these functions in one place. From a customer (student) service standpoint, this needs to be reversed. Either the present computer system needs to be changed to accommodate such integration or new computer procedures need to be implemented.

- Tuition fees for types of students need to be reviewed. Presently, undergraduate traditional students pay the most per credit hour, with graduate students paying less, and nontraditional students paying the least. This has resulted in a steady increase of graduate and nontraditional students, with a steady decrease in the number of undergraduate traditional students. Typically, most colleges charge more for graduate studies than for undergraduate. Mercy College, in fact, pays more per credit hour to adjunct graduate and nontraditional instructors than for adjunct instructors of undergraduate traditional students. The definition and rules for being a nontraditional student should also be reviewed. At present, any student who does not come directly from high school to college is considered a nontraditional student.

- Accounts receivable and collection procedures are extremely unwieldy. Typically, a college is in the enviable position of receiving payments for services up-front prior to providing the service. This not only is effective from a cash conversion focus but also allows for the minimization (or elimination) of accounts receivable. Mercy College actually encourages students not to pay their bills in advance by their liberal policies of financing and collecting. There should be flexibility for students registering and paying in advance, with a substantial discount (actually, the total amount paid in advance after the discount should be the fee desired, and those paying at the time of registration or financing, their payments would receive a penalty) and the avoidance of the on-site registration process.

- The Accounts Receivable/Purchasing Coordinator spends most of her time maintaining student accounts receivable records and attempting to collect from those students who are financing their payments through an outside financial institution. Many of these students do not have the resources to pay the amounts due and possibly should never have been accepted to the college. The college may want to revise its philosophy of making payments easier for the student as a way of attracting students and place more emphasis on student services. The college may also want to develop relationships with other financial institutions that would be willing to provide such student financial arrangements whereby the college receives its money up front and the financial institution takes over the accounts receivable and collection functions. This would not only decrease the need for the Accounts Receivable/Purchasing Coordinator position at the college but also refocus the college on student services rather than financial concerns.

CASHIER. The Cashier is the main control point over all cash receipts (cash and checks) received by the college, especially student payments. The major duties of the Cashier encompass the following tasks:

- Setting up and administering the cashier window on a daily basis. The Cashier works with a $2,000 cash imprest fund, which is reimbursed on the 10th and 20th of the month.

- Acceptance of all student payments by cash and check and entering all payments received on a daily basis.

- During the student registration period, verifying that each registration form is properly authorized and amounts due properly calculated by all college departments. If the calculations do not balance or are incorrect, the Cashier coordinates the proper correction with the Accounts Receivable/Purchasing Coordinator.

- Controlling and distributing student meal tickets upon proper payment by the student.

- Controlling and distributing the five-part student registration form and a three-part receipt form as follows once proper payment is made:
  - #1 Gold—to the student with #3 Pink receipt
  - #2 White—to the Registrar's office
  - #3 Pink—to the Financial Aid office
  - #4 Yellow—with #2 Yellow receipt to the Accounts Receivable/Purchasing Coordinator for entry into the computer system and then filed in the student's file folder
  - #5 Light Blue—Cashier's file copy with #1 White receipt

- Processing student add or drop forms to verify proper Registrar approval and collecting funds due or processing a refund.

- Filing student receipts, drop and add forms, and other cash out documentation on a daily basis.

- Reconciling all daily cash receipts, which includes the following:
  - Manually preparing daily cash register report
  - Preparing adding machine tapes with totals of all cash receipts per account

- Reconciling all cash money in the Cashier's drawer: beginning balance, plus cash receipts, minus cash disbursements, equals ending balance and cash on hand

- Preparing Daily Cash Reconciliation Form, which reconciles all physical cash and checks received to the records posted

- Preparing deposit slips for each bank account and making deposits to the bank

- During payroll periods, stuffing each pay envelope with checks and any other correspondence and filing them in alphabetical order for subsequent pickup by the employee. Upon issuance of each check to the employee, the Cashier ensures that the employee properly signs for the check.

- Processing checks received in mail by the Comptroller's Secretary. The checks are first routed to the Accounts Receivable/Purchasing Coordinator, who records the payment to the student's record and prepares a check transmittal form. The checks and the check transmittal forms are then processed by the Cashier as part of the daily cash receipts. A three-part cash receipt form is prepared for each check receipt, with #1 copy mailed to the student, #2 copy to the Accounts Receivable/Purchasing Coordinator, and #3 copy filed by the Cashier with the check transmittal form.

- Processing the monthly checks received from the lending financial institution for those students paying off their bills. The checks are received by the Accounts Receivable/Purchasing Coordinator, who posts each payment to the student's records. Each check with a manually prepared check transmittal form is routed to the Cashier, who processes each one as part of the daily cash receipts as above.

- Receiving miscellaneous cash receipts, such as conference fees, room rentals, admissions to theater and other special events, and cash disbursements, such as departmental cash expenses, travel reimbursements, and petty cash payments, and processing these transactions as part of the daily Cashier routines.

It appears that Mercy College has made a cumbersome procedure out of a simple cashiering function. Some of our comments regarding these activities are as follows:

- The college should establish the cashiering function only for miscellaneous cash receipts and cash disbursements. There is no reason to involve the Cashier in an already complicated student registration process or in the payroll function.

- All student mailed checks should go directly to the bank, with the bank providing the detail electronically for automatic computer updating to student records. All on-site checks paid by students during registration can be processed and controlled directly by the Registrar's office.

- Students who pay off their bills on a ten month basis should send their checks directly to the financial institution, who would provide for direct depositing and electronic submission of payment data for automatic updating of student records.

- The outside payroll processor should provide for electronic direct deposit of paychecks to the extent possible, with direct mailing to employees of pay stub information. Those employees who still request an actual paycheck would have their paychecks mailed directly by the payroll processor.

GENERAL COMMENTS

During the course of the operational review of Mercy College's business office operations, we noted seven general or college-wide concerns that should be brought to the attention of College management.

1. Computer systems need to be integrated within the college (and with outside processors, such as those used for payroll and student loans) for both student, academic, departmental, and accounting functions. Although the college is using microcomputer networking technology, the pertinent student and accounting software is not integrated. Each subsystem operates on its own with little computer integration. As a result, many functions are still being conducted on a manual basis in spite of the existence of relevant computer records. Although this is a business office concern, it affects all operations of the college. The present hardware and software systems need to be modified to take advantage of such integration while at the same time college management explores more effective hardware and software upgrades.

2. Organizationally, the college appears to be working on a model that provides superfluous managerial levels in each operational area. For

instance, we found a Comptroller, an Assistant Comptroller, and a Business Operations Manager in the area under review. If the college desires to have and pay someone at the Comptroller (or more normally titled Vice President of Business and Administration) level to provide a higher level financial assistance, the college require this person to also be the day-to-day manager over business operations. This internal business advisor function could also be provided through outsourcing on an as needed basis, providing possibly greater expertise at less overall cost. The college also needs to address the need for both an Assistant Comptroller and a Business Operations Manager. It appears that what is needed is really a working accounting supervisor.

3. Furthermore, the college needs to look at its practice of providing a secretarial support person for each managerial position as well as for each departmental entity. There are other less expensive methods for providing such services, such as making all employees responsible for their own word processing and using a central word processing center for additional requirements.

4. Viewing each function as comprising an individual employee is also costly and inefficient. Some employees are overwhelmed with work, while others have little to do at times. The organization of work should be based both on the work requirements and on the best way to handle such work. Consideration must be given to more effective use of computer systems, part-time versus full-time employees, contract services on an as-needed basis, outsourcing functions, and so on. There is always a best form of organization and distribution of work for each area. It does not have to be the same for each.

5. There should be a greater focus on student service rather than forcing the students to conform to ineffective and outdated methods, for example, having the students go from one office to another during the registration process. Even without drastic computerized changes, much can be done in these areas, including providing for prepayments, consolidating payments, electronically transferring data such as monthly loan payments, and so on.

6. Planning (long-term, short-term, and detail planning) appears to be almost nonexistent. Although the Board of Trustees working together with the President identifies areas for emphasis on an annual basis

(e.g., property improvements, tuition policies, personnel changes, and so on), that is the extent of any real planning. With the current state of private liberal arts colleges in the country today and many such colleges going out of existence or greatly curtailing their programs, it is exemplary that Mercy College has been able to maintain its independence and continue with its mission. This is the case even with steadily decreasing student enrollments and retention and greatly increasing costs of operations in many private liberal arts colleges. No longer can student payment concessions and payment plans alone continue to make the college viable in the marketplace. Without proper planning, Mercy College's problems will only increase.

7. Effective planning procedures also need to be integrated with effective budgeting procedures. At present, only nonsalary expenses are budgeted and controlled. The college not only has to effectively budget revenues to maximize revenue contributions by each academically related area, but also has to plan and budget the use of personnel (which represents approximately 80 percent of overall operating expenses) so as to maximize net profit contributions for each program. Through such effective planning and budgeting procedures, college management will be better able to decide which programs to retain, change, eliminate, and add. College management must learn to balance the business end of operating a college with concerns for fulfilling their mission and providing the correct level of student service.

OPERATIONAL REVIEW REPORT

Based on the operational review of Mercy College's business office, we presented our findings as discussed above with college management. Subsequently, we prepared and distributed our final formal written report as shown below.

Mercy College Business Office Operational Review Report

Dr. Lynn Anderson, President
Mercy College
College Boulevard
College, XX 99999

Dear Dr. Anderson:

Reider Associates is pleased to submit this report to Mercy College relative to our comments, findings, and recommendations as a result of our review and analysis of your business office systems and procedures. During the course of our review, we:

- Interviewed all business office personnel at your central administrative location about their roles and functions.
- Reviewed business office systems and procedures set up to accomplish these functions.
- Performed a general review of manual and computerized systems to determine whether such systems were being used most efficiently and effectively.
- Identified areas that indicated more pervasive operating inefficiencies in other areas or throughout the college.
- Reviewed the use of personnel to determine if they are being used most effectively.
- Identified areas for positive improvements and implementation of best practices in overall functions as well as individual operating areas and use of personnel.

Specifically, we performed the following four work steps:

1. Analyzed present business office systems and procedures.
2. Assisted operations personnel in implementing our best practice recommendations of an immediate and short-term nature as the start of the college's program of continuous improvements.
3. Documented the methodology for implementing long-term improvements.
4. Identified areas of personnel staffing economies in conjunction with recommended efficiencies of operations

BACKGROUND

Mercy College has made major strides in the past few years, resulting in increased student enrollments and the development and growth of a number of academic programs. However, basic systems and methods have remained relatively the same, with many of these no longer being geared toward the college's and students' needs. In fact, even with such growth, the college has been operating at a monetary operating deficit.

Mercy College is in existence to provide quality education and services to its students. However, the college is in a very competitive marketplace both within the state and around the country. With the present state of the economy, potential students are looking more intently at alternative options, both from an economic and a quality education standpoint, prior to choosing a college. Mercy College, as a small private college, must work harder both to recruit potential students and to retain them. This means developing a uniqueness in the marketplace and establishing systems for maintaining academic and student service excellence. This, of course, costs more money.

To accomplish such a mission and meet its goals in the present environment of scarce resources, Mercy College needs to plan for and manage its resources more effectively. There are two main ways to increase monetary resources: either by increasing revenues or by decreasing expenditures (or eliminating some spending). There needs to be effective planning both for revenue maximization and for use of funds. Typically, it costs something to create additional revenues, which sometimes delays doing what needs to be done, particularly with limited funds. However, a dollar not spent, without sacrificing what needs to be done to achieve desired results, goes directly to the fund balance or reserves. Accordingly, scarce resources need to be planned for and managed so as to use them most effectively based on a system of priorities and effective allocation.

We performed our operational review of business office operations to address these issues as well as to be responsive to the present needs of Mercy College. As we discussed, our comments, suggestions, and recommendations are for your review and consideration. You and the Board of Trustees ultimately must decide the direction that Mercy College must take and whether these suggestions and recommendations are helpful in getting you there.

You and Mercy College senior management have been aware of the need for an operational review and analysis of business office procedures. While the scope of business office activities has greatly expanded in response to changing internal and external requirements, basic procedures have remained relatively stable. Additional procedures have been implemented solely to address specific situations. This method of operation has produced an operating environment characterized by individualized procedures that do not always efficiently meet operating and reporting needs. In recognition of this gap, Mercy College management engaged Reider Associates to assist management in performing an operational review of such business office procedures.

SCOPE OF OUR REVIEW

For the purpose of identifying areas for improvements, our review and analysis of present business office systems and procedures included the following functions:

- Comptroller responsibilities and activities, including the Comptroller, Assistant Comptroller, and Comptroller's Secretary
- Business Operations Manager
- Payroll Technician
- Accounts Payable Coordinator
- Business Office Secretary
- Restricted Funds Accountant
- Accounting Technician
- Accounts Receivable/Purchasing Coordinator
- Cashier

We reviewed the above functions according to the following general work steps:

Personnel Interviews

We met with business office management and operations personnel to analyze present operating procedures and associated areas for improvement, as well as to determine future requirements. These discussions and reviews provided us with a working knowledge of:

- Present operating procedures
- Timing and flow of current data
- Problem areas, particularly the critical ones
- Coordination and related communication networks between functions
- Information requirements, present and future needs

Functional Activities

We reviewed systems and procedures presently required to perform such business office–oriented functions as:

- Business office organizational structure and related functional job descriptions, including responsibility and authority relationships
- Business office planning systems, including the establishment of goals, objectives, and detail plans and the integration of such plans with overall college planning systems

- Personnel practices, including employee hiring, orientation, training, evaluation, promotion, and firing
- Business office policies and operating procedures

OBJECTIVES

The objectives of this operational review were to identify the work being performed by Mercy College business office personnel in order to formulate future operational requirements as well as to make observations and recommendations about the manner in which immediate and short-term improvements could be realized. The principal focus of our efforts was toward developing operating procedures that would provide optimum efficiencies in meeting Mercy College's requirements. We did not attempt to evaluate present personnel or their performance but only to evaluate the tasks and functions being performed.

OUR APPROACH

Our approach to reviewing business office operating procedures involved an analysis of operations according to the existing organizational structure. Accordingly, we divided our review into the business office functional activity areas:

- Management and supervision
- Payroll processing and coordination
- Accounts payable coordination
- Business office operations
- Accounting procedures and internal record keeping
- Management and operating information system
- Restricted funds accounting
- Purchasing coordination
- Accounts receivable coordination
- Cashiering function

At the conclusion of each of the above stages of analysis, we prepared a review of findings and recommendations, which were submitted to appropriate Mercy College management and operations personnel in oral presentations, together with written documentation. Accordingly, these presentation materials are not being included in this report. Basically, our review of findings discussed present deficiencies, suggested methods of improvement, and identified areas in which economies and efficiencies could be achieved immediately or as a result of additional work efforts.

SUMMARY OF FINDINGS AND RECOMMENDATIONS

We are summarizing our major findings below for your review. The details of each finding have been submitted under separate cover for your information. We believe that should you implement all of these recommendations, Mercy College could realize an estimated annual savings of $410,000.

General Areas

During the course of our operational review of the business office operations, we identified various areas that have an impact on other functions or on the college in general. Many times, in conducting an operational review, we pick up indications of inefficiencies or improper practices that are more pervasive than just the functions and activities being looked at. We call these "the tip of the iceberg" situations. We would like to bring them to your attention, as follows:

Organization

The organizational structure appears to be set up in the typical top-to-bottom hierarchy based on the need to police and control, review and redo, rather than on the need to achieve results based on clear expectations and criteria for accountability. Theoretically, it is better to develop a workplace where all individuals know what is expected of them and each is motivated by clearly understood, helpful systems as part of a self-motivated discipline system. To make this type of system work most effectively, you need to have clear performance and evaluation criteria as well as the ability to determine whether effective results are being achieved. Within your constraints of limited resources, this allows you to accomplish desired results at less cost and to reward on a merit basis, rather than an across the board or years in service basis, those individuals who contribute most positively.

The art of management is to accomplish desired results with the least amount of resources, using the most efficient methods. Based on our observations, there appears to be too much time being spent on day-to-day crises and on just getting through the day and less emphasis on real management. For example, in the business office, there is a Comptroller, an Assistant Comptroller, and a Business Operations Manager, all with responsibilities for supervising other business office personnel. Not only is this a costly duplication of efforts but also such a practice tends to create a demoralizing and confusing atmosphere for employees. In addition, there are a number of other positions, such as Payroll Technician, Accounts Payable Coordinator, Restricted Funds Accountant, and Accounts Receivable/Purchasing Coordinator, in which a great deal of time is taken up with clerical or mechanical functions rather than functional management and analysis tasks.

Systems and Procedures

The business office is presently using a XXXXXX minicomputer system with XXXX software for its accounting processing functions. This software is fairly old and does not incorporate many of the standard features to be found in currently available college accounting systems, such as an integration of systems (e.g., accounting, student registration, financial aid, plant funds, and so on) and accounting data files (e.g., Payroll, Purchasing, Accounts Payable, student charges, budgets, Accounts Receivable, and general ledger), ability to manipulate data for user needs, capacity to generate reports, and effective provision of management and operating data. Accordingly, business office personnel are spending a relatively large amount of time performing manual and clerical functions to make the system work as well as develop necessary and requested information. In fact, management's compiling of most special reports requires an inordinate amount of time and often requires the development of microcomputer spreadsheet and/or database procedures.

There are many college accounting and financial software packages presently available for operation on microcomputers. Most of your business office work stations are presently using microcomputers as data terminals into your present XXXX system. To support a new system, hardware costs can be kept to a minimum by using existing microcomputers and purchasing a file server (basically a microcomputer CPU and large hard disk storage unit) and network software. Before looking at software packages, you should develop your own system's specifications as to what you want the system to do, module by module and by each data file. Then make sure the preferred software package can give you the flexibility required to meet your defined needs and can be ultimately integrated with other operating functions. We believe the cost of necessary hardware and software will be far less than the costs of present processing methods and the time required to provide operations and management information. In addition, it will provide the information necessary to manage and control college operations.

Planning and Budgeting

A review of the college's budget process shows it to be more of a line item mathematical-type exercise (using last year as a base) than an effective budgeting system based on long-term, short-term, and detail planning concepts. It seems that management personnel are spending their time developing budgets based on incremental increases from last year's budget and actual spending regardless of what is actually needed to achieve agreed-upon goals and results.

The budget should be the allocation of resources to ensure success of the detail plans and depict the manner in which scarce monetary resources will be acquired and used over a period of time. The budget is the quantitative manifestation of the next year of the college's strategic or long-term plan. The strategic plan is the defined direction from top management of where the college should be heading considering factors such as:

- Makeup of the student body—in-state, out-of-state, undergraduate, graduate, continuing education, and so on
- Expansion and contraction of programs
- Use of facilities
- Student services
- Community outreach

The strategic plan should be backed up by organizational and departmental short-term plans that identify the results to be accomplished in the coming period. Once such planning goals and objectives have been agreed on by management and operations personnel, departmental personnel are then responsible for developing detailed operating plans identifying the resources and activities necessary to accomplish these results. Until such detailed plans are developed, there is no effective way to prioritize desired results and then allocate resources. This is budgeting. Such a planning and budgeting system does not exist at Mercy College.

Budgeting should include both revenue and expenditure planning, so that management at all levels agrees to the approach to be taken to produce revenues and expend funds to accomplish desired results. Some advantages to Mercy College of such a planning-oriented budget process include:

- Requires managers and others to focus on planning, and become proactive rather than reactive
- Provides for communication of plans throughout the organization, creating an understanding of priorities and allocation of resources, thus fostering cooperation rather than competition
- Reduces doubts as to what each employee, function, and activity is expected to accomplish, how the function or activity is to be performed, and what results are expected
- Provides specific goals and objectives and detail plans, which serve as benchmarks for the subsequent evaluation of results achieved

- Provides objective criteria for accountability in that each manager is evaluated based on working the plan and achieving results rather than spending or not spending his or her budget dollars

The present budget system does not appear to relate results to resource allocations, in turn creating an atmosphere in which some or all of the following budget games appear to be present:

- The hammer or punitive tool—blaming the budget or someone else when things go wrong
- The operational straitjacket—providing minimum freedom or flexibility to operating management
- The excuse for inaction—It's not in the budget
- The spending game—If it's in the budget, I can spend it
- Other games such as high/low negotiating, hoarding, cushioning, and management harassment or gotchas

The budget process in its proper place at the end of the planning process should be used as a positive force to assist Mercy College management in establishing expectations, measuring results, working toward long- and short-term goals and objectives, and identifying operational areas in need of improvement. In this context, Mercy College should consider the following steps in making the present budget process work for it:

- Implementing revenue planning, which defines revenue targets and develops detail plans as to how to reach the targets in all areas of Mercy College, such as academic departments, facilities use, development fund raising office, outreach programs, noncredit continuing education, conferences, seminars and workshops, and so on.
- Prioritizing and allocating expenditure resources so that such funds are spent where they are most needed rather than on an incremental (usually across the board) increase system based on last year's budget.
- Adapting flexible budget concepts that take into account the fact that conditions change and that neither plans nor budgets are static but ever-changing. In fact, typically as soon as the budget is set, it is already obsolete and it can hardly be set for the entire year.
- Using the automatic budget adjustment, which allows for budget changes as conditions change that are not in the control of the specific manager, for example, a price increase on items that are needed to achieve results, or a planned expenditure that is no longer needed.
- Evaluating budgets based on movement toward achievement of detail plans, goals, and objectives. This eliminates the present need to monitor

the detail spending related to line items and the consistent movement of dollars from one line item to another. The approved budget should not be permission to spend. However, agreed-upon plans are authority to take action.

- Focusing on results rather than numbers focus. Because 70 percent or more of most of your departmental budgets consist of personnel-related costs, which are set by contract, there is really little else to be concerned about. What is more important is how each department will use its personnel and what additional resources are needed to achieve results.

Management Information System

The present accounting and financial system does not contain the flexibility to provide the information to monitor and control operations effectively. It is not fully integrated between subsystem modules and the general ledger and is not designed to provide the following necessary operating statistics on an exception basis:

- Cash requirements—excess cash to invest or needs for borrowing
- Accounts payable—overdue accounts with automatic notices
- Accounts receivable—accounts becoming due or overdue
- Revenue shortfalls—present or future conditions
- Personnel statistics—absenteeism, overtime, overloads
- Cost analysis—by department, program, class, function

Key operating indicators (KOIs) should be defined for all academic and operating functions and investigated with an eye toward what is possible with the present system and what is desired when you look at new software packages. The effective use of such KOIs and related exception reporting is usually much more effective than trying to analyze a universe of data, which many times operational personnel and accountants do not fully understand.

Committees and Meetings

It appears that management and other personnel are involved in numerous committees and meetings. This not only disrupts the main purposes for which these individuals are employed but also indicates that the one calling the meeting as well as those attending may have time that needs to be filled. Sometimes it also indicates the inability to know what to do with one's time. Furthermore, the overuse of such committees and meetings keeps other people from getting their jobs done and also either requires them to work additional hours or means someone else must be employed to perform their functions or that secretaries and administrative assistants step in to maintain the employees' schedules. Although there are many legitimate purposes for committees and meetings, it does not appear that many of these meetings at Mercy College are really needed, particularly in your present condition. The necessity of each committee and the abuse of meetings are issues that should be investigated.

Specific Areas

The following comments, suggestions, and recommendations relate to our review of the specific functions within the business office. They are presented for your consideration, understanding that they emanate from a general review and need to be tempered with actual conditions, such as present systems and personnel. They are presented in the order of the business office organization chart.

Comptroller

The Comptroller is responsible for all business office operations and is the Director of Support Services, with authority over physical plant, computer center, central mail operations, and the bookstore and indirect responsibility for the financial aid office. This appears to be a strange mixture and overburdening of responsibilities. In light of the amount of work that needs to be done, coupled with the number of meetings the Comptroller is required to attend, it appears that he has been put in an impossible position. Typically, the responsibilities of a college comptroller at a college of your size include the following:

- Financial analysis and planning—helping to set the future direction of the college and identifying the financial impact of the plans.
- Accounting and auditing—maintaining accurate books and records, analyzing results, and evaluating performance.
- Financing and capital structure—investigating and deciding on sources of funds to meet ongoing capital needs.
- Controlling and reporting—establishing methods for maintaining financial control over operations and informing management about results (both favorable and unfavorable) and what, if anything, needs to be done to make improvements.
- Asset management and protection—controlling and managing cash, accounts receivable, accounts payable, and fixed assets to ensure that assets are being properly used to benefit the college.

- Information systems—managing and monitoring the information system to ensure that the system provides the operational data necessary for effective decision making.

Based on discussions with the Comptroller and a review of his responsibilities, it appears that these priorities have been shifted into other areas and his time is being grossly compromised. Priorities need to be readjusted in order for positive improvements to be made to support the growth of the college.

Comptroller's Secretary

The Comptroller's Secretary performs traditional secretarial duties such as typing correspondence using word processing software and doing related filing. In addition, she maintains the Comptroller's calendar and appointments in a manually maintained schedule book. This function could easily be computerized and shared between the two individuals, eliminating clerical time and the possibility of double or conflicting entries.

The Comptroller's Secretary is also involved in other clerical duties, such as picking up and sorting the departmental mail, which appears to be a waste of high-priced and valued secretarial assistance. Instead, this duty could be accomplished by a mail delivery system. We also noticed that accounts receivable checks were included as part of the mail, which requires the Comptroller's Secretary to date stamp, record each item on a check log, and then submit these materials to accounts receivable. You might consider providing a pre-addressed return envelope, which could alert the mail room to bring these receivable items directly to a control point for processing and immediate deposit. The returned portion of the billing statement would then be used to record the receipt against the accounts.

It appears that the Secretary could be used to better advantage as more of an administrative assistant to the Comptroller than as a more typical clerical secretary.

Assistant Comptroller

The Assistant Comptroller is responsible for managing the various business office functions and assisting the Comptroller. After reviewing and discussing her functions, it does not appear that either of these responsibilities is being performed adequately. In fact, we are not quite sure why both a Comptroller and an Assistant Comptroller are necessary, particularly with a Business Operations Manager as well. You might want to consider whether the Assistant Comptroller can be used to straighten out these operations and develop more helpful systems and procedures.

Business Operations Manager

There appears to be some confusion between this role and that of the Assistant Comptroller. The other business office employees are not quite sure to whom they should go when they have a problem. There is also confusion with regard to who has decision making powers. It appears that the Accounts Payable Coordinator, Payroll Technician, and Business Office Secretary are to report to the Business Operations Manager, while the Accounts Receivable/Purchasing Coordinator and the Cashier report to the Assistant Comptroller. This is an expensive division of management and is probably unnecessary.

The Business Operations Manager pointed out some problems with the present accounting software, which need to be addressed because they are indicators of unnecessary manual efforts created by a nonresponsive system:

- Record keeping and printing of Form 1099s at the end of the year.
- Vendor balance report—total dollars spent by each vendor for the year for purchasing purposes and Form 990 (over $30,000).
- Nonintegration of the purchasing system with accounts payable, requiring separate entries for disencumbering.
- Inability to print purchase orders, causing the Business Office Secretary to hand-type purchase orders and then enter them into the system.

The Business Operations Manager is also involved in the ongoing budget system by:

- Comparing purchase requisitions to a computer produced budget report because the computer system is unable to make such a budget check, and printing the report on the 15th and the 30th of the month. Although this comparison may catch some requisitions that should not be processed, this manual checking misses any interim transactions and encumbrances and possibly could be stopped until new systems are implemented.
- Preparing and processing budget amendments, which appear to be mainly line item changes where a specific department has overspent on a line item. We are not sure what this accomplishes other than keeping the total departmental budget in line. Time could be better spent analyzing whether the purchase is necessary in the first place.
- Reviewing check requests (helping accounts payable) for proper account approval, backup documentation, authorization, and so on. Oddly, these are not checked against the budget and are an area in which personnel could be bypassing the purchasing system.

The Business Operations Manager also manually prepares various journal entries based on computer-produced data in areas where the system does not automatically make the entries:

- Payroll transactions from the outside payroll processor. These entries are manually prepared and could total as many as 12 pages. The information is available from the payroll processor but not in machine usable form. Investigation should be made as to whether the payroll processor could either telecommunicate this data or provide a computer-usable data file.
- Off-site programs accounting transactions. This is another area in which computerization could automatically transmit these transactions as they occur.
- Plant, restricted, and endowment fund transactions, which also could be easily computerized.
- Accounts receivable collection fees, which are computer entered against accounts receivable records; but this practice does not create corresponding entries to the general ledger.

Because of the overload of paperwork and the present systems being used, the Business Operations Manager is presently spending time assisting the accounts payable operation with tasks such as reviewing check requests, reconciling large-vendor transactions, processing prepayments, and so on. You should consider best practice systems for reducing the number of check requests, purchase orders, and accounts payable transactions, such as elimination of low-dollar purchases (e.g., under $200) with a direct cash system, purchase credit cards, vendor charges, and the like; elimination of repetitive check requests, purchase orders, and vendor transactions through blanket purchase order releases; and direct vendor purchases for approved budget purchases.

The Business Operations Manager is also involved in closing out the accounting system subledgers to the general ledger because the system is unable to close automatically. Cash receipts are closed out daily, accounts payable twice a month to update budget reports, and accounts receivable monthly. Note that with a fully integrated system, each of these subsystems and the general ledger would be up to date with each entry.

The Business Operations Manager and the Comptroller review the budget reports on a monthly basis looking for questionable items resulting in budget line item adjustments based on an "overspent" message. This appears to be chasing mice to keep total departmental budgets in line as opposed to identifying what is happening and taking corrective action. Keep in mind that under flexible budget concepts, many times budgets need to be increased based on activity level changes, and the charge may be actually an automatic budget adjustment.

In summary, the Business Operations Manager is performing many unnecessary clerical and computer routines due to present systems and the lack of an integrated computer system. It would be more advantageous to free up his time for more systems analysis and evaluation tasks.

Payroll Technician

The Payroll Technician works part time (20 hours a week) coordinating payroll processing with an outside payroll processor. An on-line submission system to and from the payroll processor does not exist, which means data must be manually fed by preparing various input forms. Through discussions with the payroll processor, it was determined that such on-line processing is possible and is used by many of the payroll processor's other customers. Such on-line processing should be implemented immediately.

The Payroll Technician still maintains certain data files in the college's accounting system, such as the master payroll file, deduction file, and vacation and sick leave file. This is a duplication of efforts with the service provided by the outside payroll processor. A move to on-line processing would allow access to these files maintained by the payroll processor.

The Payroll Technician prepares a budget salary schedule monthly using a computer spreadsheet routine. This procedure should be incorporated into the college's systems specifications for a new computer system.

Accounts Payable Coordinator

Purchases emanate either from a purchase requisition or a check request from the various departments as they see fit. This has created a larger number of purchases than appear to be necessary. There is no central purchasing function to exercise overall control to take advantage of purchasing economies such as:

- Blanket purchase orders for large volumes of items or dollars where prices can be negotiated downward and releases processed against a single purchase order (e.g., maintenance supplies, copy paper, office supplies, and the like).
- Traveling requisitions for repetitively ordered items rather than individual purchase requisitions each time the item is ordered.
- Preapproved purchases based on agreed-upon plans and budgets, eliminating the need for purchase requisitions.

- Telephone ordering system whereby the user can order for small purchases and repetitive items without having to go through the purchasing and accounts payable systems.
- Combined purchases for items like books, which increase volume discounts based on the total order and reduce the number of purchase orders.

As a result of the present system, particularly with the inability of the system to computer produce a purchase order, the volume of clerical work required greatly exceeds what should be necessary. In effect, the Accounts Payable Coordinator is being overwhelmed with paper. The Business Operations Manager is providing some assistance, and the Business Office Secretary is typing and entering purchase order data and assisting in filing. All of this is a waste of time, which could be used better in the analysis and evaluation function.

Compounding these problems is the lack of a centralized receiving area, which results in items being delivered to each and every area. Because payments cannot be processed until receipt is verified, vendor invoices are waiting in accounts payable, increasing processing volumes and problems. The Accounts Payable Coordinator estimates this entails about 30 to 40 percent of all vendor invoices. Conversely, there are receipts without invoices caused by departments requesting the vendor to submit its invoices directly to the department because many departments maintain their own private budget control systems, due to the lack of confidence in central accounting functions.

This entire purchasing and accounts payable area needs to be streamlined and better controlled. Mercy College is not achieving meaningful purchasing economies, and the present system is not providing adequate controls and is causing an overburden of clerical activities and paperwork.

Business Office Secretary

The Business Office Secretary provides basic secretarial-type duties to the business office, such as telephone receptionist, word processing, mail sorting, and the like. She is also presently processing purchase requisitions into the computer purchasing system. However, she is first typing the purchase order using a typewriter and then entering the data into the computer system because the present software does not produce a purchase order. This is not only a duplication of effort but also provides the opportunity for picking up the wrong data. For the time being (until new computer procedures are implemented), a mock printout from the present system should be used as the purchase order.

Restricted Funds Accountant

The Restricted Funds Accountant is responsible for maintaining and controlling the college's restricted funds, such as:

- Multicultural Education Program
- Upward Bound
- Center for Academic Development
- Financial Aid
- Other private restricted grants and gifts

He is responsible for preparing all necessary federal reports (e.g., those required by the Department of Education) for grant reimbursement as well as any other necessary reporting.

Mercy College does not have an approved indirect cost allocation plan. Presently, indirect cost rates are set for each program within the individual federal contract. This may be adequate for the present level of federal contracts. However, the college should actively go after more federal monies, because once in the federal system, you are obligated with reporting, record keeping, and audit requirements. The more federal funds, the greater the economy of scale in charging indirect costs to federal programs. Furthermore, each dollar paid for by the federal contracts releases the same amount to the college for other purposes.

The Restricted Funds Accountant is also responsible for student loan funds (e.g., Stafford loans with independent lenders and Perkins revolving funds). In addition, he is responsible for the endowment fund, of which about 55 percent is unrestricted and 45 percent restricted (mostly for scholarships). It does not appear that records as to restrictions (i.e., specific purposes) are complete.

This entire area of restricted and endowment funds needs to be defined as to its requirements and incorporated into the college's systems specifications for more sophisticated computer systems.

Accounting Technician

The Accounting Technician is responsible for a number of functions that help support business office operations, such as:

- Reviewing cash receipts as processed by the Cashier
- Maintaining the cash balance via a manual log, which again should be provided by the computer system.
- Reconciling cash accounts to monthly bank statements

- Preparing the cash flow report weekly using a spreadsheet, a responsibility that should be computerized. In the interim, determine how useful this is. Can it be eliminated?
- Using a spreadsheet or database system for special projects when the present system cannot provide the information.

The Accounting Technician should be spending more time analyzing and less time doing.

Accounts Receivable/Purchasing Coordinator

Accounts receivable mainly consist of student payments that are due. The student registration, student account, financial aid, and payment system appears to be more than just cumbersome, with the student being shunted from one area to the other. Because Mercy College is in the student service business, this entire process should be evaluated so that it is more student oriented.

The Accounts Receivable/Purchasing Coordinator is now seeing all students at the time of registration to determine the amount of tuition based on each student's registration form. She then records room and board charges manually and prepares a financial aid voucher. This information is then entered into the student account system, and the amount due is calculated. The student then goes to the Cashier to make payment.

Mercy College presently has differential rates per credit for traditional students, graduate students, nontraditional students, and off-site students, each with different payment terms. For instance, traditional students pay on the front end with a three percent discount or in 10 monthly payments with an extra $40 fee. Graduate, nontraditional, and off-site students can pay all up front or in three installments. With Mercy College's present cash position, these pricing and payment policies should be reviewed. The one advantage that colleges in general have related to cash flow is that they receive the bulk of their money prior to providing the services. Mercy College is losing some of this advantage.

Those students not paying immediately are required to sign a promissory note, which is kept in a loose-leaf binder. These notes are not on the computer system and require the Coordinator to manually post to the note. In addition, the book must be reviewed manually to determine who has not paid or is delinquent. The Coordinator also prepares the accounts receivable monthly aging schedule using a spreadsheet application as well as manually aging each receivable.

The Accounts Receivable Coordinator is also recognized as the Purchasing Coordinator. It appears that what she does in the latter role is to handle the ordering of departmental envelopes, stationery, and business cards as well as advising departments about and possessing catalogs with regard to business furniture, business equipment, and office supplies. This should, of course, be part of a central purchasing function, and the operating departments should have more autonomy.

Cashier

The Cashier is responsible for recording and receiving all payments. These include student payments at registration, subsequent payments made in person, and payments received in the mail. As the present system is set up, this requires the Cashier to check for a number of items at registration, such as signatures (e.g., accounts receivable and financial aid), installment payment approval, overload conditions, and amount due. If the student pays in full, the Cashier calculates the three percent discount and writes up a payment slip for accounts receivable to enter. It appears that all this can be integrated through a well-designed computer system, not only making the registration process easier for students but also providing greater control over cash receipts.

Mail receipts for subsequent student payments are processed by accounts receivable against the student records and then sent to the Cashier for cash receipts processing. It would appear that these types of transactions can be captured as received, allowing direct deposit of the funds into the bank.

Other receipts and checks are also funneled through the one Cashier. Again, the goal is to get such cash receipts deposited as quickly as possible. It does not appear that present procedures are accomplishing this, so other alternatives need to be investigated.

Summary

We believe through cross-training and redefinition of job responsibilities, business office personnel can be better used for both processing type functions as well as analysis and control. Presently, clerical functions are being performed by more highly paid and capable people, and skilled accounting personnel are being used as computer data entry clerks rather than as analyzers, evaluators, and controllers. Through the appropriate use of personnel, and the implementation of systems improvements, the business office can be operated at less cost, more efficiently, and with increased results.

OTHER AREAS

During the course of our review, we identified eight other areas that were not necessarily part of business office operations but that we believe should be brought to your attention.

1. The chart of accounts appears to be extremely cumbersome. You might want to look at a simpler system that makes it easier for users to provide account coding, to input the data into the computer system, and to prepare reports.
2. With regard to price, cost, volume issues, we want to make the following points. The college presently has different prices for credit courses (e.g., traditional, graduate, nontraditional, and off-site). These should correspond to the college revenue plan based on expected number of students and costs for providing such services. Sound cost principles require that such tuition pricing recover direct costs, indirect costs, allocated costs, overhead costs, and a contribution to fund balance or reserves. Such cost principles should be based on expected student volumes or a break-even point concept.
3. Centralized services, for example, centralized purchasing, copying (with large copying better controlled at less cost), word processing, and centralized secretarial and administrative services (as opposed to the proliferation of such personnel throughout the college), might provide the college with some economies.
4. The registration system and related payment options needs to be revamped so that the college gets its money as quickly as possible on the front end without causing inconvenience to the students. Rather than a three percent discount for paying all at once, consider a larger discount with a stiffer penalty (e.g., more than just a $40 fee) based on the cost of money for installment payments. The cash tuition paid after the discount should represent the tuition revenues desired, with penalties for time payments representing the time value of money to the college.
5. As concerns external reporting and special requests, there appears to be a large amount of manual spreadsheet and database manipulation to provide such reporting. Until such time as these requests can be incorporated into a more flexible computer system, the college should evaluate each such request with regard to its benefit versus the time and cost involved. It appears that sometimes, even with such efforts, the data is still inaccurate and may cause improper decisions.
6. You presently require a federally mandated organization-wide type of external audit because you receive more than the threshold amount of federal awards. The present audit fees are not being paid with these federal funds to the extent possible. As previously mentioned, the college should be going after more federal monies and then developing an indirect cost allocation plan. The trick here is to get federal monies to pay as much as possible so that the college can free up these non-unexpended funds for other purposes.

In addition, a review of the past audit report showed that although all of the required reports for federal purposes were there, the college does not appear to be getting any worthwhile operational suggestions and recommendations. The auditor's findings and comments all relate to internal controls over federal moneys. The college should be clear in negotiating the next audit contract that it expects to receive such suggestions and recommendations as part of the audit process.

7. Revenue planning seems to be deficient, with little backup in terms of expected revenue numbers. For instance, what is the college's plan to provide the number of students by department, program, off-site, and so on? In addition, what are the fund raising and development office's detail plans as to federal and other grants, gift giving, wills, insurance beneficiaries, fund raising, and so on?

As in most purely line item budget systems, revenues tend to be overestimated with minimal backup support, and expenditures tend to be underestimated after much justification and calculation efforts. A more effective integrated planning and budgeting system will allow Mercy College to better manage its needs more effectively through proper prioritizing and scarce resource allocations. Such a system will also allow the college to control ongoing operations more effectively and permit flexibility based on continuing changing requirements throughout the year.

8. We propose that the college implement an integrated computer system. The computerized integrated financial and accounting control and management reporting system that we are proposing involves a communications process in which data are recorded initially, and revised as needed, in order to support management and staff decisions for planning, operating, and controlling college operations. Our conceptual design attempts to maximize the use of common data to satisfy the information requirements of Mercy College staff at various levels. It attempts to strike an economic balance between the value of the information to be carried and the cost of operating the system. Accordingly, our objective is not simply to mechanize but rather to design an effective computerization plan that will provide Mercy College personnel with the necessary data to manage and operate.

Proposed computerization will also afford the opportunity for additional personnel cost savings in the purchasing, accounts payable, payroll, accounts receivable, general ledger, and management and operating analysis and reporting functions. We believe that the business office should be able to function with a Comptroller, a data-base analyzer, and one data entry support person (three personnel) instead of the present level of 11 personnel. This will result in considerable dollar savings as well as greatly increasing the efficiency of operations and the level of operating data provided.

Mercy College management should review future departmental and personnel functions for possible eliminations, combining, shifting, and downgrading. A personnel plan should be developed to coordinate procedural changes with personnel requirements on an ongoing basis as changes are implemented.

We believe that successful and timely implementation of the proposed computer systems, while simultaneously completing our other computer processing–related recommendations, will require that at least one additional experienced computer programmer be hired.

We also believe that the most efficient and practical course of action for Mercy College management to take, with regard to computer processing, is to establish the following priorities:

- Implement our recommended business office function improvements, based on the priorities previously established.
- Simultaneously program and implement the financial and accounting systems presently being designed.
- System design and program the proposed integrated college computer system.

We believe that the present computer system hardware (with some additional file servers and data terminals) is capable of performing the processing described above. Computer usage is relatively low at present and can be appreciably increased with minimal impact on overall computer operations. Additionally, manual control functions should be reduced, providing for a streamlining of operations. After the recommendations described above have successfully been accomplished and are operational, Mercy College management should reappraise computer equipment needs with respect to total processing.

We appreciate the courtesies and cooperation extended to us by Mercy College management and business office personnel during the course of this operational review. We are, of course, prepared to discuss any aspects of this review or specific items mentioned in this report with you, should you so desire. In addition, we are available to provide additional consultative assistance in the operational review of other functional areas, as well as to work with you in the implementation of the recommendations mentioned in this report. We appreciate the opportunity to assist Mercy College management in accomplishing its goals and objectives as they relate to the results of this operational review and look forward to continued good relations between Reider Associates and Mercy College.

Very truly yours,

Rob Reider, President
REIDER ASSOCIATES

---

*Operational Reviews
Are the Cornerstone
to Best Practices
in a Program of Continuous Improvements*

CHAPTER FIVE

Development of Review Findings

The operational review team, considering the critical areas identified in the field work phase for further analysis, begins to develop its significant findings. During the course of the operational review, the review team may have identified certain findings that required no additional analysis. In those instances, the review team would have prepared its findings and presented them directly to management. It is not good practice to hold such findings for the final report. As findings are identified and/or developed, they should be reported to management, so that if management agrees, remedial action can be taken as soon as possible.

Every operational review finding, whether requiring additional analysis or not, has certain common structural characteristics, just as every building, no matter how different from other buildings, has a roof, walls, floor, and so on, which can be regarded as building blocks. The operational reviewer must use these basic building blocks to construct a complete finding, one that gives the reader all the information needed to understand the finding and the reason for the recommendations.

> **All Review Findings Have Common Structure**

This chapter discusses the development of effective and convincing operational review findings. Using the work steps performed in the field work phase, the operational review team identifies those findings it believes to be most significant. For these findings, the team develops the necessary elements to convince management that a deficiency exists and that there is need to take corrective action. These findings are not intended to be critical, but to help management improve its operations. Establishing a constructive atmosphere helps to ally management with the review team and to ensure greater receptiveness of such findings. Moreover, if operations people are part of the review team, the findings will be more binding. This chapter reviews the attributes of a well-developed, convincing operational review finding and how the operational review team can put the relevant principles into practice.

This chapter will address four main topics:

1. Increase understanding of the importance of the proper development of an operational review finding.

2. Familiarize the reviewer with the five operational review attributes (statement of condition, criteria, cause, effect, and recommendation) and their significance in the development of review findings.

3. Increase knowledge as to how to use proper review finding presentation as an effective reporting tool.

4. Provide hands-on experience in the development of operational review findings.

The most important single element of the operational review is the development of specific findings. This is the heart of the operational review. Furthermore, the acceptance and implementation of these findings by management is the yardstick for operational review success. A good rule of thumb is that if the review team can persuade management to accept at least 50 percent of its findings and recommendations, then the team has been successful. Developing review findings involves:

- Data collection, to get as much pertinent, significant information about each finding as is realistic

- Evaluation of the finding; in terms of cause, effect, and possible courses of corrective action

In developing such specific review findings and conclusions, the reviewer must do the necessary amount of analytical work, along with accumulating all appropriate evidential supporting data.

ATTRIBUTES OF A REVIEW FINDING

To develop a specific operational review finding, the reviewer should be aware of, and use effectively, the following attributes or building blocks: statement of condition, criteria, cause, effect, and recommendations. These attributes are summarized below in the following five categories.

1. *Statement of Condition*

   What did you find?

   What did you observe?

   What is defective, deficient, or in error?

   This is the what-when-where-how step.

2. *Criteria*

   What should it be?

   What do you measure against?

   What is the standard procedure or practice?

   This is the comparing what is with what should be step.

3. *Cause*

   Why did it happen?

   What is the underlying cause of the deficiency?

   Why have operations become inefficient or uneconomical?

   This is the identification of the cause and not the symptom step.

4. *Effect*

   So what?

   What is the effect of the finding?

What is the end result of the condition?

This is the present or potential impact on the operations step.

5. *Recommendations*

What is recommended to correct the condition?

What recommendation is practical and reasonable for acceptance?

Who should implement the recommendation?

This is the what needs to be done to correct the situation step.

Statement of Condition

In determining the present condition of an operational review finding, the reviewer should address the following questions:

- What was found?
- What was observed?
- What is defective, deficient, or in error?
- Is the condition isolated or widespread?

All operational reviews involve initial fact finding in the field work phase. When fact finding is used to determine the statement of condition, the reviewer examines and verifies as much of the operations and related data as necessary to establish clearly all pertinent facts. The work steps performed are those that best fit the situation. In an operational review, this fact finding process is really the "what-when-where-how" step. The statement of condition provides a reference point to the finding as it relates to established criteria.

One difficulty in performing operational reviews is that the condition disclosed by the detailed work in the field work phase often does not turn out to be quite the same as initially indicated in the planning phase. Thus, developing the finding sometimes turns out to be an evolutionary process in actual practice, which requires the work program to be evolutionary as well. It is in the field work phase that these changes take place, causing the work program to be revised as facts are discovered.

The reviewer should be able to reach agreement with appropriate management on the correctness of the facts; even though there may be disagreement on the reasons, significance, and need for corrective action. The reviewer's failure or inability to agree on the facts with management does not, however, stop the review team from reporting a finding if team members are reasonably certain that the information developed is correct. Although it may be reported to top management and financial management, the operational review finding is really intended for operations management.

Note, too, that the condition (or the problem or the finding itself) is always in the singular. However, the related criteria, causes, effects, and recommendations may be multiple in nature. Although there is no absolute order, the attributes of an operational review finding are normally presented in this order; condition, criteria, cause, effect, and recommendation. The reviewer may decide to present operational review findings in a different order, but always starting with condition and ending with recommendation.

Criteria

In analyzing present conditions, the operational reviewer must be aware of what conditions are expected to meet organizational goals and objectives. In determining the proper criteria for a specific condition, the reviewer looks at such areas as relevant legislation and laws, existing contracts, policy statements, systems and procedures, internal and external regulations, responsibility and authority relationships, standards, schedules, plans and budgets, and principles of good management and administration. In determining the correct criteria for a specific finding, the reviewer answers the following questions concerning the stated condition:

- What should it be?
- What is it measured against?
- What is the standard procedure or practice?
- Is it a formal procedure or an informal practice?

This is the comparing what is to what should be step.

In evaluating procedures and practices, the reviewer should be aware that procedures are formal methods of doing things. Such procedures are documented, usually in writing, and prescribed by management. Practices are the actual ways in which work activities are performed and are rarely documented in written form.

Essentially, in developing the finding criteria, the reviewer compares what is with what should be. The review team has taken the first step toward developing a review finding when it has identified a difference between what actually exists and what should be or what the reviewers think is correct or proper.

Examples of criteria that can be used for such comparison purposes include:

- Written requirements, such as laws, regulations, instructions, policies and procedures manuals, directives, and so forth.

- Stated goals and objectives of the organization and/or department or work unit.

- Verbal instructions.

- Independent opinion of experts.

Some other measures or standards that are used to compare an operational condition with what it should be are shown in Exhibit 5.1.

ALTERNATIVE CRITERIA.   In many cases, criteria may not be available, and must be developed. This is one of the operational reviewer's challenges. In the absence of standards or other effective criteria with which to evaluate performance, three alternative approaches are available to the operational reviewer:

1. Comparative analysis

2. The use of borrowed standards

3. The test of reasonableness

Comparative Analysis.   Where there are no specific standards for comparison, comparative analysis can be used to compare the reviewed circumstances with similar situations. This analysis can be accomplished in the following ways:

EXHIBIT 5.1   Operational Review Criteria Standards

---

a. *Internal to the Organization:*
- Organizational policy statements
- Legislation, laws, and regulations
- Contractual arrangements
- Funding arrangements
- Organizational and departmental plans: goals and objectives
- Budgets, schedules, and detail plans

b. *Developed by the Operational Reviewer:*
- Performance of similar individuals or functions (internal benchmarking)
- Performance of similar organizations (competitive benchmarking)
- Industry or functionally related statistics (industry benchmarking)
- Performance of functions outside the company (best-in-class benchmarking)
- Past and present performance of the organization
- Engineered standards
- Special analysis or studies
- Reviewer's judgment
- Sound business practices
- Good common business sense

Example:
Objective: To provide meaningful, accurate, and timely financial information.

Criteria:
1. Information provided is relevant to management's needs.
2. Information supplied is accurate.
3. Information is received in sufficient time after the reporting period to be useful for its intended purpose.
4. Information is easily understood.

- Current performance can be compared between individuals within the same function or similar functions within the company (internal benchmarking).

- Current performance can be compared to past performance (historical comparison).

- Performance can be compared with that of a similar organization(s) (competitive benchmarking).

Comparing current performance between individuals within the same function can provide a yardstick as to what the performance standard can be. However, the reviewer must be careful not to adapt an unrealistic standard for the others working within the same function. They may be inadequately trained, inappropriate for the job, or need coaching assistance. It may be equally important to determine the cause for the disparity in individual performance and what corrective action may be necessary.

Comparing similar functions (e.g., various purchasing units within the company at different locations) within the company, using internal benchmarking techniques, again may provide internal criteria to use. The reviewer must be careful, however, not to use a standard that is merely the best of inefficient practices. In the development of a program for continuous improvement directed toward implementing best in class practices, the reviewer should also look at the comparison of these functions with those of other companies (competitive and best in class benchmarking).

Comparing current performance with that of past periods has the advantage of possibly disclosing trends in performance. For example, if the cost per employee procedures manual rises from year to year, the reviewer might question whether prices have risen, inefficiencies in manual preparation have increased, employees are being given larger quantities, or a better quality of material is being used. The reviewer can then analyze the situation further to determine exactly why the cost per procedures manual has increased. In this example, the criteria by which actual performance is evaluated are not part of a predetermined plan or a formal set of performance standards, but simply derived from what was done in prior years. Using such comparisons does not provide sufficient data to tell whether the rise in procedures manual prices per employee is good or bad, or whether costs are too high. This method does, however, identify the causes so that management can judge performance as it occurred. Although trends can be noted and examined by this method, meaningful comparisons of alternative methods or procedures cannot usually be accomplished.

The comparison of two or more similar organizations normally provides the opportunity for the reviewer to evaluate different approaches to operations management. By determining the results of different operational approaches, the reviewer can make some helpful recommendations for improving efficiency and effectiveness. Such comparison can be made separately as part of the operational review or as part of a formal external benchmarking study (competitive or best in class) connected to the operational review.

There are, however, some disadvantages in comparing two separate but similar organizations. The major disadvantage is the reviewer's possible failure to recognize factors that justify differences between the two organizations. For example, it is difficult to compare two manufacturers, because no two manufacturers have exactly the same type of manufacturing systems, hire the same type of employees, use the same type of equipment, or have the same proximity to materials and other essentials. Most manufacturers would, however, have many of the same types of problems, regardless of their differences. The similarity of problems can enable the operational reviewer to analyze how each management group handles them. The reviewer can then analyze alternatives for improving the efficiency and effectiveness of operations, and the resultant recommendations can reflect his or her judgment, based on the results produced by each alternative.

Borrowed Standard. Many groups and organizations throughout the country such as manufacturers, hospitals, and banking associations, provide uniform and comparable standards for evaluating performance. These borrowed standards can then be used to compare performance of organizations in similar endeavors. Although such comparisons may make performance evaluation quicker and easier for the operational reviewer, there are some disadvantages to this procedure as well.

One disadvantage is that national averages and broad-based statistics hardly ever relate to specific situations. Thus, although such standards and statistics provide some indications of the organization's performance, they cannot be used for precise measurement or evaluation. Another disadvantage is that very few national averages or uniform statistics actually exist. In those cases where such standards and statistics do exist, such as by standard industry code, for hospitals, banks, service industries, schools, and libraries, they either relate to only a small portion of the areas subject to operational review or are limited to very restricted areas and are of minimal use to the reviewer.

Such borrowed standards and statistics can be used as the starting point for external benchmarking, either competitive or best in class, in the establishment of yardstick criteria. If the review team desires to develop such standards in more detail, it may decide to conduct a full-scale external benchmarking study, looking at competitors' specific operations and functions or at other organizations from a best in class functional standpoint. Such borrowed standards or benchmarking study results can not only provide criteria standards to compare against but can also provide the basis for best in class recommendations. The reviewer should be more critical when thinking of using these borrowed standards or statistics than when using the performance standards established by the organization itself. The reviewer should use borrowed standards only when and if they are found to be relevant and appropriate.

Test of Reasonableness.   When there are no internal standards, and comparisons with other organizations are not practical or borrowed statistics are unavailable, the reviewer can still test organizational performance on the basis of reasonableness. Through experience, reviewers have become familiar with how things are done economically, efficiently, and effectively in other organizations (and other locations within their own company, for instance the accounting function at various company locations). The reviewers should be able to relate these experiences to the current operations under review.

Accordingly, the reviewer can often spot operational irregularities and weaknesses that might escape the notice of others without such a background. In operational reviews, perceptions of a situation are in the eyes of the beholder; in this case, the cumulative experience of the individual operational reviewer. In addition, there exist what may be termed "general standards of society" that apply to good management in any field, public or private. For example, the reviewer can often spot work being done in a loose, unsatisfactory, and inefficient manner, even in the absence of specific standards. Often this work has been considered acceptable because "that's the way we've always done it."

Obsolete inventory, excessive supplies, personnel who are continually absent from work, abuse of resources such as automobiles and expense accounts, and negligence in processing documents or handling cash funds, all are examples of items that can be evaluated through the test of reasonableness.

The reviewer can also use the test of reasonableness as an appropriate tool to quickly review operating areas not subjected to detailed analysis. Even where the review team has analyzed in detail, the reviewers should still examine their conclusions for reasonableness. This ensures that the reviewers have not become so engrossed in statistics that they have overlooked important items or put too much weight on minor ones. The test of reasonableness can also be viewed as the operational reviewer's application of good common sense or prudent business practice to the situation.

Cause

The operational review finding is not complete until the reviewer has fully identified the cause or reason for the deviation from the criteria. To analyze the cause, the operational reviewer must answer the following questions:

- Why did it happen?

- What are the reasons for the operational deficiency?

The most important factor of an operational review finding is the underlying cause of the deficiency. This cause is the reason that operations have become inefficient or uneconomical. The reviewer's responsibility is to report what must be done to correct the situation and prevent recurrence of the adverse effect.

Developing the underlying cause of a review finding requires a good amount of judgment on the reviewer's part. If the reviewer analyzes the cause of a problem too deeply, the conclusion may be impractical. Moreover, the reviewer must make sure to identify the cause, not the symptom.

Review tests and procedures should normally be sufficient to show whether the condition is isolated or widespread. This determination is necessary to:

- Reach a proper conclusion about the significance of the deficiency

- Propose adequate recommendations for corrective action if the condition is widespread and/or likely to recur

The reviewer must be careful in identifying a specific cause, as the cause often appears to be specific individuals. Normally, the reviewer's responsibility is to identify the underlying reasons for resultant deviations from expected criteria, not specific individuals. The review team is wise to avoid identifying specific individuals as the cause of a problem. The real cause could be such things as improper orientation or training, unclear instructions and expectations, poor hiring practices, ineffective supervision and management, or inappropriate systems and procedures. Remember, the operational reviewer is to help achieve positive improvements in the operation, and finger pointing at employees may jeopardize the review team's ongoing credibility.

The following are some possible types of causes:

- Ineffective or lack of adequate planning systems and procedures

- Confusing, ineffective, or faulty organizational structure

- Superfluous or unwieldy organizational hierarchy

- Lack of effective delegation of authority, commensurate with related responsibilities

- Inability or unwillingness to change, as exemplified by resistant attitudes: "We've always done it that way"; "It's industry practice."

- Lack of effective or sufficient management or supervision

- Inadequate, misleading, or obsolete policies, procedures, directives, or standards

- Lack of effective personnel procedures relative to hiring, orientation, training, evaluation, promotion, and firing

- Ineffective use of computerization

- Inadequate management and/or operational reporting systems

- Lack of effective communication

- Personal inadequacies such as negligence, carelessness, unfamiliarity with expected requirements, failure to use good sense or judgment, dishonesty, lack of effort or interest, and the like

- Inadequate resources, including people, equipment, materials and supplies, and facilities

- Ineffective operating systems and procedures

- Deviation from expected standards or criteria

- Lack of knowledge that a problem or condition exists

Effect

One of the primary goals in conducting the operational review is to persuade operations management to take positive action to correct the findings of operational deficiencies the review team has identified. To help management determine just how seriously the condition affects its operations, the reviewer should quantify the effect to the extent possible. As discussed earlier, economy, efficiency, and effectiveness are good measures of effect. They can usually be stated in quantitative terms such as dollars, time, production, number of items or transactions, and so on. Sometimes, when past effects cannot be fully determined, the reviewer may want to present future effects. In determining an operational review effect, the reviewer should answer the following questions:

- So what?

- What is the effect of your finding?

Effect represents the end result of the condition, actual and/or potential. Effect should convince management either that its policies are working out well and its goals are being achieved, or that its goals are not being achieved, and therefore something needs to be done.

The operational reviewer should, whenever possible, quantify the financial effects or loss. Such determinations demonstrate to management the need for corrective action, as well as help convince management in the operational review finding report. Such quantification may consist of the following:

- Actual or estimated monetary losses or potential cost savings,

- Uneconomical or inefficient use of resources,

- Actual or estimated loss of potential income,

- Not achieving as effective operating results as possible,

- Job expectations not being met as well as they could be,

- Information system not useful or meaningful, resulting in poor decision making, and

- Decrease in employee morale and organizational atmosphere.

A list of possible indicators for quantifying effect is shown in Exhibit 5.2.

Recommendations

The successful completion of the operational review finding is the development of recommendations as to the action that should be taken to correct the present undesirable condition. The recommendations should logically follow an explanation of why the present condition exists, the underlying causes, and what should be done to prevent its recurrence. The reviewers' recommendations should be practical and reasonable, so that management will easily see the merits of adopting them.

In developing recommendations, the reviewer should answer these questions:

- What could be recommended to correct the situation?

- Is this recommendation based on a logical connection to the present condition, criteria, and causes?

- Is the recommendation practical and reasonable for implementation?

In many cases, a workable recommendation seems to suggest itself, but at other times the reviewer may need some ingenuity to come up with a recommendation that is sensible and has a reasonable chance of being adopted. Operational review recommendations should be as specific and helpful as possible, not simply that operations need to be improved, controls need to be strengthened, or planning systems need to be implemented. Review team members should do their best to make certain that their recommendations are practical and acceptable to those responsible for taking action.

Each recommendation should be directed to a specific management member, so that it is clear who should take the necessary action to implement the recommendation. In addition, the reviewer should always weigh the cost of carrying out a recommendation against its expected benefits.

REVIEW FINDINGS DEVELOPMENT

The operational review team is responsible for the effective development of the review findings. As an aid in developing adequate and complete review

EXHIBIT 5.2   Effects of Operational Review Findings: Possible Indicators

1. *Management and Organization*
   - Poor planning and decision making
   - Too broad span of control and/or poor channels of communication
   - Badly designed systems and procedures
   - Excessive crisis management
   - Excessive organizational changes and/or inadequate delegation of authority
2. *Personnel relations*
   - Inadequate hiring, orientation, training, evaluation, and promotion procedures
   - Lack of clearly communicated job expectations
   - Idle, excessive, or not enough personnel
   - Poor employee morale
   - Excessive overtime and/or absenteeism
   - Unclear responsibility/authority relationships
3. *Manufacturing and Operations*
   - Poor manufacturing methods excessive rework, scrap, or salvage
   - Inefficient plant layout and/or poor housekeeping
   - Idle equipment and/or operations personnel
   - Insufficient or excessive equipment
   - Excessive production or operating costs
   - Lack of effective production scheduling procedures
4. *Purchasing*
   - Not achieving best prices, timeliness, and quality
   - Favoritism to certain vendors
   - Lack of effective competitive bidding procedures
   - Not using most effective systems such as blanket purchase orders, traveling requisitions, electronic and telephone ordering, and so on
   - Excessive emergency purchases
   - Purchase of unnecessary expensive items
   - Unmet delivery schedules
   - Excessive returns to vendors
5. *Financial Indicators*
   - Poor profit/loss ratios
   - Poor return on investment
   - Unfavorable cost ratios
   - Unfavorable or unexpected cost/budget variances
6. *Complaints*
   - Customers: bad products or poor service
   - Employees: grievances, gripes, or exit interview comments
   - Vendors: poor quality or untimely deliveries
   - Production: schedules not met, material not available, deliveries not on time, quality poor, and so on

findings, reviewers can use a checklist addressing the following seven questions:

1. Are any of the finding attributes (statement of condition, criteria, cause, effect, recommendation) missing? Why? What can or should we do about it? Is it a presentation defect or a symptom of an incomplete review?

2. Are attributes mixed up with one another in a way that impedes clarity? Are facts distinguishable from opinions?

3. Is the *condition statement* valid? Have we indicated that it is a fact or that it was told to us?

4. Are the *criteria* unclear or unconvincing? Are they weak or unsound from a professional standpoint? Do they contain subjective bias?

5. Have we explained the *cause*? Have we given the real cause, or is it a symptom? Is the information on the cause incomplete? Superficial? Does it get to the heart of the matter?

6. Has *effect* been understated? Exaggerated? Quantified when possible?

7. Is the *recommendation* unnecessarily vague? Too rigid? Does it take care of the past but not the future? Is it punitive rather than constructive? Is it out of harmony with cause?

**The More Complete the Finding,
the More Complete the Acceptance**

IDENTIFYING ATTRIBUTES

Operational reviewers who do not use an approach such as that based on the operational review finding attributes, as suggested, tend to prepare confusing and incomplete findings. This contributes to management's resistance and lack of follow-through on findings. To ensure greater success in acceptance, reviewers should become proficient in identifying and documenting finding attributes.

APPROACH TO DEVELOPING REVIEW FINDINGS

There are, of course, many different and varied operational review situations. Thus, there is no one approach to use consistently to perform the operational review and develop findings. However, the following six steps can be considered as a basic approach:

1. Review and analyze operating policies, systems, and procedures and the practices actually being followed to determine whether they will produce the desired results if performed correctly and adequately. If they will not, the operational reviewer can proceed directly to quantifying the effect and determining the cause.

2. Accumulate valid evidence on the operational area under review and its corresponding transactions. This is done by gathering available documentation such as written correspondence, contracts, authorized forms; through interviews with management and operations personnel; and systems analysis such as via systems flowcharts, layout flow diagrams, work observation, and so on.

3. Compare actual transactions with systems and procedures to determine whether procedures are being followed correctly and desired results achieved. If so, the reviewer stops here and ceases spending any more time in reviewing this area. If procedures are not being followed and results are not being achieved, then the reviewer continues with the development of the finding and identification of the attributes.

4. Quantify the effect in terms of dollars lost, or ineffectiveness resulting from the failure to achieve desired results. If the effect is insignificant, the reviewer curtails spending more time in finding development. Nevertheless, the reviewer may decide to report the area to management and may spend some additional time to develop reporting details.

5. If desired results are not being achieved, determine the cause, together with appropriate and sufficient evidence. Note that it is possible that the policy or procedure is faulty and the practice correct, in which case it may be that the policy or procedure should be changed.

6. Develop recommendations on improving the situation for economy, efficiency, and effectiveness. If the cost of a proposed recommendation exceeds the projected dollar savings, the reviewer may conclude that the recommendation is not warranted. This situation is not usually the

case. Operational review recommendations are not always considered solely on an economical basis. They may also provide for increased operational effectiveness, improved decision making, increased organizational efficiency, higher personnel morale, and so on.

Having completed the steps in this approach, the operational reviewer is then ready to present the finding to management, using the finding attributes. This approach to developing operational review findings is summarized in the following six steps.

1. Review and analyze policies, procedures, and practices.

   a. Determine whether policies are appropriate, consistent with goals and objectives.

   b. Determine whether procedures and practices are appropriate, resulting in attaining desired goals and objectives.

2. Accumulate evidence and determine its validity.

   a. Analyze a number of different types of transactions.

   b. Analyze a number of individual transactions.

   c. Ascertain results: statistical sample, decision making, questioning, and so on.

3. Compare transactions to prescribed procedures.

   a. Test transactions versus procedures.

   b. Are procedures followed properly?

   c. Analyze results of following or not following procedures.

4. Quantify the effect.

   a. Calculate the dollars lost (amount of savings).

   b. Determine other factors such as ineffectiveness, and so on.

   c. Establish total effect.

5. Determine cause.

a. Determine why results are not being achieved.

b. Document with appropriate and sufficient evidence.

6. Develop recommendations.

a. Determine how to improve the situation using economy, efficiency, and effectiveness.

b. Document how to implement recommendations that are practical and reasonable.

A Well-Developed Finding
Moves Management to Action

REVIEW FINDING DEVELOPMENT: EXAMPLE COMPANY

In the planning and field work phases, the reviewers learned that the Example Company's purchasing department processed 18,100 regular purchase orders annually, and that the policy is not to issue a purchase order where the cost to process a purchase is greater than 25 percent of the value of the purchase. It was also found that this policy has not been changed since it was issued 12 years ago, when the cost to process a purchase order was $11.80. In the field work phase, the reviewers found the present cost to process a purchase order to be approximately $51. In addition, two sample groups of purchase orders were analyzed, and it was found that approximately 23.5 percent of all purchase orders, amounting to only 1.23 percent of the total cost of purchases, were for $200 or less.

Based on existing Purchasing Department policy, all of these purchases should be eliminated from regular purchase order processing, as the cost to process each purchase order would be greater than 25 percent of the value of the purchase. ($200 divided by 4 = $50.)

Given these data, the reviewer needs to quantify the effect of this practice: what it is costing to process purchases that, economically, should not be going through the central Purchasing Department. This is done by calculating the annual cost to process purchase orders for $200 or less by the

Purchasing Department. The facts needed to perform this calculation are as follows:

Data:

18,100	Regular purchase orders processed annually
$51	Cost to process a purchase order
23.5%	of all purchase orders are for $200 and less

Analysis:

18,100	Purchase orders (annual)
23.5%	% of orders for $200 and less - from sample
4,253	Purchase orders for $200 and less (estimate)
$ 51	Processing cost of a purchase order
$216,903	Annual processing cost for purchase orders of $200 and less

In the process of quantifying the economical effect of processing purchase orders for $200 or less, the review team determined that at least 75 percent of the present processing costs of $216,903 (or $162,677) could be saved by diverting their processing from the Purchasing Department. Reviewers should always state their effects (and savings) on the conservative side and be able to prove them easily. This approach has a psychological advantage in that it avoids overwhelming and putting managers on the defensive. It also ensures the ease of managers' achieving such savings by setting them up to beat the reviewers' estimates and make them look good. Normally, there are more than enough savings and inefficiencies to cite to persuade management to take action without having to overstate the situation.

The review team now has sufficient data to develop and document an operational review finding using the five basic attributes: statement of condition, criteria, cause, effect, and recommendation. It is good practice to submit such findings as they are developed, and to request management's response. If agreed upon, action should be started immediately. If findings are reported this way, the final report becomes mainly a summary of the review and its accomplishments. The actual operational review finding related to the annual cost to process purchase orders for $200 and less is documented in the five steps below.

1. *Statement of Condition* (What did you find?)

   - 23.5% or 4,253 of 18,100 purchase orders were for $200 or less (based on our sample).

   - $51 cost to process a purchase order.

   - $216,903 estimated annual processing cost for purchase orders of $200 or less.

2. *Criteria* (What should it be?)

   Based on present Purchasing Department policy, purchase orders should not be issued where the cost to process a purchase is greater than 25% of the value of the purchase. Accordingly, since the present cost is $51 to process a purchase order, all purchase orders under $200 should be processed in a more efficient and economical manner.

3. *Cause* (Why did it happen?)

   Present purchasing policy states that all purchases for items charged to specific accounts for more than $50 should be processed as a regular purchase order. This policy has been continued since it was effected 12 years ago, when the cost to process a purchase order was calculated at $11.80. This cost has not been recalculated since that time, and the policy has remained the same.

4. *Effect* (So what? What is the effect of the finding?)

   The processing of purchase orders for under $200 results in unnecessary purchasing procedures and resultant costs. As a result of present practices, it is costing an estimated amount of $216,903 to process these purchase orders. We believe we can realize at least 75%, or $162,677, of this $216,903 in savings as well as increase the efficiency of purchasing systems and procedures.

5. *Recommendation* (What is recommended to correct the situation?)

   We recommend that the policy be changed to process all purchase orders under $200 either as petty cash or direct purchases, as appropriate.

   Note: The details for the cost to process a purchase order, amount of savings claimed, and the recommended direct purchase system would be documented in the reviewer's work papers and reviewed with management. They need not be part of the actual documented finding, which would tend to clutter the finding.

DEVELOPING RECOMMENDATIONS

As mentioned earlier, the development of review findings is the most critical element of the operational review. Furthermore, the development of practical and reasonable recommendations that persuade management to implement them is sometimes the most difficult element of the finding. Good, workable recommendations are a result of the review team's collective experience. The more alternative systems and procedures team members are aware of, the better the chance to arrive at the optimum recommendation. In developing recommendations, the review team should consider all sources: review team members, outside consultants, departmental personnel, other employees, other review staff, other organizations, professional associations, results of internal and external benchmarking studies, and so on.

Often the best recommendations come from operating personnel, who need only the reviewer's channel of communication to be heard by decision making management. In these instances, the reviewers must make sure that such operating personnel are given credit for identifying and/or developing the recommendation. The more involved operation personnel are in developing recommendations, the more committed they will be to make them work most effectively. The reviewer's goal is to identify the systems and procedures for recommendations that will optimize savings, be least costly and most efficient to use, and achieve maximum results, regardless of where they come from.

Review team members also need to be aware that management may ask them to assist in implementing their recommendations. Whether or not this is possible in a given situation, the review team should use this situation as a test of their recommendations; that is, the reviewers might ask themselves: "If we are asked to implement our recommendations, would we be able to?" If the reviewers document their recommendations adequately as to the process for implementation and the results to be expected, there is a good chance for success. On the other hand, if recommendations are stated in general terms, not only will management tend to shy away from them, but there is a good chance that results will be sabotaged.

The review team should work toward developing a working together atmosphere with management and operating personnel, whereby the reviewer's role becomes that of helping and change agent. In such a working relationship, there is a much greater likelihood that management will accept the reviewers' recommendations. Operational reviewers will be much more successful in this situation than in the typical reviewer versus management adversarial relationship.

> *Developing Practical and Reasonable*
> *Recommendations Is Sometimes*
> *the Most Difficult Element*

RECOMMENDATIONS THROUGH INTERNAL BENCHMARKING

As part of the operational review and the development of findings, the reviewers may use internal benchmarking concepts to acquire an understanding of how different individuals or functions within the company perform similar tasks. Where significant differences are noted, the reviewer may spend additional time to determine the cause of the difference and how the other individuals or functions might perform at this standard. Such differences may also be an indication that further work is necessary to determine whether even better best practices might be achievable. This could result in some form of external benchmarking study or additional research into best practices.

The successful completion of the internal benchmarking study (considering individuals and/or functions) is the development of recommendations as to the action that should be taken to correct the present undesirable condition. The recommendations should logically follow an explanation of why the present condition is happening, the underlying causes, and what should be done to prevent it from recurring. The reviewers' recommendations should be practical and reasonable, so that management easily sees the merits of adopting them. In developing recommendations, the reviewer should answer these three questions:

1. What is recommended to correct the situation?

2. Is the recommendation based on a logical connection to the present practice?

3. Is the recommendation practical and reasonable for implementation?

Often, a workable recommendation seems to suggest itself, but in other cases the reviewer may need some ingenuity to come up with a recommendation that is sensible and has a reasonable chance of being adopted. Internal benchmarking recommendations should be as specific and helpful as possible, not simply that operations have to be improved, controls have to be strengthened, or planning systems must be implemented. The review team should do its best to make certain that their recommendations are practical and acceptable to those responsible for taking action. Remember, in considering and developing recommendations, the reviewer is moving toward best practices and a program of continuous improvements.

> *Internal Benchmarking May*
> *Provide Simple Recommendations*

Examples of Internal Benchmarking Recommendations

The operational review team should present its internal benchmarking conclusions and findings as to deficient practices together with workable recommendations, orally and then in a more formal reporting system, either deficiency by deficiency or at the end of the study. For example, as part of the operational review internal benchmarking study, the Purchasing Department activities at the Example Company headquarters facility were reviewed to identify those areas of deficiency where positive improvements could be made in terms of economy, efficiency, and effectiveness. The following areas for operational improvement were noted for management's review:

- Purchase requisition procedures

- Budgetary controls

- Buyer functions

- Competitive bidding procedures

- Value analysis program

- Vendor analysis

- Standard specifications unit

- Personnel practices

PURCHASE REQUISITION PROCEDURES. Purchase requisitions are not prenumbered and effectively controlled, resulting in instances in which items are ordered more than once or needed materials or services go unordered. At other locations, it was found that a system of direct ordering was in effect, which allowed each requisitioner to order low cost (under $200) and preapproved budgetary items directly from the vendors.

BUDGETARY CONTROLS. Purchase requisitions are not being checked against approved plans and budgets. Accordingly, purchases are being processed for many items within the company that knowingly exceed existing budgetary approvals. There is a combined problem in this situation; ineffective organizational planning and budget procedures (using static rather than flexible budgeting) together with the lack of budgetary controls at the time of purchase requisitioning. One subsidiary was found in which the functional area was held accountable for working its plans and related budget within a flexible budgeting framework. In this system of self-accountability, there is no further need for outside budget approval and checking.

BUYER FUNCTION. The buying function is presently performed by seven Buyer II's and four Buyer I's. Upon analysis of their functions it was found that the workload is distributed by commodities. Accordingly, there is uneven distribution of the workload as to vendor relations and negotiations, processing of purchases, and so on. By distributing work based on activity levels (as done for commodity class 300), the company should be able to eliminate at least four of these positions. This area should also be looked at for all other locations in an effort to standardize such best practices at other locations and in other functions.

COMPETITIVE BIDDING PROCEDURES. Although the present purchasing procedures state that competitive bidding procedures must be used for each purchase over $2,000 and at least annually for repetitively ordered items, such procedures are rarely applied. At the eastern facility, reviewers found a system of ongoing vendor (present and prospective) review, which eliminated the need for repetitive competitive bidding procedures. The company might also want to put more emphasis on vendor reliability (quality and on-time delivery) than on competitive pricing. These factors can be more significant than pricing in many instances.

VALUE ANALYSIS PROGRAM. There is no value analysis program whereby purchasing analyzes the items to be purchased to determine whether an item needs to be purchased, whether the quantity is excessive, whether less expensive items can be used, and so on. Such a value analysis program was found to be working quite effectively at two of the company's plant locations (Berwick and Southhampton). At each of these locations, the cost of materials has been reduced more than 60 percent since the inception of the program two years ago. This type of value analysis program should be initiated at all locations, including headquarters, at once.

VENDOR ANALYSIS. Reviewers found a predominant practice of habitually dealing with the same vendors. Vendor analysis is not presently being performed in an effective manner, considering such aspects as price, quality of goods, services delivered, and timeliness. In addition, many of these vendors were found to be providing deficient services and unacceptable levels of merchandise returns. At the western location, such an effective vendor analysis system was found to be in effect, which resulted in decreased costs, on-time deliveries of more than 98 percent, and almost zero goods returned. This type of program should be started immediately at all locations. However, prior to implementation, all purchasing personnel will have to be retrained in these concepts.

STANDARD SPECIFICATIONS UNIT. This unit was originally established when the company first started in business 12 years ago. At that time, purchasing specifications were required for all production materials, which were to be developed from engineering bills of material. However, at this point, there are very few new products requiring new purchasing specifications and the unit is primarily responsible for maintaining existing specifications. All other locations are using an outside organization for this purpose on an as needed basis. This has resulted in savings of more than 90 percent. This system should be implemented at the company's headquarters location as well. Other functions of the organization that may fit into the category of no longer being necessary should also be analyzed for possible elimination, reduction, outsourcing, and so on.

PERSONNEL PRACTICES. A review of personnel practices related to hiring, orientation, training, evaluation, promotion, and firing found no policies or procedures in existence. Such practices were implemented by individual managers/supervisors based on their own criteria and expertise. As a result of these deficient practices and inconsistencies of application, employees are confused, staff and management are improperly trained, and qualified employees are leaving while undesirable personnel are being retained. At the company's Cottman location, where such practices were found to be the best in the company, personnel costs were approximately 30 percent less than at other locations adjusted for volume. In addition, there was minimal turnover at this location. It is recommended that the company look at the Cottman location personnel practices as a starting point for a program of continuous improvements in this area. There appears to be a general weakness in this area throughout the organization, and it should be addressed on a planned step-by-step basis. The goal in this area should be to implement best practices not only within the company, but the best possible overall.

Conclusion: Internal Benchmarking

Using internal benchmarking procedures as part of the operational review allows the reviewer to identify the company's critical problem areas and opportunities for positive improvement, maximizing positive aspects of existing procedures and focusing external benchmarking on those most critical areas. Through the coordination of activities of various areas, the reviewer uses internal benchmarking to achieve positive changes within a function or among functions simultaneously. The process also allows these individuals or functions to work together in the analysis of present practices and the implementation of new systems and procedures. In this manner, all areas learn with less reinventing and change within the same time period.

Internal benchmarking can be part of the operational review or a standalone project to identify critical problem areas and provide standardized improvements. It can also minimize the practice of reinventing good procedures that already exist in another part of the organization or that have been unsuccessful. Internal benchmarking can consist of simple comparisons between how different people perform the same task in the same area, or a comparison of performance across different work units within the company. It also provides the knowledge of operations that is essential to the success of an external benchmarking project.

RECOMMENDATIONS THROUGH EXTERNAL BENCHMARKING

Another avenue for seeking best practice recommendations is external benchmarking. External benchmarking is normally thought of as a comparison to others, either competitors, industry, or best in class by function. Such competitive evaluation techniques have been around for a long time, related to such things as costing and pricing. External benchmarking, however, also looks at the processes used by others together with industry and functional trends to identify opportunities for continuous improvement. It is not just a process of bringing the company up to the level of others' incompetency (although better than the company's), but of identifying and implementing the best practices. The reviewer's goal should not be to compare the company with others and then match them, but to surpass others that are after the company's stakeholders and profits.

Competitive Benchmarking

Competitive benchmarking directs attention to competitors' key systems and procedures that affect competitive advantage. It is similar to traditional competitive evaluation, but is quite different in many ways. For instance, the reviewer may learn that the company's main competitor is manufacturing the same product in less than 10 days, whereas the company takes more than 20 days, providing the competitor with a competitive advantage. Knowing this, the review team could recommend that the company get rid of the plant manager as a solution, thereby fixing the blame rather than the cause. Such change, although constituting action, still leaves the company's processes inferior, and the manufacture of the product still takes 20 days.

Competitive benchmarking, on the other hand, looks for causes in the way the work is done, without blaming the people involved. Its goal is not only to match competitors but to surpass them. External benchmarking is a continuous improvement process using present employees' knowledge, creating a learning organization, and resulting in continued innovation and change.

Industry Benchmarking

Industry benchmarking is a process used to identify industry performance and trends. While competitive benchmarking may include a limited number of competitors (three or four), industry benchmarking focuses on identifying general trends across a larger industry grouping. Industry benchmarking is a more general procedure that looks at other companies with similar interests to identify trends in customer service, products/services, personnel, processes, sales/marketing, and so on.

Best-In-Class Benchmarking

Best-in-class benchmarking is a process of identifying best practices across a variety of industry settings. It is based on the belief that best practices can be applied across different types of organizations. As many organizations are stuck in the mental model whereby they believe that they know their own business best, for best-in-class benchmarking to be most successful, members of management must change their thinking to accept that someone else can do something different and better than their company. The reviewer must seek to find the best of the best practices, no matter where it comes from, and then innovatively change the company's processes.

CHOOSING A BENCHMARKING APPROACH

Internal benchmarking has been discussed as a process whereby a company can compare and standardize internal operations as well as identify opportunities for positive improvements and areas for external benchmarking. Such external benchmarking techniques can be used to measure and compare the company's performance in both financial and non-financial operating practices with that of competitors (i.e., competitive analysis), an industry (i.e., industry trends), and across functional areas (i.e., best in class).

Internal benchmarking as part of the operational reviews can be both a tool for continuous company improvement and the initial movement toward a more encompassing external benchmarking study.

Competitive benchmarking helps to identify and prioritize those critical areas of the company to be subjected to more intense review and improvement efforts. Industry benchmarking helps to identify trends and how these trends can be best used by the company. Best in class benchmarking targets the identification of best practices across specific functional areas with companies in other industries and settings. The objective is to match the processes performed rather than the type or structure of the companies involved. The objective of all of these benchmarking procedures is not to rate the company against others, but to use review findings as an organizational learning tool to support continuous growth, learning, and improvement. Benchmarking provides targets to move toward as part of strategic, long-term, short-term, and detail planning.

Benchmarking techniques have become identified with the development of internal and external scorecards that allow others to review comparable performance of the leaders in best practices. Sometimes such best practices are followed blindly, with little regard to applicability to the specifics of the review situation. Benchmarking, however, is more concerned with continuous and future improvement. It focuses on future operating and performance goals, setting the stage for strategic and short-term planning directed toward achievement of such goals. As part of the benchmarking process, performance drivers and constraints are identified, such as outmoded mental models, management assumptions, and belief systems. By reducing or eliminating these barriers, internal improvements become more possible, leading the way to internal best practices.

A performance driver is an underlying characteristic or factor of the company or its environment that determines the amount and type of activities performed to meet stakeholder demands. Performance drivers can be embedded in the organizational environment (e.g., conservative banking), part of the organizational culture (e.g., dress code), company or industry tradition (e.g., paperwork), or performance-related (e.g., customer complaint responses). Performance drivers provide the answer to "Why?" in the operational review and/or benchmarking process. Part of the reviewer's organizational analysis, then, must encompass a company's unique idiosyncrasies or management preferences, locational constraints, and other non-negotiable areas.

For the reviewer to effectively use these internal and external benchmarking techniques to identify gaps in performance and results, and to identify best practices, the reviewer must be familiar and understand the impact of the company's performance measures, quantitative, and qualitative benchmarks. Some examples of performance drivers are shown in Exhibit 5.3. Quantitative measures are shown in Exhibit 5.4, and qualitative measures are shown in Exhibit 5.5.

EXHIBIT 5.3   Examples of Performance Measures

- Organizational environment
- Company policy
- Management and employee skills and abilities
- Market constraints (e.g., price, quality)
- Product constraints (e.g., labor/material intensive)
- Technology (e.g., high, low, innovative)
- Organizational structure
- Management philosophy
- Organizational culture
- Type of structure
- Single product/diversified
- Locations/number of facilities
- Upward/downward/horizontal communication patterns
- Control elements (e.g., strong central versus delegated)
- Job and behavioral expectations
- Embedded value system
- Evaluation and reward systems
- Performance related
- Hiring, orientation, training, evaluation, and promotion practices and criteria
- Turnover or lack thereof
- Delegation of authority and responsibilities
- Unwieldy organizational hierarchy
- Overlaps of responsibility and job functions
- Emphasis on economy, efficiency, and effectiveness
- Quality and use of information systems

BENCHMARKING DATA COLLECTION

Should the reviewer decide to use benchmarking techniques in the identification of operational areas in need of improvement and best practice recommendations, the reviewer should pursue all avenues of information. The benefits of the benchmarking process are maximized by the amount and accuracy of objective data collected from a variety of sources. As part of the benchmarking study, the reviewer must analyze all related publications (competition, industry, and function) such as books, magazines, trade journals, professional associations' materials, databases (Internet, World

EXHIBIT 5.4   Quantitative Benchmarks

Productivity:
- Productivity/number of employees
- Cost per good unit produced
- Total productivity/total cost
- Orders processed per hour by employee
- Orders shipped per hour by employee
- Increase/decrease in inventory by item
- Inventory turnover ratios

Quality:
- Number of good pieces/scrap
- Amount and cost of rework
- Amount and cost of quality inspection
- Amount of vendor rejects
- Number of customer returns/complaints
- Warranty claims
- Returns and allowances
- Good units produced/material in
- Parts availability
- On-time deliveries
- Sales forecast accuracy

Timeliness:
- On-time deliveries
- Design time: customer to finished design
- Production lead time
- Purchasing to vendor delivery time
- Shipping time
- Number of late orders
- Number of late deliveries
- Number of back orders
- Set-ups: number and time
- Inspections: number and time
- Nonproductive time
- Order processing time

Accounting:
- Number of items: invoices, payments, payroll time cards
- Number bills at time of shipment
- Number of payments at terms time
- Accuracy of processing
- Number of accounts payable debits
- Number of accounts receivable credits
- Employee productivity statistics
- Timeliness and accuracy of reporting

EXHIBIT 5.5   Qualitative Benchmarks

Product/Service:
- Number of products/services
- Number of activities/moves
- Number of total parts/activities
- Number of options
- Number of products/services produced: by unit, equipment, location
- Number of stockouts
- Amount of delays/time promised changes

Facilities/Capacity:
- Number of work units
- Number of personnel
- Number and location of bottlenecks
- Number of changes
- Amount of preventive maintenance
- Number of quality control inspections

Customer Satisfaction:
- Amount of repeat business
- Satisfaction: with what
- Actual performance vs. promises
- Referrals to others
- Perceptions: quality, price, ease of use, features

Marketing/Sales:
- Number of salespeople
- Amount of marketing effort
- Increases in sales: number, profits, by customer, by salesperson
- Customer support provided
- Amount of flexibility
- Product success rates
- Sales to existing customers
- Number and sales to new customers

Processing:
- Time to process an order
- Number of contacts per order filled
- Number of errors
- Time to get order into production
- Time to process shipping
- Time to process billing
- Collection statistics
- Number of orders in backlog
- Amount of backlog never realized

Wide Web, CD-ROM), and so on. In addition, the reviewer must talk to internal and external personnel and experts, professional association staff, professional contacts, vendors, customers, competitors, non-competitors, consultants, and so on.

The collection of user provided original data many times is the most important resource to the operational review benchmarking work step. This typically means the use of a questionnaire and/or personal interviews. For this process to be most successful, the review team must be certain that they are asking the right questions without any ambiguity. The design of the questionnaire and interview questions is the link between the reviewer's understanding of the existing critical area for improvement, identified performance gaps, and opportunities for improvement. Each area of questioning must be considered carefully, as it is extremely difficult to redo the benchmark work step.

Once the review team has agreed on the individuals, functions, or other companies with the best practices, they should revisit these sites to analyze their processes as to how they might improve the company's operations. Based on the reviewer's data collection, documentation of the detail system or process, and understanding of how the same procedures would work in this situation, the reviewer presents the recommended system to management for implementation approval. The review team, together with management and operations personnel, then develops a detail plan for system implementation.

The review team can use survey forms, questionnaires, interviews, flowcharts, layout diagrams, and other tools to collect their data during the site visit. If the reviewers are visiting more than one company to address the same practice, they must make sure that their data collection tools are consistent. Typically, the review team will document their findings in a formal written report, as well as present their findings orally, at the conclusion of their site visits.

Some examples of comparisons of best practices between the company being reviewed and other companies included in a benchmarking review are shown in Exhibit 5.6.

PROCESS COMPARISONS

Often in the operational review benchmarking work step the reviewer finds that other companies perform the same practice using a different process.

EXHIBIT 5.6   Examples of Best Practice Presentations

1. *Time to Process a Sales Order to a Manufacturing Order*

Company	Time	Rank
Our Company	4 days	3rd
ABC Company	6 days	4th
DEF Company	3 days	2nd
HGI Company	1 day	Best

2. *Cost of Sales to Sales Department Cost*

Company	Cost	Rank
Our Company	$ .45	Best
ABC Company	.57	3rd
DEF Company	.52	2nd
HGI Company	.78	4th

3. *Cost to Process a Sales Order*

Company	Cost	Rank
Our Company	$8.84	2nd
ABC Company	6.56	Best
DEF Company	10.37	4th
HGI Company	9.74	3rd

4. *Percentage of Errors in Sales Orders*

Company	% Errors	Rank
Our Company	6.8%	4th
ABC Company	2.8%	2nd
DEF Company	2.2%	Best
HGI Company	3.6%	3rd

It is always good for the reviewer to understand how different organizations solve the same problem and how such practices can be used by the company under review. In addition, this allows the review team to relate a practice (the best and others) with the process being performed by the company. Process comparison also provides a quick picture of how other companies approach similar situations and how the company under review can fill a performance gap. For example, consider the following four situations:

1. *Time From Sales Order to Manufacturing Order*

	US	A	B	C
Electronic Ordering	NO	NO	Y/N	YES
Repetitive Ordering	Y/N	NO	Y/N	YES
Integration	NO	NO	YES	YES

2. *Sales Department Operations*

	US	A	B	C
Inside/Outside Sales	NO	YES	YES	YES
Direct Write Up	YES	NO	NO	NO
Customer Sales Orders	YES	NO	YES	NO

3. *Cost to Process a Sales Order*

	US	A	B	C
Sales Desk	YES	YES	NO	NO
Electronic Ordering	NO	NO	Y/N	YES
Order Form Scanning	YES	YES	NO	YES

4. *Percent of Errors in Sales Orders*

	US	A	B	C
Computer Checking	NO	YES	YES	NO
Customer Echo Check	NO	NO	YES	NO
Standard Product Codes	NO	YES	NO	NO

Some sample benchmarking measure are shown in Exhibit 5.7.

FUNCTIONAL COST CONTROLS

Another important aspect in the development of a review finding related to the attributes of effect and recommendations is to analyze and determine the cost elements of each function of the organization, such as sales, manufacturing/service delivery, engineering/service design, computer operations, and accounting. The starting point is to review and analyze the function as it is presently being performed to identify areas for positive improvement together with recommendations for such improvements.

EXHIBIT 5.7   Sample Benchmarking Measures

Sales Forecasts:
1. Forecast to Actual: Total, by Customer, by Salesperson, by Product
2. Forecast to Real Customer Orders
3. Forecast: This Year to Last Year
4. Forecast to Lost Orders
5. Customer Contacts: Number, Type, Results

Sales Order Backlog:
1. Sales Order to Production Order: Time Processed
2. Average Time in Backlog
3. Reduction in Backlog: Current, Compared to Past
4. Backlog Statistics: Conversion To Real Orders/Lost Orders

Manufacturing Orders:
1. Average Processing Time: Sales Order Receipt to MO
2. Timeliness into Production: Per Schedule, Production Ready
3. Timeliness of Start: Materials on Time, Production Start
4. Movement through WIP: Timeliness, Queue Time, Move Time
5. Comparison to Standards: Material, Labor, Scrap, Rejects, Rework
6. Quality Control: Number of Inspections, Rejects
7. Receiving: Personnel, Time, Process
8. Shipping: Process, Timeliness, Method, Costs
9. Delivery: On Time, Customer Satisfaction, Returned Items

Inventory:
1. Raw Material: Amount JIT, Amount On Hand, Amount Decreased
2. WIP: Maximize Throughput, Schedule vs. Actual, % JIT
3. Finished Goods: Completed on Time, Shipped Directly, Amount
4. Records: Physical to Records, Type of Data/Reporting
5. Statistics: Turnover, Obsolete, Inaccuracies

Purchasing:
1. Process Type: Direct, Purchase Orders, EDT, Blanket
2. Numbers: POs, Personnel, Vendors
3. Timeliness: PR to PO, PO to Vendor
4. Vendor Relations: Number, by Personnel, Negotiations
5. Vendor Statistics: Prices, quality, timeliness, Purchase Data
6. Expediting: Open Purchases, Time/Cost, Late Deliveries

EXHIBIT 5.7 (*Continued*)

Engineering:
1. Bill Of Materials: Accuracy, Number of Changes
2. Specifications: Accuracy, Number of Specs
3. Timeliness: New Products, Change Orders
4. Costs: New Design, Change Orders, Maintenance

Billing, Accounts Receivable, and Collections:
1. Billings: Timeliness, Accuracy, Process, Cost
2. Method Of Preparation: Manual, EDP, EDT
3. Billing Cycle Time: Prep/Mail/Receipt by Customer
4. Personnel: Number, Time Per Bill, Staff Vs. Managers
5. Collections: Days Outstanding, Cost Per Dollar Collected
6. Bad Debts: To Sales, Amount
7. Cash Receipts: Process, Time to Deposit, Average Days
8. Credit: Process, Approvals, Over/Under Limits
9. Invoices Returned: Bad Addresses, Inaccuracies

Accounts Payable:
1. Process: Direct Pay, EDT, EDP, Manual
2. Payments: Number, Timeliness, Accuracy/Errors
3. Costs: Per Payment, Personnel, Distribution/Mailing
4. Payment Errors: Number, Costs
5. Discounts: Taken, Lost, Costs

Payroll:
1. Process: Method, Internal/External, Frequency, Distribution
2. Process Errors: Number, Type, Costs, Correction Methods
3. Employee Benefits: Number, Type, Costs
4. Reporting: Frequency, Media, Accuracy, Timeliness
5. Costs: Per Employee, Per Check

Accounting/Financial:
1. Reporting: Late Reports, Errors in Reports, Not Needed
2. Outside Auditors: Cost, Timeliness, Errors Found, Benefits
3. Errors: Process, Personnel, Costs to Correct
4. Data Entry Errors: Number/% by Application
5. Journal Entries: EDP, Manual, Number, Correcting Entries
6. Cost: Per General Ledger/Journal Entry Transaction

EXHIBIT 5.7 *(Continued)*

Personnel:
1. Organization: Number of Personnel, Functions
2. Costs: Departmental, per Employee, per Function
3. Processing: In House/Outside, Level of Inclusion
4. Result Statistics: Hires, Training, Orientation, Discharges
5. Employee Benefits: Type/Number, Administration

Typically, the review team assigns responsibility to an individual(s)to analyze each major function. The goal of this analysis is to get each function operating under the most economical and efficient systems and procedures possible. From that point, it becomes easier to maintain the company's program of continuous improvement.

The tool to effectively assist the reviewer in understanding and analyzing each function is the systems flowchart. A sample systems flowchart for the Purchasing/Receiving/Payables/Disbursement systems was shown in Chapter 4. The reviewer analyzes the flowchart, procedure step by procedure step, and determines which steps can be made more economical and efficient. Along with the systems flowchart, the reviewer may also want to analyze the layout flow, which how work flows within the physical space allotted for the functional activities.

Once the reviewer has identified those activities that make up the function, the next step is to develop the costs of each activity and the total function. These costs should be developed both for the present and proposed activities. Present activity and functional costs can be used to show the costs of the present system, and proposed activity costs can be used to develop savings resulting from review recommendations and target costs for the proposed system.

An example of identifying activities for the purchasing function is shown in Exhibit 5.8; an example of using functional cost to assign costs to products is shown in Exhibit 5.9. The development of costs of an inventory stockout is shown in Exhibit 5.10, the development of costs for the receiving function is shown in Exhibit 5.11, and the development of costs for the accounts payable function is shown in Exhibit 5.12.

EXHIBIT 5.8   Identifying Activities for the Purchasing Function

1. *Purchase Requisition by User*
   - Preparation
   - Review
   - Authorization
   - Submission to Purchasing Department
2. *Purchasing Department*
   - Review of purchase requisition
   - Vendor review and selection
   - Existing vendor
   - New vendor
   - Competitive bidding
   - Contracting
   - Data entry
   - Purchase requisition
   - Purchase order
   - Purchase order processing
   - Printing
   - Forms separation, distribution, and filing
   - Purchase order submission to vendor
   - Mailing process
   - Electronic ordering
   - Purchase order filing
3. *Matching Process by User*
   - Open purchase requisition file
   - Receiving purchase order copy
   - Match purchase order to requisition
   - File open purchase order
4. *Accounts Payable*
   - Receive open purchase order copies
   - File in open purchase order files: by vendor, by PO number

EXHIBIT 5.9   Using Functional Costs to Assign Costs to Products

Cost Data:
   Average cost of PO process activities = $130 (labor & materials)
   POs processed in period: 240 X $130 = $31,200 total cost
   By product item: Item #123 = 82 PO's X $130 = $10,660

Costing by Product: Purchase order processing

Product	# of PO's	%
1	183	6.6%
2	346	12.5%
3	639	23.1%
4	621	22.4%
5	468	16.9%
6	512	18.5%
TOTAL	2,769	100.0%

Total cost for Purchasing Department for period = $ 88,766.

Assigning functional costs to products:

Product	%	Cost
1	6.6%	$ 5,859
2	12.5%	11,096
3	23.1%	20,505
4	22.4%	19,883
5	16.9%	15,001
6	18.5%	16,422
TOTAL	100.0%	$88,766

EXHIBIT 5.10   Cost of an Inventory Stockout

1.   INVENTORY CARRYING COST (ICC) (.02)

   ICC X INV VALUE X # OF DAYS = .02 X 8,200 X 6 DAYS = $ 984

2.   EXPEDITING COSTS

   PERSONNEL: $15/HOUR X 22 HOURS = $ 330

   COMPUTER: $20/HOUR X 2 HOURS =   40

3.   SHIPPING CHARGES (PRIORITY)   124

4.   TIME LOST: 4 HOURS X $350 =   1,400

TOTAL COST OF A STOCKOUT $2,878

NUMBER OF STOCKOUTS: 26

TOTAL COST OF STOCKOUTS FOR THE PERIOD: 26 X $2,878 = $74,828

CONCLUSION

If the operational review team is successful, many of the findings will be accepted by management as the reviewers progress through their operational review. The reviewers present their findings to management as they are identified and developed. Management can respond to each finding by either agreeing and proceeding with the implementation of the recommended action, by agreeing but requesting further clarification, or by disagreeing. Because many, if not all, of the review findings are disposed of through this process as the operational review transpires, they do not need to be restated as part of a final report. If the operational review is conducted in this way, the final report becomes a summary of what has happened.

EXHIBIT 5.11   Receiving Costs

LABOR HOUR COST: $12 PER HOUR

ACTIVITY	TIME	COST
1. RECEIVE PO COPY FROM PURCHASING AND FILE IN OPEN PO FILE	10 MIN	$ 2
2. RECEIVE DELIVERY AND VERIFY THAT DELIVERY IS OURS: CHECK BILL OF LADING, PACKING SLIP, AND SIGN	20 MIN	$ 4
3. COMPARE DELIVERY TO OPEN PO AND RECORD RECEIPT ON PO	15 MIN	$ 3
4. COUNT PARTS, RECORD ON OPEN PO, RECONCILE TO PO AMOUNT ORDERED	15 MIN	$ 3
5. PRODUCE RECEIVING REPORT USING OP OPEN PO COPY - PARTIAL: PO BACK TO OPEN FILE - FINAL: PO TO ACCOUNTS PAYABLE - RECEIVING REPORT TO ACCOUNTS PAYABLE	30 MIN	$ 6
6. WAIT FOR QUALITY CONTROL INSPECTION	4 HRS	—
7. MOVE: STOREROOM, SHOP FLOOR, OR INTERNAL DEPARTMENT	30 MIN	$ 6
TOTAL COST OF RECEIVING		$ 24

EXHIBIT 5.12 Accounts Payable Costs

LABOR HOUR COST: $16 PER HOUR

ACTIVITY	COST ELEMENT	TIME	COST
1. RECEIVE PO FROM PURCHASING AND FILE IN OPEN PO FILE	LABOR	15 MIN	$ 4
2. RECEIVE RECEIVING REPORT FROM RECEIVING, PULL OPEN PO FROM FILE AND COMPARE HOLD IN OPEN RECEIPTS FILE	LABOR	20 MIN	$ 5
3. RECEIVE INVOICE FROM VENDOR AND MATCH TO OPEN RECEIPTS OR PULL OPEN PO AND COMPARE AND HOLD AS OPEN INVOICE	LABOR	30 MIN	$ 8
4. INVOICE/RECEIVING ERRORS	LABOR	—	—
5. COMPUTER DATA ENTRY	LABOR, EDP	10 MIN	$ 3
6. COMPUTER CHECK PREP	LABOR, EDP	10 MIN	$ 4
7. MAIL CHECKS	LABOR, ENVEL, POSTAGE	10 MIN	$ 4
8. FILE PAID PAYABLE	LABOR	15 MIN	$ 4
9. MEETINGS, PHONE, FAX	LABOR, PHONE	—	—
TOTAL COST			$ 32

> *A Successful Operational Review*
> *Is Measured by the Acceptance*
> *of Findings and Recommendations*

CHAPTER SIX

Reporting Phase

In the reporting phase of an operational review, the review team communicates the results of its work to the intended operating and management personnel. The principal objectives of the operational review report are to:

1. Provide useful and timely information on significant operational deficiencies and other matters

2. Recommend improvements in the conduct of operations

The review report is the operational review team's opportunity to get management's undivided attention, an opportunity to show management the benefits of the operational review and what the operational review team has to offer. Accordingly, the operational review report has two functions:

1. To communicate the results of the operational review

2. To persuade and, when necessary, sound a call to action

This chapter discusses the principles and techniques for good reporting in an operational review. The reviewer normally prepares both an oral and written report for management's review, based on the significant operational review findings developed during the field work and review finding development phases. As discussed in Chapter 5, specific review findings are identified and developed for management review during the course of the review. If the review has been performed correctly, the review team has already presented these findings to management during the field work phase, and operations personnel have already begun to implement those steps necessary to correct the identified deficiencies. The review report then becomes more a summary of the operational review, documenting the following four findings:

1. What the operational review team has accomplished

2. What was found during the course of the operational review

3. The extent of operational deficiencies

4. What operations personnel have done thus far to correct the situation

In some instances, however, where operational review findings have not been addressed during the course of the review, the report (both oral and written) becomes the review team's vehicle to convince and persuade management to take corrective action. This is appropriate for reviews of short duration, of perhaps less than two weeks, or for a general overview type of review, where there is not sufficient elapsed time to present findings during the course of the review. Otherwise, the review team should present its findings as they are identified.

The Report Is the Vehicle
to Convince and Persuade Management
to Take Action

This chapter reviews the principles of good operational review reporting that should ensure the review team greater success in getting operations management and staff to implement recommended operational improvements. Remember, to be successful, the review team does not have to persuade management to follow all recommendations; action on more than 50 percent of the significant findings is usually adequate.

This chapter will address the following eight topics:

1. Increase understanding as to the purpose of good operational review reporting

2. Increase knowledge of the types of operational review reporting—oral and written, informal and formal

3. Increase understanding of the basic characteristics of good operational review reporting

4. Increase ability to decide the significance of findings—what to include in the formal report and what to report informally

5. Increase understanding of the types of information to be included in the operational review report

6. Increase understanding of the relationship of developed operational review findings to the reporting phase

7. Increase knowledge of positive factors related to more effective written communications

8. Increase understanding of the format of a completed operational review report by presenting a sample letter and regular report

INTERIM REPORTING

Operational review reports may be either informal or formal, and oral as well as written. The review team should issue a signed written report to appropriate management and staff and other interested parties after the field work is completed, as a record of the completed operational review. However, there is a need for reporting the progress of the review to management during the course of the review.

These interim reports may be oral or written, depending on the circumstances, and may be transmitted formally or informally. It is a good practice to review and submit findings to operations personnel in the five attribute format as they are identified during the actual review. This can be done by using the format shown in the review finding examples in Chapter 5, either showing the actual titles (statement of condition, criteria, cause, effect, and recommendations) or by merely separating each attribute into one or more paragraphs. The review team can use a standard form or merely a free form, leaving space to record management responses and comments. This gives operations and management personnel an opportunity to respond to the findings and recommendations quickly and to take whatever appropriate action is required, either to begin to implement the recommendations or to question some part of the finding.

In either case, this approach allows action to be taken when necessary, as opposed to waiting for the formal report to be issued and reviewed. This practice also allows the review team to include the views of management and operating staff in their final formal written report, both agreeing and opposing views. In addition, for balanced reporting, the reviewers' formal written report should acknowledge any outstanding accomplishments or any corrective action that operations has taken prior to completion of the operational review and issuance of the report.

The reviewers can now refer to the detailed findings and recommendations previously issued and reviewed with operations in the formal report, or attach them as an appendix to the report. In effect, the final written report becomes a formal summary of actions already taken by operations personnel.

ORAL REPORTING

Oral reports or briefings should be given to operations and management personnel periodically, as determined by the length of the review and whether there is anything significant to report. For instance, an operational review scheduled for a three-month period might include periodic oral reporting on a biweekly basis. These progress reports should be specified in the original proposal or letter of understanding and included as part of the review team's budget. There is, of course, no need to hold such a meeting if there is nothing to report.

Oral reports are usually less formal than written reports and include a greater use of visuals such as photographs, slides, charts, and graphs. Oral reporting requires effective oral communication and presentation skills on the part of all review team members. To be most effective in communicating issues to operations personnel, those review team members involved in conducting the field work and developing the findings should make the presentation, not just review team management.

Oral reports have some distinct advantages over written reports:

- Oral reports are immediate. They give prompt attention to current information to allow for timely corrective action.

- Oral reports evoke face-to-face responses. They can evoke client attitudes and convictions that may be important to the reviewers in finalizing their findings and recommendations.

- Oral reports allow the reviewers to counter operations' arguments and provide additional information that operations personnel may require.

- Oral reports can reveal inaccuracies in the review team's thinking, which can be corrected before decisions become final.

The review team may, in some cases, give oral briefings to operations personnel at various stages of the review. In most operational reviews, the reviewers present at least one internal oral briefing in addition to the final oral presentation. These oral briefings may take the form of scheduled periodic progress meetings or be called at the option of review or operations management when there is something significant to discuss or report.

These presentations must be made professionally, as they are golden opportunities to convince management of the merits of operational reviews and the reviewers' competency. This is the reviewers' chance to persuade operations management to take the proper action to improve operations immediately without waiting for a more formal written report. Often the findings are presented at these briefings in attribute format.

WRITTEN REPORT

The review team does not generally close out the operational review with a final oral presentation alone, but normally will issue a written report as well. The more formal written report benefits operations personnel, as well as review team members. The written report provides official recognition of completion of the review and highlights, in writing, the review results. For review team members, the written report serves as a source of information concerning the work done and as a resource for future reviews.

Operations management judges the completed operational review work, in large part, by the quality of the reports. Operational review reports must be prepared according to certain basic principles to maintain high professional standards of operation and to effectively meet reporting objectives. A poor job of written reporting can discredit the reviewers' work accomplished on the operational review. It can also discredit the review staff and put them in a bad position for additional work, no matter how competently they performed the other aspects of the review.

The writer of the review report must keep in mind the intended recipients and other readers. A good rule to follow in achieving this objective is to present the report in a simpler format than the perceived reader's comprehension level. In conjunction with this principle of simplicity, the reviewers should consider using familiar words and phrases, specific descriptive examples, and visual displays such as charts, graphs, and flowcharts to enhance reader understanding.

A good way to ensure that responsible management personnel comprehend and understand the primary concerns is to develop the written report in an inverse format, that is, going from concepts to more specific details. Most people, particularly senior managers, do not want to read through all of the specific details and individual issues and concerns. They want to understand the top level considerations and what action needs to be taken to correct a given operational deficiency or make operational improvements. Therefore, the reviewers present the broad overview, the purpose and objectives of the operational review, and their opinions and the benefits to be derived, in conceptual terms.

The reviewers' findings should be specific and to the point, emphasizing the present effect and future benefits of implementing the recommendations. The reviewers' recommendations should clearly state what actually needs to be done. Ideally, the reviewers' documented findings and related recommendations should be specific enough to give the person responsible for implementing the recommendation a clear description of what needs to be done. Remember too, the reviewers may be asked to help implement the recommendation.

Whether at the oral briefing, or in the written report, each finding and recommendation should be reviewed in complete detail with operations management and staff to be sure of accuracy and understanding. This ensures mutual agreement on all reported findings and action to be taken.

CHARACTERISTICS OF GOOD REPORTING

There are many characteristics of good reporting. Among the most basic are:

- Significance
- Usefulness and timeliness

- Accuracy and adequacy of support

- Convincingness

- Objectivity and perspective

- Clarity and simplicity

- Conciseness

- Constructiveness of tone

- Organization and positivity

Significance

The matters included in the operational review report must be sufficiently significant to justify reporting them to operations and management personnel. The usefulness, and therefore the effectiveness, of operational review reports are decreased by the inclusion of insignificant matters. These tend to distract the reader's attention from the truly important matters reported. To decide what is significant enough to report, the reviewers have to consider a number of factors, including:

- The degree of interest by others in the operations or activities being reviewed

- The importance of the operations or activities, judged by such measures as the size of expenditures, investment in assets, and amounts of revenue

- The relative newness or experimental nature of the operations or activities

- The opportunity to provide useful and timely information to help staff to improve the effectiveness, efficiency, or economy of their operations

- The frequency of occurrence of an adverse condition, the possibility of its occurrence elsewhere, and the relative dollar amounts of loss or additional cost involved (actual or potential)

- The failure of operating staff members to take necessary actions to correct weaknesses or improve operations

Usefulness and Timeliness

Operational review reports must be structured to meet the interests and needs of the audience; that is, they must be useful. However, it is a mistake to assume that the audience for such reports is limited to management. The report should be written so it will be clear to any reasonably intelligent, well-informed persons, even though they may not be familiar with the particular operations, activities, or even the areas involved.

Timeliness, like usefulness, is essential to effective reporting. A brilliantly written report may be of little value to operations management if it arrives too late to fully consider, and act on, the information and recommendations being reported.

The reviewers can often trace problems that affect the timeliness of their reports to unresolved problems that they should have taken care of during the field work phase. To minimize this risk, the reviewers should have their findings completely developed before leaving the field work phase.

In most operational reviews, before the final report is written the reviewers should have already discussed the major findings and reviewed them with management and staff, who, in turn, should have taken appropriate action. In these instances, the final report becomes more a summary of what has taken place, the significance of the results obtained, and the corrective actions that have been implemented.

Accuracy and Adequacy of Support

The review team should apply all of its report preparation, review, and processing procedures to the objective of producing reports that contain no errors of fact, logic, or reasoning. In addition, all facts presented and conclusions reached must be backed up by the documentation of work done.

The need for accuracy in operational review reports is based on the need for the reviewers to be fair and impartial in their reporting, and to assure report users and readers that what is reported is reliable. One inaccuracy in the report can cast doubt on the validity of the entire report and can divert attention from the reviewer's objectives. Accuracy helps to maintain the reader's positive attitude toward the reporting and the reviewers' integrity.

All of the factual data, findings, and conclusions presented in the report must be adequately documented by sufficient objective evidence in the review work papers to support the existence, accuracy, and reasonableness of the matters reported. If operations personnel question any item being reported, the reviewers must have adequate support available.

The opinions and conclusions that are included in the report should be clearly identified as such and must be based on sufficient work to support them. In most cases, one example of a deficiency will not be enough to support a broad conclusion and a related recommendation for corrective action.

Convincingness

Review findings must be presented in a convincing manner, and the related conclusions and recommendations must follow logically from the facts presented. The information presented must be adequately supported to persuade those who read the report that the findings are significant, the conclusions reasonable, and the implementation of the recommendations important. The data presented must be convincing enough to move management to action.

The reviewers cannot substantiate their findings by saying or implying, "It's so, because we say it's so." The burden of proof is on the review team, not on those being reviewed. If findings are questioned, the review team must be able to provide sufficient support to convince operations personnel of their correctness.

Objectivity and Perspective

Every operational review report should present the findings in an objective and unbiased manner. The report should include sufficient information on the subject to give its readers proper perspective. The objective of good report writing is to produce reports that are impartial and fair, not misleading, and that emphasize those matters that need attention. The reviewers, as the report writers, must not however, exaggerate or overemphasize deficient performance.

The following are examples of the types of information that the reviewers should include in their report to provide proper report balance:

- Appropriate information as to why the reviewers made the particular examinations on which they are reporting.

- Clear statements of the nature and scope of their operational review examinations. The review reports, where applicable, should clearly state that the primary emphasis of the operational review was the analysis of matters apparently needing attention, and not an evaluation of the department's total activities or operations.

- Information on the size and nature of the operations and activities to which the review findings relate. This provides proper perspective in judging the significance of the findings.

- Correct and fair descriptions of review findings to avoid reader misinterpretation and misunderstanding. The report should identify all significant relevant factors, even though some may contradict the findings. Information on the size of review tests and the methods of selecting items to test should also be included so that readers may relate such information to the reviewed areas' total operation and the findings.

An effective way to ensure that operational review reports are complete and objective is to obtain advance reviews and comments, prior to final issuance, by personnel whose operations are discussed in the report. This enables the reviewers to produce a report that shows not only what the reviewers found and what they think about it, but also what the operations personnel think about it and what, if anything, they are going to do about it. This kind of report is usually more useful to those receiving it.

Clarity and Simplicity

Operational review reports must be presented as clearly and simply as practicable, to effectively communicate to report recipients. It is unwise to presuppose any detailed technical knowledge of the subjects by the readers. Where technical terms and unfamiliar abbreviations must be used, they should be clearly defined. Efforts at style should be aimed at clear meaning. Flowery expressions aimed at impressing the reader must be avoided.

To achieve report clarity, it is essential to properly organize the report material. The writer should be concise in stating facts, analyzing them, and drawing conclusions. The report should be so well-organized that everything that is pertinent to a given subject is covered in one place.

The use of visual aids (pictures, charts, graphs, and maps) whenever possible, can make the report more easily understood and therefore more useful. Readers are more inclined to take the time to look at such visuals than to read lengthy narrative.

Conciseness

Operational review reports should be no longer than necessary to communicate the required information. They should not contain words, sentences, paragraphs, or sections that do not clearly tie in with the report message. Too much detail detracts from the report and may even conceal the real message or confuse or discourage readers. The reader will appreciate getting the point directly.

Although there is a certain amount of judgment involved in determining the exact content of the report, the reviewers should understand that reports that are complete, but concise, are more likely to get attention. Those who receive the report are usually busy people who may not want to wade through unessential details to get to the essential points. The reviewers should try to determine the audience and what type of reporting will get the most attention.

Constructiveness of Tone

The reviewers' basic objective in performing the operational review and reporting its results is to help improve the operation of reviewed activities. Accordingly, the tone of the report should encourage favorable reaction to their findings and recommendations.

The titles, captions, and texts of the report should be stated in constructive terms. Although findings should be presented in clear, concise terms, the objective of obtaining favorable reaction must be kept in mind. This objective can best be accomplished by avoiding language that unnecessarily antagonizes those the review team is trying to help and causes them to become defensive and resistant.

Even although it is often necessary to criticize past performance to demonstrate the need for some management or operational improvement, the primary emphasis in the report should be on the needed improvements rather than on criticism.

Organization and Positivity

Two other areas of which the report writer should be aware are organization and positiveness. One of the most significant problems that report writers face is how to organize their material. The reviewers must present the information in a logical order or the reader may become confused. They must get the reader's attention immediately and retain it throughout the report. They must stimulate interest by starting with the most important findings, not burying their important comments in the middle of the report. Forcing management to hop, skip, and jump around in their thinking reduces the effectiveness of the report.

The reviewers should think and write positively. Their aim in the report is to help management improve their operations. This requires a good deal of concentration by the reviewers to keep the tone of their report positive. Reviewers tend to use negative words such as deficiencies, weaknesses, errors, delinquent, inefficient, and inaccurate to describe operating practices and procedures. Words of this type immediately put management personnel on the defensive, and so they start to defend the situation for which they feel they are being criticized. Experience has proved that people will be more cooperative if the reviewers express their opinions positively. The reviewers should try to use words such as strengthening, improving, and increasing to make it more difficult for management to disagree with their findings, recommendations, and comments.

Manager who do not favor improving their operations are not effective. Most managers will be responsive to the reviewers if they are able to describe or explain how their recommendations will help achieve the manager's objectives. Keep in mind that the operational reviewer is a helping agent and a catalyst for change, and the report (both oral and written) is the communication tool for convincing and persuading operations management to take the proper action.

Summary

It should be clear from everything stated about the need for clarity and conciseness in operational review reports that conducting and reporting on operational reviews requires effective communication skills on the part of the reviewer. However, the review team rarely has the executive authority to take the action necessary to correct the deficiencies noted. This means that the review team must communicate effectively with those who do have such authority and persuade them to take action. Then they must also be ready to assist management in making positive changes and improvements if called upon.

The report should be as brief as possible. Reviewers' comments should be factual, adequate, pertinent, and clearly and precisely worded. The report should include any statements or promises management made that pertain to the correction of the deficiencies noted. To be most effective, the report must be completed promptly after the conclusion of the field work.

REPORTING REVIEW FINDINGS

As discussed in Chapter 5, well-developed findings, regardless of subject matter, have certain common attributes (statement of condition, criteria, cause, effect, and recommendations).

Review findings can be reported separately as identified and developed in the field work phase, held for reporting until the final formal report, or both. Proper reporting practice calls for separate reporting of findings in the field work phase, with a summary of findings in the final report that either references the previously submitted individual findings or includes them as an appendix.

Some aspects for the operational review team to consider relative to these attributes and reporting review findings in the reporting phase are:

• Statement of condition

• Criteria

• Effect

• Cause and recommendations

• Inclusion of all attributes

Statement of Condition

All operational reviews involve fact-finding, but, what is a fact? Suppose someone involved in operations tells the reviewer that something has happened. Is that something a fact? Or is the fact only that the person told the reviewer it is a fact? For facts that make up the statement of condition, the reviewer must obviously make sure that the information is accurate, well-supported, and worded as clearly and precisely as possible. Each fact must be adequately supported in the reviewers' work papers to the extent that it cannot be questioned.

Criteria

The reviewer's selection of criteria in judging the statement of condition requires experience and wisdom. Many of the review findings stand or fall on the criteria used. If the review team apply or interpret the criteria incorrectly, their initial comparison process is defective and they will have compounded the problem. It is the reviewer's responsibility to convince the reader that the finding criteria are valid. The review team must make sure that they are not merely comparing to a convenient standard or one which is less inefficient than the company's present practices.

Effect

Effect is probably the most important attribute of review findings. Effect quantifies the impact of the deficiency and encourages management to take the proper corrective action. The significance of a deficiency is judged by effect.

Efficiency, economy, and effectiveness are useful measures of effect and frequently can be stated in quantitative terms such as dollars, times, units of production, numbers of procedures and processes, or transactions. In addition, where possible, any potential future effects should be presented.

Cause and Recommendations

The remaining attributes of a review finding, cause and recommendations, are normally interconnected and should be reported as such. Constructive recommendations usually depend on the correct identification of the cause of the operational deficiency. When the reviewers know why something has happened, they can more readily consider how to prevent it or continue it, as the case may be. If it is not practical to recommend a specific or best way to correct a situation, the review team may propose a more general recommendation or suggestion, but only in isolated instances.

The reviewers must make sure that the reader fully understands the reasons for their recommendation, that is, what it is correcting and what benefits will accrue through successful implementation. Most important, operations management and staff must understand and agree to the benefits to be derived so that they will see the change as necessary and act on it. Change is difficult for both individuals and organizations. In this context, it is usually necessary for the reviewers to discuss their recommendations and proposed changes with operations personnel before issuing their report (usually during the field work phase) to motivate them to take the corrective action. Often times such changes are started or have been successfully implemented prior to the submission of the final formal report to management, which then becomes a summary of what has been accomplished through the operational review.

Inclusion of All Attributes

The review team's well-developed review findings should not only include every attribute, but should also be written so that each attribute is clearly distinguishable from the others. The operational review report readers will then have no difficulty understanding what was found, what the reviewers think about what was found, why it happened, what the effect is, and how the review team believe it should be corrected. When review findings are reported with one or more of the attributes missing, the reader almost always raises questions. For no matter how skillful the reviewers are as writers, if they do not adequately cover every attribute while the operational review is in process, they will have problems when writing the report. The finding is the tool to persuade operations personnel and management to take the right corrective action.

The reviewers should decide on a report format for reporting their operational review findings to management and operations personnel. The review team can decide to include the finding attributes as documented captions (either on a preprinted form or on a free form format) for each finding presented. They can also decide to report in finding attribute sequence (i.e., statement of condition, criteria, effect, cause, and recommendation) without identifying the attribute. This is an acceptable format as long as the intended readers can differentiate between the finding attributes. Whichever method and format the review team decides to use to present their documented findings, the method must clearly document the attributes of a well-developed review finding. In addition, finding reporting procedures must allow for management and operations personnel response to the finding, and subsequent redevelopment of the finding by the reviewers where necessary.

Examples of reporting operational review findings are shown in Exhibits 6.1 and 6.2.

EXHIBIT 6.1   Reporting Review Findings: Product Design Change
Reviews

Condition (What was found by the operational review team):
Once a product design review change is approved for implementation by
senior management, the Engineering Department is to start work
immediately on redesigning the product specifications for manufacturing
and purchasing. At the same time, the Sales Department is to start
actively selling the product with the new design change to customers.
Based on our analysis of all 148 product design changes worked on by
the Engineering Department during the last year, we found it took a
minimum of 52 days, an average of 68 days, and a maximum of 146
days to complete these changes.

Criteria (What it should be):
The Example Company attempts to operate on an integrated basis;
whereby the Engineering Department, Manufacturing Department,
Purchasing Department, and Sales Department work together to
coordinate product changes with sales forecasts, production schedules,
and purchase commitments. Accordingly, company policy states that all
such product design changes must be completed and approved for
production within 25 days from initiation of the approved design change.

Cause (Why it has happened):
The Engineering Department was not meeting its product design change
schedule because it lacked the necessary information from other
departments such as sales, manufacturing, and purchasing as well as
top management. In addition, the Engineering Department assigned only
two full-time and one part-time employee (out of a staff of 12) to work on
these product design changes. Although this level of personnel was
sufficient three years ago when design changes were less than 50 for the
year, at present these individuals are not able to support the present
level of 148 changes for the year, and there is no effective system for
scheduling, monitoring, and controlling these design changes so as to
detect scheduling bottlenecks, time delays, and slippage in order that
remedial action can be taken.

Effect (What has resulted):
The impact of not meeting the 25 day schedule for product design
changes has resulted in chaos between sales forecasting and production
scheduling. Our analysis of new customer orders related to the 32 major

EXHIBIT 6.1 (*Continued*)

product design changes in the past year dis- closed that more than $300,000 in sales were canceled prior to or during actual production. In addition, for those customers who did not cancel their orders, actual shipments were made between 45 to 80 days beyond promised delivery dates resulting in greatly decreased customer satisfaction.

In addition, as a result of rushing these product design changes into production in many cases, returned goods were found to be 22 percent of total sales as opposed to a more normal 6 percent for all other products shipped. Although the overall impact could not be quantifiably measured, this situation also caused great disruption in the production scheduling and control, manufacturing process, inventory control, and the purchasing function.

Recommendation (What would you recommend to correct this situation?): The Engineering Department should establish a routing and approval schedule for all product design changes to include Sales, Manufacturing, Purchasing, and any other appropriate functions or individuals. This insures desired integration between all affected parties, as well as complete and accurate data for the Engineering Department to process the desired product design change. As the workload of product design changes is not consistent throughout the year, it is difficult to permanently assign any number of engineers to this function. We recommend that all 12 engineers be cross-trained to work on these product design changes, so that the greatest flexibility is achieved in meeting necessary commitments. In addition, temporary peak-load situations need to be taken into account where the present level of engineering personnel is insufficient to meet product design change requirements. Consideration should be given to more flexible project scheduling, the use of per diem engineering assistance, appropriate project delays, and so on.

Because not all product design changes are of the same nature and extent, the application of a standard 25-day period for completion and approval is not really workable. A more realistic approach would be to schedule each product design change using effective engineering scheduling techniques based on a system of project priority assignments and available resources. What is most important is the adherence to the agreed upon schedule and proper integration and communication with the other parties affected such as Sales, Manufacturing, and Purchasing.

EXHIBIT 6.2   Reporting Review Findings: Purchasing Department
Renovations

Condition (What was found by the operational review team):
An approved plan for the renovation of the Purchasing Department
facilities has been part of the last three years' approved organizational
plan and related budget. However, in each of these three years,
Purchasing Department management has been able to divert these
budgeted funds via approved budget change requests to its normal
operating requirements. As a result, these needed renovations have still
not been started.

Criteria (What it should be):
Proper planning calls for effective priority setting of goals and objectives
and resource allocation. If the renovations are an agreed-upon priority
and adequate resources were allocated for successful accomplishment,
then proper accountability expects the project to be done. By diverting
these funds for normal operating purposes, management erodes the
entire organizational planning and budget system.

Cause (Why it has happened):
Management has implemented planning procedures. However, adequate
control systems have not been implemented that insure plan completion.
Once organizational and departmental plans and related budgets are
agreed upon by top management, plan implementation becomes the
responsibility of each operating department. There is no overall
mechanism in effect to control all departmental plans from an organization
standpoint. Each department is then free to make whatever changes it
desires on an almost automatic basis.

Effect (What has resulted):
As a result of the current lack of monitoring and control of the
organizational and departmental planning system, the Purchasing
Department has been able to divert the funds earmarked for facility
renovations to its normal operations for the past three years. The funds
needed for these renovations have increased from $220,000 to over
$340,000 over the three-year period. In addition, since the renovations
have not been made, the deficiencies that would have been corrected
are continuing, resulting in unnecessary ongoing operating expenditures
of approximately $120,000 per year.

EXHIBIT 6.2 *(Continued)*

Recommendation (What would you recommend to correct this situation?): Planning systems and procedures should be revised to include proper monitoring and control systems. Such controls should prevent arbitrary planning and budget changes. Responsibility and authority should be delegated to an independent work unit to coordinate the implementation and reporting of results of organizational plans.

The renovation of Purchasing Department facilities should be accomplished. This is an approved and agreed-upon project with economic and operational justification. Proper project control procedures should be established to insure successful project completion.

ABCs OF EFFECTIVE REPORT WRITING

For the review team to produce more effective reports, it sometimes helps to think in terms of the ABCs of effective report writing, as exemplified by the following six attributes:

1. *Accuracy.* The reviewers should be accurate in presenting facts, spelling, punctuation, grammar, and usage. Accurate description of problems, conditions, and situations is an absolute necessity. If management is to rely on the information given by the review team, it must be accurate in all respects. The reviewers cannot shade the facts or manipulate them to their unfair advantage. If they do, they shake management's faith in their reporting.

2. *Brevity.* The reviewers should strive for brevity, using the short, concrete word and the short, simple sentence. Their report should be exactly the right length—long enough to cover the subject, short enough to be interesting. Lengthy narratives and long paragraphs are to be avoided; listings and tabulations should be used instead.

3. *Confidence.* The reviewers should be confident that they have something of value to say. If they are (and this is basic to an effective report) then they must say it confidently, positively, and sincerely, as well as simply and directly.

4. *Defense.* As the saying goes, there are two sides to every story, so the reviewers should be sure to present management's defense and reaction to their findings and recommendations. Failure to present management reactions detracts from the value of the report to management and wastes time. Management may agree with the review teams' findings and conclusions in whole or in part, or may totally disagree.

5. *Explain.* The reviewers must explain, interpret, and describe, since many times facts have to be interpreted for management. Tabulations, charts, and graphs may present the overall picture, but the reviewers have to tell management what the facts mean.

6. *Format.* In presenting the review report, there is the conflict between formatting it in free style, based on the creativity of the reviewers, or using a strict formula in which the reviewers fill in the spaces. A recommended middle ground is to define some basic directions, but to avoid strict standardization.

Exhibit 6.3 illustrates a sample report format of this kind.

EXHIBIT 6.3   Sample Report Format

Mr. John Q. Reader
ABC Department

Dear Mr. Reader:

This Guide has been prepared to simplify the task of writing and to standardize the format of operational review reports. It has been prepared in the format of an actual report.

In many ways, the introductory paragraph is the most important part of the report. It is the first thing the reader sees. The reader's reaction to these first few sentences determines whether the reader cares to read further. The reviewers must prepare the report in a manner that motivates the reader to accept and implement their recommendations.

MAJOR SIDE HEADS

The major side heads signify the major divisions. They are started at the margin, in capitals letters, and underlined. Major side heads are never numbered.

EXHIBIT 6.3 Sample Report Format

Minor Side Heads
This is an illustration of how to use minor side heads.

A Second Minor Side Head
When minor side heads are used, it is mandatory to have at least two under a major side head. Note that the minor side head is indented five spaces, underscored, and in upper and lower case.

Another Minor Side Head
Frequent use of major and minor side heads has several advantages, namely:

- They help the writer to outline the significant major and minor findings, conclusions, and recommendations for each section of the report before he or she begins to write the report.
- They assist the reader in quickly locating major and minor subjects in the report.

TWO TYPES OF REPORTS

There are two types of operational review reports: the letter report and the regular report.

1. The *letter report* is designed to be used when the subject matter requires only a few pages of discussion. As a general rule, it should not be used if the report will be more than five pages, contains exhibits or numerous appendices, covers a complex subject, or contains a group of different ideas or topics.
2. The *regular report* contains the introductory letter, in the form that you are presently reading, plus a table of contents and several report sections, each covering a major subject.

LISTINGS AND TABULATIONS

Listings (see "Two Types of Reports") and tabulations (see "Another Minor Side Head") can be used. Note that the items are single-spaced but have a double space between items. Listings are numbered. Tabulations are preceded either by a "bullet" or a "dash."

REPORT DATE

The report is dated as of the date it is delivered to operations management as a final product. It is, however, a good practice to provide

EXHIBIT 6.3   (*Continued*)

a draft of the report beforehand and to include management's and staff's comments in the final report.

PAGE NUMBERS
The first page of the letter report or introductory letter is not numbered. Succeeding pages are numbered at the top or bottom (left, center, or right) of the page. For the long or regular report, the first and succeeding pages of the sections are numbered in Roman numerals-Arabic numerals (I-1, I-2, etc.).

CONTENTS
Contents of the letter report or introductory letter will have the following typical major heads:

Background
Scope of Our Review
Objectives
Our Approach (how you made the study)
Summary of Findings and Recommendations
Concluding Paragraph (expressing your appreciation)

In both the letter report and the regular report the section "Summary of Findings and Recommendations" would include a brief description of the reviewers' findings and related recommendations. The reporting of all of the attributes (statement of condition, criteria, cause, effect, and recommendation) directly associated with these findings have either been submitted and reviewed with management previously and/or can be included as an appendix with the report.

   In the long regular report this section in the introductory letter is called "Summary of Findings and Recommendations," and only the major or significant findings and recommendations would be included. A final sentence is added indicating that details of the major recommendations, plus all other findings and recommendations, are located in the following sections of the report, such as:

I. PURCHASING UNIT PROCEDURES
II. VENDOR RELATIONS AND ANALYSIS
III. STANDARD SPECIFICATIONS UNIT
IV. COST TO PROCESS A PURCHASE ORDER
V. SHIPPING AND RECEIVING OPERATIONS
VI. PROPOSED INTEGRATED COMPUTER SYSTEM

EXHIBIT 6.3 (*Continued*)

* * * * * * * *

At the close of every report, it is suggested to include a comment regarding the cooperation (or lack of cooperation) of the reviewed organization's staff and to state that the review team can be contacted for any additional information relative to the findings in the report. Remember, another important purpose of the operational review report is to acquire additional or follow-up work and to convince management of the merits and benefits versus cost of having other operational reviews performed by the review team organization.

TABLE OF CONTENTS

EXHIBIT 6.3 *(Continued)*

I. SECTION HEAD

The introductory paragraph introduces the reader to the section. From this introduction the reader should learn what this section is about.

Note that each section has a section heading, which is centered in upper case and underlined. Each section should be prefixed with a Roman numeral (as in "I" above), followed by a very brief, descriptive, interesting subject heading.

MAJOR SIDE HEAD

The long report should extensively use major side heads and minor side heads.

TABLE OF CONTENTS

The table of contents of the report is comparable to the table of contents of a book. It lists every section head, major side head, and minor side head in the report. The purpose of the table of contents is to help the reader find a topic in the report. It also gives the reader a summary of the organization of the report and the topics covered.

The table of contents is prepared after the report has been completed. It is placed between the introductory letter and the first major section.

SAMPLE REPORTS

Strict standardization is not recommended for operational review report formats. However, without some basic directions, there would be as many variations of reports as there are operational reviewers. The suggested sample report format shown in Exhibit 6.3 can be used effectively by operational reviewers, intact or with their own modifications.

Exhibit 6.3 describes these two types of reports, the letter report and the regular report, as follows:

1. The *Letter Report,* or short report, is used when the subject matter requires only a few pages. As a general rule, it should not be used if the report will be more than five pages, contains exhibits or numerous appendices, covers a complex subject, or contains a number of different ideas or topics.

2. The *Regular Report,* or long report, is used for more lengthy reporting, particularly when a number of different areas or subjects are covered. It typically contains an introductory letter, plus a table of contents and several report sections, each covering a major subject or area.

A sample letter report and a sample regular report for the Example Company Purchasing Department case study materials covered in preceding chapters are presented in Exhibits 6.4 and 6.5. These sample reports contain many of the elements discussed and recommended for good operational review report writing. These materials should be reviewed and then used as a guide for preparing operational review reports.

Note in the letter report that there is a Summary of Findings and Recommendations section, which gives a general description of each finding and the estimated savings. The detailed findings have either been presented previously, or are documented separately or as an appendix to the report. In the regular report introductory letter, the Summary of Findings and Recommendations section merely references the findings and states the total amount of savings. The major findings are then summarized by section, as referenced in the table of contents. Attachment A to the report is a Summary of Major Findings and Recommendations, which provides a capsulized view or scoreboard for management. Attachment B, Other Areas for Review, describes nonmajor areas noted by the reviewers in which management can either take action on their own or enlist the review team to help them (see Exhibit 6.5).

CONCLUSION

The purpose of this chapter is to present principles and techniques for effectively preparing operational review reports and presenting them to operations management and staff. Operational review reporting can be accomplished in either an informal or a formal manner. The actual reporting can be oral, written, or a combination.

The operational review report communicates the results of the operational review work to the intended recipients. The principal objectives of the report are to provide useful and timely information on significant operational deficiencies and to recommend operational improvements.

The reporting phase provides the reviewers with an opportunity to obtain management and staff's undivided attention and prove to them the benefits

EXHIBIT 6.4   Sample Operational Review Letter Report

Mr. George Worthington
Vice President—Operations
The Example Company
Example Boulevard
Example, XX 99999

Dear Mr. Worthington:

   Reider Associates is pleased to submit this report to The Example Company relative to our findings and conclusions as a result of our review and analysis of Purchasing Department procedures. During the course of this consulting engagement, we:

1. Analyzed present purchasing procedures.
2. Assisted The Example Company personnel in implementing our recommendations of an immediate and short-term nature.
3. Documented the methodology for implementing long-term improvements.
4. Identified areas of personnel staffing economies in conjunction with recommended efficiencies of operations

BACKGROUND

Prior to our review, The Example Company Purchasing Department work unit consisted of 16 employees associated with the following functions:

- Purchasing Supervisor
- (7) Buyer II's
- (4) Buyer I's
- Clerk Stenographer
- Clerical Supervisor
- (2) Clerk Typists

The Example Company senior management has been aware of the need for an operational review and analysis of Purchasing Unit procedures. While the scope of purchasing activities has greatly expanded in response to changing internal and external requirements, basic procedures have remained relatively stable. Additional procedures have been implemented solely to address specific situations. Accordingly, this method of operation has produced an operating environment characterized by individualized procedures that do not always efficiently meet purchasing, operating, and

EXHIBIT 6.4 (*Continued*)

reporting needs. In recognition of this need, the Example Company management engaged Reider Associates to assist them in performing an operational review of Purchasing Unit procedures.

SCOPE OF OUR REVIEW

For the purpose of identifying areas for improvements, our analysis of present Purchasing Unit procedures included the following tasks:

1. *Personnel Interviews*
Met with Purchasing Department management and Purchasing Unit operations personnel to analyze present operating procedures and associated areas for improvement, as well as to determine future requirements. These discussions and reviews provided us with a working knowledge of:

- Present operating procedures.
- Timing and flow of current data.
- Problem areas, particularly the critical ones.
- Coordination and related reporting and communication networks between departments.
- Information requirements, present and future needs.

2. *Functional Activities*
Review of systems and procedures presently required to perform such purchasing-oriented functions as:

- Purchasing Department organization structure and related functional job descriptions, including responsibility and authority relationships.
- Purchasing Department planning systems, including the establishment of goals, objectives, and detail plans; and the integration of such plans with overall organizational planning systems.
- Personnel practices including employee hiring, orientation, training, evaluation, promotion, and firing.
- Purchasing Department policies and operating procedures.

OBJECTIVES
The objectives of this engagement were to identify the work being performed by Purchasing Unit personnel in order to formulate future operational requirements, as well as to make observations and recommendations as to the manner in which immediate and short-term

EXHIBIT 6.4 *(Continued)*

improvements could be realized. The principal focus of our efforts was toward developing operating procedures which would provide optimum efficiencies in meeting the Example Company's requirements.

OUR APPROACH

Our approach to reviewing Purchasing Unit operating procedures involved an analysis of operations according to the existing organization structure. Accordingly, we divided our review into the Purchasing Unit functional activity areas:

- Purchasing supervision
- Buying and vendor relations
- Purchase requisition and purchase order processing
- Open purchase order control and expediting
- Internal record keeping
- Purchasing information system

At the conclusion of each of the above stages of analysis, we prepared a review of findings and recommendations which were submitted to appropriate Example Company management and operations personnel in oral presentations, together with written documentation. Accordingly, these presentation materials are not being included in this report. Basically, our review of findings discussed present deficiencies, suggested methods of improvement, and identified areas where economies and efficiencies could be achieved immediately or as a result of additional work efforts.

SUMMARY OF FINDINGS AND RECOMMENDATIONS

We are summarizing our major findings below for your review. The details of each finding have been submitted under separate cover for your information. We believe that should you implement all of these recommendations, the Example Company could realize an estimated annual savings of $410,000.

1. *Purchase Requisition Procedures*
Purchase requisitions are not pre-numbered and effectively controlled, resulting in instances in which items are ordered more than once or in which needed materials or services go unordered. Based on our analysis of this situation, we believe you can realize at least $120,000 in annual savings, as well as maintain more effective controls as to purchasing only those items that are necessary.

EXHIBIT 6.4 *(Continued)*

2. *Budgetary Controls*
Purchase requisitions are not being checked against approved plans and budgets, resulting in purchases being processed for many items that exceed budgetary approvals. There is a combined problem in this situation: ineffective planning and budget procedures (using static rather than flexible budgeting) and the lack of budgetary controls. We analyzed this situation and found that an estimated annual savings of $80,000 could be realized through the elimination of unnecessary purchases.

3. *Buyer Function*
The buying function is presently performed by (7) Buyer II's, and (4) Buyer I's. We analyzed their functions and found that the work load is distributed by commodities. Accordingly, there is uneven distribution of the workload as to vendor relations and negotiations, processing of purchases, and so on. By distributing work based on activity levels, you should be able to eliminate at least four of these positions, resulting in an estimated annual savings of $164,000, without sacrificing the effectiveness of operations.

4. *Value Analysis Program*
A value analysis program does not exist whereby purchasing analyzes the items to be purchased to determine if less expensive items can be used to meet the same needs. Based on a limited review of 120 selected items, we found that more than $46,000 could have been saved through the use of such a value analysis program. The total savings which could be realized from a full value analysis program would, of course, be much greater than this.

* * * * *

We appreciate the courtesies and cooperation extended to us by Example Company personnel during the course of this operational review. We are, of course, prepared to discuss any aspects of this review or specific items mentioned in this report with you, should you so desire. In addition, we are available to provide additional consultative assistance in the operational review of other functional areas, as well as work with you in the implementation of recommendations mentioned in this report. We appreciate the opportunity to assist Example Company management in accomplishing the results of this operational review and look forward to

EXHIBIT 6.4 (*Continued*)

continued good relations between Reider Associates and the Example
Company.

Very truly yours,

Rob Reider, President
REIDER ASSOCIATES

EXHIBIT 6.5 Sample Operational Review Regular Report

Mr. George Worthington
Vice President—Operations
The Example Company
Example Boulevard
Example, XX 99999

Dear Mr. Worthington:

Reider Associates is pleased to submit this report to the Example
Company relative to our findings and conclusions as a result of our
review and analysis of Purchasing Department activities. During the
course of this operational review, we:

1. Analyzed present systems and methods.
2. Conceptualized new manual and computerized procedures.
3. Identified those areas not susceptible to mechanization.
4. Assisted the Example Company personnel in implementing our
   recommendations of an immediate and short-term nature.
5. Documented the methodology for implementing long-term
   improvements.
6. Instituted a system for setting project priorities and monitoring
   progress on an actual versus scheduled basis.
7. Identified areas of personnel staffing economies in conjunction with
   recommended efficiencies of operations.

BACKGROUND

Prior to our review, the Example Company Purchasing Department
consisted of 23 employees, associated with the following functions:

EXHIBIT 6.5   (*Continued*)

Purchasing Unit
- Purchasing Supervisor
- (7) Buyer II's
- (4) Buyer I's
- Clerk Stenographer
- Clerical Supervisor
- (2) Clerk Typists

Standard Specifications Unit
- Standard Specifications Supervisor
- (2) Procurement Technicians
- (2) Management Trainees
- Clerk Stenographer
- Clerk

The Example Company senior management has been aware of the need for a comprehensive operational review and analysis of Purchasing Department management and operating systems and methods. While the scope of purchasing activities has greatly expanded in response to changing internal and external requirements, basic manual and mechanized systems and procedures have remained relatively stable. Additional procedures have been implemented solely to address specific situations. Accordingly, this method of operation has produced an operating environment characterized by individualized systems that do not always make efficient use of common data to meet purchasing, operating, and reporting needs in the most economical and efficient manner. In recognition of this need, Example Company management engaged Reider Associates to assist them in making (1) a detailed review and analysis of Purchasing Department operations, (2) a study of personnel efficiencies, (3) a definition of data processing requirements, and in (4) developing an implementation priority list and schedule to achieve desired results.

SCOPE OF OUR REVIEW

For the purpose of identifying areas for improvements, our analysis of present Purchasing Department systems and methods included the following tasks:

1. *Personnel Interviews*
Met with Purchasing Department management and operations personnel to analyze present operating systems and procedures and associated

EXHIBIT 6.5 (*Continued*)

areas for improvement, as well as to determine future requirements. These discussions and reviews provided us with a working knowledge of:

- Present operating procedures, both manual and computerized.
- Source document forms and their use.
- Timing and flow of current data.
- Problem areas, particularly those critical to future computerization.
- Coordination and related reporting and communication networks between departments.
- Information requirements, present and future needs.

2. *Functional Activities*
Reviewed systems and procedures presently required to perform such purchasing-oriented functions as:

- Purchasing Department organization structure and related functional job descriptions, including responsibility and authority relationships.
- Purchasing Department planning systems, including the establishment of goals, objectives, and detail plans, and the integration of such plans with overall organiza- tional planning systems.
- Personnel practices, including employee hiring, orientation, training, evaluation, promotion, and firing.
- Purchasing Department policies and operating procedures related to areas such as:
  - Forecasting commodity and service needs.
  - Vendor relations and analysis.
  - Purchasing specifications development and use.
  - Purchase approval and requisition procedures.
  - Purchase order processing and control.
  - Open purchase order follow-up and control.
  - Purchased items receipt controls.
  - Purchasing information system.
  - Computer processing procedures.

OBJECTIVES

The objectives of this engagement were to identify the work being performed by Purchasing Department personnel in order to formulate future operational requirements, as well as to make observations and recommendations as to the manner in which immediate and short-term improvements could be realized. The principal focus of our efforts was

EXHIBIT 6.5 *(Continued)*

toward developing an approach for an integrated system that would provide optimum efficiencies in meeting the Example Company's requirements. Such an integrated system would provide for (1) a purchasing information and control system, within internal and external purchasing guidelines, which would provide all necessary data for proper record keeping, analysis, and control of all purchase requisitions and orders, and (2) a meaningful planning and control system for purchasing management, operational analysis, evaluation, and general control. Accordingly, an additional objective was to define methods that would enhance the effectiveness of purchasing operations and staff by providing personnel at all levels with more timely information to enable them to make improved management and operational decisions.

OUR APPROACH

Our approach to reviewing purchasing operations involved an analysis of operations according to the existing organization structure. Accordingly, we divided our review into the existing purchasing functional activity areas:

- Purchasing supervision.
- Buying and vendor relations.
- Purchase requisition and purchase order processing.
- Open purchase order control and expediting.
- Internal record keeping.
- Purchasing information system.
- Purchasing specifications.

At the conclusion of each of the above stages of analysis, we prepared a review of findings and recommendations, which were submitted to appropriate Example Company management and operations personnel in oral presentations together with written documentation. Accordingly, these presentation materials are not being included in this report. Basically, our review of findings discussed present deficiencies, suggested methods of improvement, and identified areas where economies and efficiencies could be achieved immediately or as a result of additional work efforts.

In addition, we presented a conceptualized plan for an integrated purchasing operating and information computer system that was designed to meet Example Company's requirements as determined through our operational review and analysis. The proposed system would

EXHIBIT 6.5 *(Continued)*

include all present purchasing-oriented manual and computer applications effectively integrated with:

- Manufacturing control systems; including production and inventory control procedures.
- Cost accounting systems.
- General ledger accounting system, particularly the budget and accounts payable modules.

Such an integrated computer system would use common data sources, many of which exist presently, to efficiently update the system.

SUMMARY OF FINDINGS AND RECOMMENDATIONS

We are summarizing our major findings in the following sections of this report for your review. The details of each finding have been submitted under separate cover for your information. We believe that should you implement all of these recommendations, the Example Company could realize an estimated annual savings of $1,775,000. We are also attaching a list of other findings identified during the course of our review that we believe should be brought to your attention for remedial action to achieve increased economies, efficiencies, and effectiveness of results in the purchasing-related areas.

*   *   *   *   *

We appreciate the courtesies and cooperation extended to us by Example Company personnel during the course of this operational review. We are, of course, prepared to discuss any aspects of this review or specific items mentioned in this report with you, should you so desire. In addition, we are available to provide additional consultative assistance in the operational review of other functional areas, as well as to work with you in the implementation of recommendations mentioned in this report. We appreciate the opportunity to assist Example Company management in accomplishing the results of this operational review and look forward to continued good relations between Reider Associates and the Example Company.

Very truly yours,

Rob Reider, President
REIDER ASSOCIATES

Attachments

EXHIBIT 6.5 *(Continued)*

THE EXAMPLE COMPANY
PURCHASING DEPARTMENT OPERATIONAL REVIEW REPORT
TABLE OF CONTENTS

EXHIBIT 6.5 (*Continued*)

I. PURCHASING UNIT PROCEDURES Page I-1

We reviewed operating procedures of the Purchasing Unit to identify those areas of deficiency where positive improvements could be made in terms of economy, efficiency, and effectiveness. The following major areas for operational improvement were noted for your review:

1. *Purchase Requisition Procedures*
Purchase requisitions are not pre-numbered and effectively controlled, resulting in instances in which items are ordered more than once or in which needed materials or services go unordered. Based on our analysis of this situation, we believe that you can realize at least $120,000 in annual savings as well as maintain more effective controls as to purchasing only necessary items by using such controls.

2. *Budgetary Controls*
Purchase requisitions are not being checked against approved plans and budgets. Accordingly, purchases are being processed for many items within the company, which are known to exceed existing budgetary approvals. There is a combined problem in this situation: ineffective organizational planning and budget procedures (using static rather than flexible budgeting), together with the lack of budgetary controls at the time of purchase requisitioning. We analyzed this situation and found that an estimated annual savings of $80,000 could be realized through the elimination of unnecessary purchases. In addition, with the implementation of effective planning and budgetary systems, you should realize other monetary and operational benefits.

3. *Buyer Function*
The buying function is presently performed by (7) Buyer II's and (4) Buyer I's. We analyzed their functions and found that the workload is distributed by commodities. Accordingly, there is uneven distribution of the workload as to vendor relations and negotiations, processing of purchases, and so on. By distributing work based on activity levels you should be able to eliminate at least four of these positions, resulting in an estimated annual savings of $164,000, without sacrificing the effectiveness of operations.

4. *Open Purchase Order Control*
The control over open purchase orders is presently being accomplished on a manual basis. Purchase order copies are used as the control

EXHIBIT 6.5 (*Continued*)

mechanism. We found that there are approximately 1,200 open purchase orders at any one time, so that this has become a difficult task for the one Clerk Stenographer to handle on a manual basis. Our proposed computerized system will eliminate this problem by providing mechanized control over the expediting of open purchases, resulting in an increased degree of on-time vendor deliveries. We estimate that the present large number of late deliveries is costing you more than $245,000 annually in canceled customer orders and manufacturing delays and stoppages.

5. *Competitive Bidding Procedures*
Although your present purchasing procedures state that competitive bidding procedures must be used for each purchase over $2,000 and at least annually for repetitively ordered items, we found such procedures rarely applied. Based on our analysis, we estimate that you could save a minimum of $342,000 by effectively exercising such bidding procedures.

6. *Value Analysis Program*
A value analysis program does not exist, whereby purchasing analyzes the items to be purchased to determine whether less expensive items can be used to meet the same needs. Based on a limited review of 120 selected items, we found that more than $46,000 could have been saved through the use of such a value analysis program. The total savings that could be realized from a full value analysis program would, of course, be much greater than this.

II. VENDOR RELATIONS AND ANALYSIS Page II-1

As part of our operational review of Purchasing Department functions and activities, we analyzed those systems and procedures related to vendor relations. Our major findings and recommendations are summarized below:

1. *Dealing With Same Vendors*
We found a predominant practice of habitually dealing with the same vendors. Although this makes it easier for the buyers to perform their functions, it is a costly practice from the standpoint of achieving the best possible pricing. On this basis, we found that it is costing the company an estimated annual amount of more than $224,000 for the purchase of manufacturing raw materials. This does not include all other purchases.

EXHIBIT 6.5 (*Continued*)

2. *Vendor Analysis*
Vendor analysis is not presently being performed in an effective manner, considering such aspects as price, quality of goods, services delivered, and timeliness of deliveries. This is presently accomplished on an exception basis, as the result of a specific complaint. However, we found no evidence of effective vendor action or of any vendor being replaced as a result of such actions. Although we could not quantify the cost of such inefficient procedures, as adequate records do not exist, we have documented for you a number of such incidences in previous reporting.

3. *Leased Car Procedures*
We analyzed the procedures used by the Buyer II responsible for negotiating and assigning leased cars to employees. We found that for the 87 cars being leased, 24 were being used insufficiently to justify the lease payment. In addition, we found 37 other employees who presently use their own cars and are reimbursed at 30 cents per mile, whereby the actual reimbursements exceed the cost of leasing. The reassignment of these leased cars, based on actual usage, will result in an annual savings of over $44,000 per year.

III. STANDARD SPECIFICATIONS UNIT Page III-1

The Standards Specifications Unit is responsible for maintaining the detailed specifications as to what to purchase. As this is an extremely critical function, particularly for the Example Company manufacturing operations, we included a review of its activities in our operational review. Our major findings and recommendations are presented below.

1. *Staffing Requirements*
The Standard Specifications Unit was originally established when the Example Company first started in business more than 12 years ago. At that time, purchasing specifications were required for all production materials, which needed to be developed from engineering bills of material. The staffing level of one Supervisor, (4) Procurement Technicians, and (2) Clerical Support personnel was established at that time. The same positions still exist, although two Procurement Technician jobs are being done by Management Trainees. However, at this point, there are very few new products requiring new purchasing specifications, and the unit is primarily responsible for maintaining existing specifications. Based on these present requirements and our analysis of existing systems and procedures, we believe that you can

EXHIBIT 6.5   *(Continued)*

accomplish the present level of activity with one Procurement Technician and one Clerical person. This should result in the displacement of five employees, for an estimated annual savings of more than $150,000.

2. *Reporting Relationship*
Based on the above proposed reorganization of the Standard Specifications Unit, we believe that the revised unit of two employees can report directly to the Purchasing Supervisor, resulting in increased control and efficiency within the unit.

IV. COST TO PROCESS A PURCHASE ORDER Page IV-1

As part of our operational review we determined that it was advisable to establish appropriate policies relative to the amount of a purchase that should be processed by the central Purchasing Department. To arrive at what this amount should realistically be, we calculated the present cost to process a purchase order. Our findings are stated below.

1. *Present Purchase Order Processing Costs*
We determined that it presently costs approximately $51 to process a purchase order. This cost has not been calculated since you first started operations more than 12 years ago, when it was calculated to be $11.80. Based on this calculation and your policy that purchase orders should not be issued where the cost to process the purchase is greater than 25% of the value of the purchase, your rule has been that all purchases over $50 go through the Purchasing Department. However, based on our calculation of $51 to process a purchase order and your 25% of value policy, we believe that all purchases under $200 should circumvent the purchasing system.

2. *Purchases Under $200*
We analyzed present purchases and found that 23.5% of all purchase orders were for $200 and less. We estimated that it costs about $216,903 to process these purchases. We believe you can realize an annual savings of over $160,000, as well as increase the efficiency of the Purchasing Department, by having all purchases under $200 processed as petty cash or direct purchases.

V. SHIPPING AND RECEIVING OPERATIONS Page V-1

During the course of our operational review of Purchasing Department operations, we identified some major operational deficiencies in the

EXHIBIT 6.5 (*Continued*)

shipping and receiving areas. Based on our review of these areas with you, it was mutually agreed that we should spend the necessary time to analysis these operations. Our findings in these areas are presented below.

1. *Shipping Procedures*
Our analysis of shipping procedures disclosed that you are presently storing finished goods on pallets in your warehouse. However, at the time of shipping, you use forklifts to take the items to the shipping area. Work crews then unload the pallets by hand onto trucks or rail cars. We were told that this policy was instituted owing to the large number of pallets lost in shipment in the past. We contacted your 12 major customers (accounting for more than 80% of total sales) and found that 10 of them would be willing to provide pallets to you.

2. *Receiving Procedures*
Receiving procedures were found to be working in just the opposite way, whereby your major suppliers were shipping unpalletized. Your receiving personnel then have to remove the goods from the trucks or rail cars and place them on pallets for the forklift operators to store them in the raw material warehouse. We checked with your four major suppliers and found that each of them would be willing to palletize your shipments if you would provide in-transit pallets.

3. *Palletized Shipments and Receipts*
The net cost savings of revising shipping and receiving procedures, as described above, is estimated at more than $200,000 annually. In addition, the use of palletized shipments and receipts for other customers and suppliers should result in even greater annual savings.

VI. PROPOSED INTEGRATED COMPUTER SYSTEM Page VI-1

The computerized integrated purchasing control and management reporting system that we are proposing involves a communications process in which data are recorded initially, and revised as needed, in order to support management and staff decisions for planning, operating, and controlling purchasing operations. Our conceptual design attempts to maximize the use of common data to satisfy the information requirements of the Example Company staff at various levels. It attempts to strike an economic balance between the value of the information to be carried and the cost of operating the system. Accordingly, our objective is not simply

EXHIBIT 6.5 (*Continued*)

to mechanize, but to design an effective computerization plan that will provide the Example Company purchasing personnel with the necessary data to manage and operate.

1. *Proposed Computerization*
Proposed computerization will also afford the opportunity for additional personnel cost savings in the purchasing, inventory control, and warehousing functions. Example Company management should review future departmental and personnel functions for possible eliminations, combining, shifting, and downgrading. A personnel plan should be developed to coordinate procedural changes with personnel requirements on an ongoing basis as changes are implemented.

2. *Additional Personnel*
We believe that to successfully implement the proposed computer systems in a timely manner, in addition to simultaneously completing our other computer processing-related recommendations, will require at least one additional experienced computer programmer to be hired.

3. *Computer Processing Priorities*
We also believe that the most efficient and practical course of action for Example Company management to take, with regard to computer processing, is to establish the following priorities:

- Implement our recommended purchasing function improvements, based on the priorities previously established.
- Simultaneously program and implement the production and inventory control systems presently being designed.
- System design and program the proposed integrated purchasing computer system.

4. *Computer Equipment Requirements*
We believe that the present computer system is capable of performing the processing described above. Present computer usage of approximately 50 hours a month is relatively low at present and can be appreciably increased with minimal impact upon overall computer operations. Additionally, manual control functions should be reduced, providing for a streamlining of operations. After the recommendations described above have successfully been accomplished and are operational, Example Company management should reappraise computer equipment needs with respect to total processing.

EXHIBIT 6.5   (*Continued*)

THE EXAMPLE COMPANY   ATTACHMENT A

SUMMARY OF MAJOR FINDINGS AND RECOMMENDATIONS A-1

Description	Estimated Annual Savings
1. *Purchasing Procedures*	
a. Purchase requisition controls	$ 120,000
b. Purchasing/budgetary controls	80,000
c. Redistribution of buyers' workloads	164,000
d. Control over open purchase orders	245,000
e. Competitive bidding procedures	342,000
f. Value analysis program	46,000*
2. *Vendor Relations and Analysis*	
a. Dealing with same vendors	224,000**
b. Vendor analysis	Can't quantify
c. Employee leased cars	44,000
3. *Standard Specifications Unit*	
a. Personnel displacement	150,000
b. Reporting to Purchasing Supervisor	—-
4. *Cost to Process a Purchase Order*	
a. Purchases over $200	—
b. Purchases under $200	160,000
5. *Shipping and Receiving Operations*	
a. Shipping procedures	—
b. Receiving procedures	—
c. Revised shipping/receiving procedures	200,000
Total Estimated Annual Savings	$1,775,000

*Based on a limited review. Total annual savings should be much greater.
**Includes manufacturing raw materials only.

EXHIBIT 6.5   (*Continued*)

THE EXAMPLE COMPANY   ATTACHMENT B

OTHER AREAS FOR REVIEW Page B-1

Based on the work performed during our operational review of the Purchasing Department, we identified additional operational areas that we believe should be brought to your attention for further review and analysis. These additional areas include:

1. *Organizational planning and related systems*
We found that presently the Example Company operates on a reactive basis, that is, in response to specific situations and crises. Steps should be taken to implement effective planning techniques which encompass:

- Sophisticated sales forecast procedures which allow management to determine the related production requirements based on planned customer demand.
- Effective production scheduling systems that provide for controlling manufacturing operations based on planned customer orders rather than for inventory demands.
- Formal planning procedures that would include organizational and departmental goals, objectives, and detail plans, as well as an effective reporting and control system to ensure compliance to agreed-upon plans.
- Development and implementation of departmental and work unit budgets that use established plans as their basis and are reported on a flexible basis as related to activity levels.

2. *Review and analysis of organizational structure*
This review should be directed toward making the organization more responsive to current demands. Areas to look at could include reporting relationships, responsibility/authority relationships, management/supervisory assignments, work load distributions, and so on. For example, based on our review of the Purchasing Department, we suggested you review the following areas:

- Purchasing Department reporting to the Vice President of Operations; under the direct supervision of a Purchasing Supervisor.
- Functions, responsibilities, and authority of staff positions such as Market Analyst and Administrative Analyst.

EXHIBIT 6.5 (*Continued*)

- Use of clerical staff such as two Clerk Stenographers reporting to the Vice President of Operations, four clerical staff in the Purchasing Department, two clerks in the Standards Specifications Unit, and three in the Inventory Control unit.
- Work units such as Inspection, Inventory Control, and Warehouse reporting to the same individual as the Purchasing function—the Vice President of Operations.

3. *Review of personnel practices*
Personnel practices should be reviewed related to hiring, orientation, training, evaluation, promotion, and firing. We found no policies or procedures related to these personnel practices in existence at the Example Company. Accordingly, such practices are implemented by individual managers/supervisors based on their own criteria and expertise. Accordingly, in all of these areas, procedures are weak and inconsistent, resulting in employee confusion, improperly trained staff and management, loss of qualified personnel, and retention of undesirable employees.

4. *Review of operating systems and procedures*
Operating systems and procedures should be reviewed so as to perform necessary functions in the most economical and efficient manner without sacrificing expected results. For instance, our review of Purchasing Department functions identified operational areas for positive improvements, such as the following:

- Well-defined organization structure with defined responsibilities and authority relationships.
- Agreed-upon goals, objectives, and detail plans.
- Accurate and up-to-date position descriptions.
- Effective personnel practices to ensure well-qualified staff.
- Workable and practical operating policies and procedures.
- Integrated management and operating information system.
- Use of efficient operating techniques, such as:
- Traveling purchase requisitions.
- Blanket purchase orders.
- Integration of manufacturing and vendor deliveries.
- Vendor analysis as to price, quality, and timeliness.
- Competitive bidding procedures.
- Value analysis program.

EXHIBIT 6.5 *(Continued)*

5. *Computerized techniques*
More efficient use and integration of computer processing techniques with actual operations. You have had your computer system operational for more than eight years; however, you are still performing manually many functions that lend themselves to effective computerization. A major reason for this is the lack of direction over computer activities by top management. Accordingly, computer personnel are presently maintaining those systems that were originally designed and implemented with the help of outside consultants at the time the computer system was installed. Accordingly, you are using these resources minimally, although there is sufficient personnel and equipment capacity within your organization to achieve maximum use. Our recommended integrated purchasing system is an excellent first step. However, other areas should be looked at as well, such as sales forecasting, production scheduling, production control, inventory control, and billing and collections.

of operational reviews and the reviewers' related expertise. Although the final report marks the official close of the present operational review, it is also an effective vehicle for selling the concept of operational reviews for additional reviews.

Moreover, if the reporting is done effectively, the reviewers will not only be able to communicate the results of this operational review and persuade management to take the proper corrective action, but may also be able to sell management on the benefits of additional operational reviews. Each successful operational review should develop the demand for the next one.

Another purpose of this chapter is to increase the knowledge and understanding of effective operational review reporting principles and techniques. In relation to the operational review reporting phase, the operational review report should be viewed more as a summary of operational review results than as a call to action.

To be most effective, the review findings and recommendations should have been presented to and accepted by management as the review team proceeded through the review. It must be remembered that the primary goal of the review team is to assist in improving operations as expeditiously as possible, as a helping agent or catalyst, and not to hold back until the final report so as to receive personal recognition for the review organization.

AFTERWORD

This guide to performing the operational review for results has addressed various concerns relating to the phases of an operational review:

- Planning the operational review

- Developing the work program

- Performing field work steps

- Developing review findings and recommendations

- Reporting the results of the review

The techniques presented should be of particular interest and value to those who are presently or are desirous of providing operational review services as external consultants for clients, as well as those who provide such operational review services internally for specific work areas or for others within their organizations.

Because of the unique characteristics of individual firms or internal organizations, the materials covered and the situations presented may not all apply directly to each specific situation. Each reader should, therefore, use his or her own professional judgment as to which suggestions and recommendations to use in a given situation. However, the adoption of the systems and procedures covered in this guide should help in the development of effective operational review practices, thus effecting more economical, efficient, and effective operations.

> *The Application and Techniques*
> *of Operational Reviews*
> *Is Everyone's Business*

Index

Printed in the United States
82864LV00002B/21/A